President Brown –

May the Spirit empower
you for every good work
and give you wisdom as
you lead!

D Sul

Where the Spirit Is

Where the Spirit Is

Pentecostal Worship, Affect, Ritual, and Liberative Praxis

R. Shea Watts

PICKWICK *Publications* · Eugene, Oregon

Pickwick Publications
An Imprint of Wipf and Stock Publishers
199 W. 8th Ave., Suite 3
Eugene, OR 97401

www.wipfandstock.com

PAPERBACK ISBN: 978-1-6667-3508-6
HARDCOVER ISBN: 978-1-6667-9180-8
EBOOK ISBN: 978-1-6667-9181-5

Cataloguing-in-Publication data:

Names: Watts, R. Shea, author.
Title: Where the spirit is : pentecostal worship, affect, ritual, and liberative praxis / R. Shea Watts.
Description: Eugene, OR : Pickwick Publications, 2023 | Includes bibliographical references and index.
Identifiers: ISBN 978-1-6667-3508-6 (paperback) | ISBN 978-1-6667-9180-8 (hardcover) | ISBN 978-1-6667-9181-5 (ebook)
Subjects: LCSH: Pentecostal churches—Doctrines. | Worship.
Classification: BX8762.Z5 W38 2023 (print) | BX8762.Z5 W38 (ebook)

FEBRUARY 28, 2023 1:59 PM

To all those in my life who vehemently refused to let me give up,

this project is made possible by

your relentless love and encouragement

To Kathryn Watts, who has been my greatest companion

and source of support

Contents

Acknowledgments

NONE OF THIS—THE DISSERTATION nor all the work culminated and reflected in it—would be possible without the unwavering support and resources of the faculty and staff at Chicago Theological Seminary, including our PhD program director, Dr. Emily Vogt, as well as my dissertation committee members and mentors: Drs. JoAnne Marie Terrell, Ken Stone, Christophe Ringer, BoMyung Seo, Scott Haldeman, and Zachary Moon. This committee pushed me to take my line of inquiry deeper and to consider how this work is "my work." To my advisor, Dr. Ken Stone: your guidance and advice has been a constant before and especially throughout the PhD process, and I have gleaned much from your example as scholar, teacher, advisor, and dean. Thank you, Reverend Dr. JoAnne Terrell. I fondly remember the moment you kneeled and prayed with me as I considered applying to the PhD program. Making music with you has been an honor. Thank you, Reverend Dr. Susan Thistlethwaite, for all you have taught and continue to teach me. Your embodied public witness in the world reminds of the importance of putting scholarship into action.

I am fortunate to have faithful friends, family, and companions who have served as interlocutors along the way. In particular, my dads, the Reverend Tim Wolfe and Walt Watson Swift; my two dearest companions, Katie Kinnison and Jacqui Buschor; as well as my academic confidants, Tyler Tully and Jason Frey. For all of the questions, conversations, encouragements, and recommendations—thank you. My work is marked by your brilliance, graciousness, and influence. I have made it to this point only by the grace of God and the goodness of these friends. Neil, you are the person who walked beside me on this unpredictable journey, and you have stood with me when times were hard. Our friendship shows the power of love, curiosity, and generosity.

ACKNOWLEDGMENTS

Finally, I acknowledge the many, like me, who have felt like a stranger in your own home. Always wedged "between something real and something wrong," as Brian McLaren once said, this project stems from my own attempts to find a place within the Pentecostal tradition. For those who share in the isolating pain of bewilderment and estrangement, this is for you.

Introduction

The Pentecostal power, when you sum it all up, is just more of God's love. If it does not bring more love, it is simply a counterfeit.

—WILLIAM J. SEYMOUR, THE APOSTOLIC FAITH

Religions are little nourished by disembodied reflection, and it is a mistake to assume that dancing one's religion precludes thinking about it.

—RONALD GRIMES, RITUAL CRITICISM

Introduction

UNDER A BLUE STREET sign that bears the name Azusa, in a boisterous LA neighborhood just Northeast of Downtown, a smaller square brown sign reads, "AZUSA ST. MISSION. Site of the Azusa St. Revival from 1906–1931. Cradle of the Worldwide Pentecostal Movement."[1] The site, once a dynamic religious destination that drew curious visitors from across the world, is now humbly marked above a white LAPD sign indicating the neighborhood is under video monitoring. The "fire" that once burned intensely on Azusa St. was tempered locally but not extinguished. Its flame has spread across the globe. Led by William Seymour, a Black pastor from Louisiana, Pentecostalism is widely understood to have its origins in the Azusa St. Revival. Initially, the revival was noteworthy for its egalitarian ethos of worship vis-à-vis race and gender. Eventually, the movement collapsed and fragmented, proving that such an egalitarian vision of race and gender was "too radical a departure from prevailing social norms"[2] at that

---

1. There are varying dates for the Azusa St. Revival, most of which are significantly shorter than this twenty-five-year timeline.
2. Lewin, *Filled with the Spirit*, 6.

time. As a result, the Pentecostal movement subsequently splintered into divisions along racial lines, evidenced by the two largest traditions: The Black Church of God in Christ (COGIC) and the (predominantly) white Assemblies of God. There exist interracial movements within the offshoots of Pentecostalism; but generally speaking, these two large denominations are more racially homogenous.

Yet and still, the fires of Pentecostalism continue to kindle globally. With an estimated 35,000 people joining per day, Pentecostals constitute 25 percent of Christians and represent the fastest growing sect of Christianity.[3] Interestingly, the gender dynamics of Pentecostalism suggest an empowerment of women in places such as Africa, where it is estimated that 75 percent of Pentecostals are female. This highlights the presence of matriarchal ecclesial leadership. While Donald Miller and Tetsunao Yamamori have given significant attention to "Progressive Pentecostalism" as a complex social movement in *Global Pentecostalism: The New Face of Christian Social Engagement,* I focus on the a/effects of what they refer to as "exclusions."[4]

Broadly, this project is the result of my interests, both as a lifelong Pentecostal and a doctoral student in the study of theology. It encompasses my experiences growing up in the Pentecostal church, the ways in which they marked, shaped, and wounded me. It is also representative of my academic pursuits, which have given me the necessary tools to explore, prod, and interrogate these experiences. Over the past few years, these two streams have flowed together into one. The moment of their coalescence has been burned into memory: July of 2017, when I attended the Fellowship of Affirming Ministries' (TFAM)[5] yearly gathering. In a hotel ballroom in New Orleans, sounds of ecstatic worship and spirited preaching filled the spaces of the room. Though skeptical, I found myself moved to tears in unexplainable and uncontainable ways. From the depths of my body,

---

3. Van der Haak and Vijgen, *Atlas of Pentecostalism.*

4. They note that their work "intentionally exclude(s) Pentecostal and charismatic Christians who have aligned with right-wing repressive governments. We also exclude churches from our definition of Progressive Pentecostalism that focus exclusively on faith healing or 'health and wealth' without connecting their Christian faith to socially beneficial programs for their community. And, finally, we exclude Pentecostal churches that emphasize conversion as their only mission to the community" (quoted in Miller and Yamamori, *Global Pentecostalism,* 2).

5. The Fellowship of Affirming Ministries is a predominately Black LGBTQIA Pentecostal tradition founded by Bishop Yvette Flounder.

in the innermost places, it felt as if something was bubbling up and out. As the dynamics of the singing and shouting ebbed and flowed, so too did my body's responses to the sounds—evidenced by shaking, goosebumps, a rush of blood to the head, crying, and a warm, overwhelming sense of the special sacredness of those moments. Moved and moving, the more I tried to restrain the feelings, the more intense my bodily reactions became. What bubbled up eventually burst out of me.

There, surrounded by Black LGBTQ church leaders, many of whom have been historically chastised and rejected by their own traditions, I was confronted by the familiar feelings of my religious upbringing in ways I could neither explain nor deter. I felt like a child once again, exploring the wonder and awe of being engulfed in a dense atmosphere of feeling. These overwhelming sensations were made tangible in the collective connectedness of the group—the hugs, kisses, warm greetings, tears and laughter, and ecstatic communal worship. The atmosphere of each session was electric, charged with an open-ended excitement of what is possible, i.e., what "the Spirit" would and could do in that particular space and time. The sights and sounds of the worship experience were more than an observational event; they constituted ways of knowing that are felt, but seldom spoken; absorbed, but not fully cognitively registered at the time. I was only aware that "something" was happening to me, to my body, in my person. Some years later, I am still processing the effects of all that transpired.

Where the Spirit Is moves in two directions. It is at once a reference to the Pauline passage "where the Spirit of the Lord is, there is freedom"[6] and also a nod to a theology of embodiment or enfleshment (of the Holy Spirit), extended beyond the one-time incarnation of Jesus, which I consider foundational for and archetypal of liberative Pentecostal spiritualities. This shift of understanding in the Word-becoming-flesh is inherently material and analogous to the notion of "deep incarnation," that is, that the Spirit incarnates all things. As Elizabeth Johnson has argued, deep incarnation is a "new radical embodiment, in which the Wisdom/Word of God joins the material world to accomplish a new level of union between Creator and creature."[7] Building on the work of Niels Henrik Gregerson, Johnson extends the notion of deep incarnation to include all flesh: "The flesh assumed in Jesus connects with all humanity, all biological life, all soil, the whole

6. 2 Cor 3:17 NRSV.

7. Quoted in Edwards, *Deep Incarnation*, 5.

matrix of the material universe down to its very roots."[8] If all humans are incarnated by the Spirit and fashioned in the *imago Dei* (God's image and likeness), then all people are endowed with infinite and irrevocable worth. Such is the vision that Seymour carried—a vision espoused by TFAM. By centering the Fellowship of Affirming Ministries (TFAM), a Black LGBTQ Pentecostal tradition, this project connects Seymour's original egalitarian vision of Azusa St. with TFAM's radical inclusivity as liberative praxis. Central to Seymour's theology was the belief that Azusa Street was an outpouring, or "Pentecost," in which the Spirit would be poured out on all flesh, in accordance with the vision of Joel the prophet and reiterated by the apostle Paul.[9] Seymour steps into the prophetic tradition, pioneering a new order of Christian leaders. It is also perhaps why Bishop Yvette Flunder, founder and leader of TFAM, declares the movement as a "Third Pentecost."

Where the Spirit Is underscores people and movements consonant with Seymour's vision through their embodiment and espousal of a spirited, egalitarian, and inclusive ethos—not all of whom were or are self-avowed Pentecostals nor exclusively Christian. Therefore, a theology of deep incarnation, i.e., that the Spirit incarnates all created things, is precursory to the divisions and demarcations of religion (*this* God and not *that* one, *this* holy book and not *that*, *these* people but not *them*). Insofar as spirited practices are lived out for and toward liberation—in responding to the vicissitudes and exigencies of the social milieu—these are instances and loci of the Holy Spirit's work, or "where the Spirit is." As James Cone compellingly argues in *A Black Theology of Liberation*, "Christian theology is a theology of liberation. It is a rational study of the being of God in the world in light of the existential situation of an oppressed community, relating the forces of liberation to the essence of the gospel, which is Jesus Christ."[10] Forces of liberation evidence God's work in the world, both through the Holy Spirit and the gospel of Jesus Christ, both of which inform the daily life of the Christian. And when Christians live in proximity to the good news through a heightened awareness of the in-dwelling of the Holy Spirit, they begin to live out their spirituality in ways of endless possibilities, wholly embracing Walter Rauschenbusch's sentiment that "the kingdom is always but coming."[11] This turn of phrase distorts traditional, binary breaks between

8. Johnson, *Ask the Beasts*, 196.

9. Joel 2:28–29; Acts 2:16–18.

10. Cone, *Black Theology of Liberation*, 1.

11. Rauschenbusch, *Christianity and Social Crisis*, 338. I prefer the term *kin-dom* to

the here and now and eschatological futurity: the kin-dom of God is here and now, but not yet fully. The kin-dom is the domain where the radical inclusive and liberative life in the Spirit is lived out. The kin-dom is the cosmos that binds all creation together like muscle and connective tissue. One etymology of the word *religion*, argued by various thinkers, including Lactantius, Augustine, and Thomas Aquinas, comes from the Latin root *religio*, which means to "bind" or "connect."[12] Of course, religion can be a way to behold how everything is already bound together—the universe and all life within it. To understand the degree to which we are bound, and consider whether these bindings are liberative, therefore becomes the work at hand, prompting one to ask if there is indeed freedom, where the Spirit of the Lord is.

More specifically, this work is a critical study of the Pentecostal movement and its bodily epistemologies through the bifocal lenses of theories of affect and ritual studies toward spiritualities of liberation. Gustavo Gutierrez, considered as the father of Latin American liberation theology, lifted up the "need for a spirituality of liberation."[13] Gutierrez saw theology as an expression of spirituality. Theology, in his work, is the secondary and mediating act between a primordial spiritual experience (mystical, contemplative, silence) and the only appropriate response to this experience: to share or announce it (annunciation). Because Gutierrez saw conversion as always to both God *and* neighbor, spirituality is the process of living out that coming-together or alignment. Another word for this is: justice. There is a Trinitarian-like flow evident in Gutierrez's spirituality in which God, neighbor (world or cosmos), and self are fundamental relations. Christ, universal and personally incarnated, becomes the presence and energy binding all things together, making the path to wholeness and harmony possible.

Looking beyond liberation theologies discourses to their underlying spiritual practices vis-à-vis theories of affect and ritual studies offers tools necessary to peel back the layers of worship experiences—the apex of Pentecostal theology—to expose their social ramifications, asking whether

kingdom, as such a change emphasizes the familial aspects of Jesus's teachings and de-centers the male body from the top of gendered hierarchies. The use of kin-dom is from Ada María Isasi-Díaz, who gives credit to Georgene Wilson, OSF.

12. Taking his cue from Lactantius, St. Augustine changes his understanding of the word religion, arguing away from an understanding of recovery to the notion that religion "binds us" to God in Augustine, *Retractions*.

13. Gutiérrez, *Theology of Liberation*, 74.

and how Pentecostal ritualizing can be liberative. Through "epistemological vigilance,"[14] i.e., embracing subjectivity, harnessing introspection, and
cultivating communal theologies, Pentecostalism has the power to subvert
the monolith of theological fundamentalist doctrines. However, while Pentecostal ritualizing ostensibly opens bodies to boundless freedom in Christ,
not all Pentecostals are fully free in expression or identity. Rather, many
live legalistic lives, enclosed by theologies meant to suppress, fashion, and
master subjects of desire into desired subjects. Miller and Yamamori iden-
tify four different emphases which cut across different expressions of Pentecostalism: 1) Pentecostal churches that are legalistic and otherworldly;
2) Prosperity Gospel movement, or health-and-wealth churches; 3) Progressive Pentecostalism, referred to as the "integral" or "holistic" gospel;
4) routinized Pentecostalism, which are churches that are have shed their
sectarian heritage and embrace contemporary culture. TFAM, the focus
here, fits most appropriately in number 3.

In *Blackpentecostal Breath*, Ashon Crawley describes his project as
"*a*theological-*a*philosophical," positing that black aesthetics of worship
are produced against "the grain of liberal logics of subjectivity."[15] Deeply
entrenched in "liberal logics of subjectivity," Western ways of knowing
(epistemologies) are always already racialized. It is particularly present in
theological and philosophical projects—insidiously embedded in mechanisms and strategies of power—that rose to prominence during the Enlightenment. M. Shawn Copeland notes:

> When confronted with the writings on race by major thinkers
> of the European Enlightenment, contemporary philosophy too
> often blinks, dismissing these texts as minor or unrepresenta-
> tive. Yet, as Emmanuel Eze argues, "Enlightenment philosophy
> was instrumental in codifying and institutionalizing both the
> scientific and popular European perceptions of the human race."
> In an age that has become synonymous with criticality, major
> Enlightenment thinkers—including Georges Léopold Cuvier, Jo-
> hann Friedrich Blumenbach, David Hume, Immanuel Kant, and
> Georg Wilhelm Friedrich Hegel—played a role in shaping white
> European sensibilities of national, cultural, and racial superiority
> vis-à-vis non-white non-Europeans. Indeed from the eighteenth
> century until well into the twentieth, their ideas about race served
> to reinforce proslavery attitudes, to sustain racial segregation and

14. Isasi-Díaz, *Mujerista Theology*, 76–77.
15. Crawley, *Blackpentecostal Breath*, 1–10.

discrimination, and to exert subtle, perhaps devastating, influence on metaphysics and ethics. . . . The enervating dimensions and underside of Enlightenment evaluations that correlated white skin with reason, intelligence, civilization, goodness, and creativity also correlated non-white skin, black skin with unreason, ignorance, savagery, depravity, and mimicry. . . . These evaluations insinuated the idea that white skin functionally accorded absolute supremacy to white men over non-whites and women and legitimated imperial brutality, extermination, slavery, racism, and biology as human destiny.[16]

Crawley's work builds upon Copeland's argument—adding theology to the philosophical project—and exposes a tension, specifically, the possibility that Pentecostal ritualizing is also its liability insofar as the dynamism of Pentecostal religious experience authorizes and elevates certain types of authority and logics. Power, in this manner, is at once productive, restrictive, and destructive. Power produces a vulnerability that can be exploited through the conflation of divine and human authority. The relationships among chance, authenticity, and manipulation are at the core of Pentecostal spiritualities. With that in mind, I suggest considering Pentecostal worship and spiritualities as irreducible, in the spirit of their refusal to conform or be reduced to the singular.

Theories of affect and ritual, together, constitute my main methodologies. The former are approaches to history, culture, politics, and other forms of embodied life that highlight para- and noncognitive forces,[17] while the latter focuses on a wide range of embodied practices and actions that move, teach, and orient bodies in particular, often intended and repetitious ways. Neither affect nor ritual are homogenous categories, but each offers varying genealogies and divergent approaches. Within both broad fields are broader inquiries: queer, feminist, Black radical, womanist, ecological, critical race, critical theory, and decolonial studies. Additionally, I engage in theological discourse and Scripture interpretation. Like complementary languages, affect and ritual talk to each other, interpret one another, and interface in ways that can enrich conversation around Pentecostal culture. By invoking the slippery word *culture*, I am intimating how affect and ritual play out in the social through everyday phenomena.[18] The malleability and

16. Copeland, *Enfleshing Freedom*, 9–10.

17. See Schaefer, *Religious Affects*.

18. Kathleen Stewart has broached the subject of everyday affects in Stewart, *Ordinary Affects*, and her work with Lauren Gail Berlant in Berlant and Stewart, *Hundreds*.

capaciousness of these theoretical fields will allow me to suggest what is lacking in each, mainly, critical conversations on racism and the racist implications of knowledge production. Thus, when I speak of affect and ritual, I will demonstrate how womanism and Black radical thought are complementary and supplementary to the theoretical fields, often filling in the interstices that exist.

A recurring medium that I highlight for the coalescence of affect and ritual is religious experience in general and worship music in particular. I argue that worship music, as sound, organizes bodies in spaces (i.e., ritualization), transmits affect, produces unique ways of knowing, and shapes subjects. The dynamics of music play a vital role in interpellation, that is, the process in which the culture's values (including theology) are internalized at the level of the subject.[19] The worship experience is central to Pentecostal culture and on par with preaching in terms of importance, influence, and authority. Worship, as dynamic communal exercise, though seemingly ephemeral, has long-lasting a/effects beyond the event—a/effects that blur the lines of consciousness and notions of subjective autonomy as they push and pull and compel bodies through the world. As an affective assemblage that brings together things disparate and alike, music can organize and constitute an archive of feelings.[20] In Pentecostal worship, the participant always practices and performs, individually and collectively, as they strive to cultivate an epistemological framework that makes sense (sense-making) and *feels* right. A kind of resonance seeks to resolve any perceived dissonance. However, at times, such as a song built around a minor scale, dissonance is the point.

All to say, worship music offers a unique entry point into the affective and ritualistic components of Pentecostal worship, which can be liberative, exploitative, improvisational, manipulative, and perhaps even accidental. How one understands and wields power makes the difference. Power, throughout this dissertation, is explored on two intersecting and overlapping planes, the religious and the secular, both of which are enveloped in the cultural. Thus, I speak of power through the work of Michel Foucault, whose interest is in how power is always simultaneously produced and restricted/opposed, how it is systemic and governs all social life, on the

19. This theory was developed by French Marxist Louis Althusser (1918–1990) in Althusser, *On Reproduction of Capitalism.*

20. This is a reference to the work of queer affect theorist Ann Cvetkovich, particularly her work *An Archive of Feelings*, cited in Bray and Moore's *Religion, Emotion, Sensation*, 10.

one hand, and power, as *dunamis*, found in Acts 2 as the fulfillment of the prophecy found in the book of Joel about God's Spirit being poured out on all flesh, on the other. Below, I map out each chapter, tracing their key arguments and placing them within the scope of this work and within Pentecostal culture generally. Each chapter takes the former chapter as its predecessor, building upon its contributions and nuances.

In chapter 1, "A Move of the Spirit: Exploring the Interarticulations of Affect and Ritual," I parse out these different approaches, mapping out 1) my approach and 2) the importance and usefulness of using the two—affect and ritual—as a broad hybrid methodology. I explore a working definition of affect and its usefulness for theological studies. This necessitates tracing the genealogies of two primary strands of affect theory (on the one hand, that associated with Baruch Spinoza, and developed by Deleuze, Massumi, etc., and on the other hand, that associated with Silvan Tomkins, and developed by many thinkers such as Schaefer, Sedgwick, Ahmed, Chen, Berlin, etc.). Theories of affect are not monolithic, and I draw out ideas and insight from various scholars across both genealogies accordingly. While each genealogy offers an entry point into the conversation, ultimately the phenomenological strand (found in queer and feminist scholars' elaboration of Silvan Tomkins's research) is most amenable to embodiment, and therefore most pertinent to this project. To that end, I hope to create a rhythm of "feeling and doing" throughout the project. It is always both—how we *feel* affects what we do and what we *do* affects what or how we feel. I consider religion to be a primal and instinctual phenomenon; it is a product of the queer animacy[21] of our bodies.

Next, I introduce a problem with affect: that because of its potentiality as unconscious and para-and nonlinguistic, it can be difficult to find appropriate discursive vehicles for analysis. Thus, I introduce ritual studies as a methodology for exploring "what bodies do," as Schaefer notes about

21. For my purposes, I will not be engaging affect as "animal," as do Schaefer and others. To say humans have animal bodies is not untrue, per se, but doing so creates a tension—albeit, unintended—between certain bodies that have been dehumanized through animalization in various degrees. People of color, especially black people in the US, have been victims of this type of human hierarchy and so using the term *animality* is sometimes unhelpful with regard to race and other affective economies of embodiment. Chen uses *animacy* as a way to queer the binaries of life/death, human/animal distinctions. In Sara Ahmed's work, animacy can be used to evince how the phenomenological approach to affect splits the binary between affect and emotion, a distinction that is clearly made in the Deleuzian and Massumian strand of affect. It is precisely this queering work, this in-betweenness, that I believe affective analyses proliferate. See Chen, *Animacies*, 7–12.

affect, including how bodies are "impelled by forces other than language and reason." Schaefer uses the example of "the waterfall dance," an observation made by Jane Goodall in which the chimpanzees of the Kakombe valley community arrive at a magnificent waterfall, to show how affect and ritual focus on how bodies experience religious phenomena. While they watch, Goodall observes that they make sounds and perform gestures, what Goodall calls *dance*, that are *sui generis* and not repeated in any other part of their embodied lives. Goodall reflects:

> Is it not possible that these performances are stimulated by feelings akin to wonder and awe? After a waterfall display the performer may sit on a rock, his eyes following the falling water. What is it, this water? . . . If the chimpanzees had a spoken language, if they could discuss these feelings among themselves, might not they lead to an animistic, pagan worship of the elements?[22]

Schaefer's appeal to Goodall's work proposes that spoken language, i.e., human language, is not the only or ultimate grounds or prerequisite for the legitimacy of ritualizing or spirituality. As a continuation of the work in *Religious Affects*, ritual is a fertile framework that tracks Pentecostalism through ecstatic, animated worship, through moments of awe and unintelligible sounds, and through the signaling of para- and nonlinguistic cues. A problem arises from Schaefer's emphasis on the animality of affect, mainly, the complicated nature of animality with the history of race. To the same extent that words *primitive*, *magic*, and *savage* have been used in anthropology and ritual to distinguish between higher and lower forms of ritual, the word *animal* and other dehumanizing words have been deployed toward other-than-white forms of worship in comparison to whiteness.

Finally, I lift up Pentecostalism as a theological example of how phenomenological affect theory and ritual studies work together, sketching out the scope of the dissertation. Drawing on the work of Sara Ahmed vis-à-vis affective economies and the recursive impressions that constitute the subject and shape their horizon of feeling (i.e., orientation), I argue for an affective analysis of racism through how power interfaces with bodies in cultural contexts.

In chapter 2, "Dance-Possible Epistemologies of Sound and Space," I offer and interpret three vignettes: Pentecost in Acts 2, the spirituals that emerged under the horrors of slavocracy in the South, and finally, the sound produced at Azusa. Sound is an affective language, and music is a

22. Goodall, "Primate Spirituality," 1304.

compound of sonic affects.[23] It resonates within, reverberates, and bounces off bodies. Bodies—like sponges—soak up sound and affects in the room and are thus marked and shaped by the impressions other bodies make as they brush up against each other, shaping the horizon of what is possible.[24] The upper room narrative provides such a case, as the Spirit manifests and spills over in power-ful, sensate ways: the sound of a violent rushing wind, tongues divided—distributed, spread—as of fire, and the ability to speak new languages. Finding its origin in Acts 2, I note the sound in the upper room and how it established "otherwise" hermeneutics for Pentecostal bodies—unpredictable, dynamic, capricious, against the norm. The observers are amazed and ask, "What does this mean?" The writers must pen down the story because they hear their own language but are unsure of the meaning. Speaking in other languages or tongues, *glossolalia*, is consonant to affect theory's supplementation of language—words without reference, signification without universal signifiers. No one knows what this language means, yet it does something, accomplishes something, has a/effect. Additionally, *xenolalia* in Acts 2 tells of an ability to speak languages without learning them. It is a supernatural empowerment to communicate with others. Whereas the Babel story in Genesis uses language to confuse, Acts reverses this, using language to universalize God's message in other native tongues.

Next, I move to an exploration of the spirituals as affective ritualizing antecedent to Pentecostal worship experience. Emerging from the daily lives of the enslaved in the antebellum South, I consider this tradition a forerunner for ecstatic, embodied worship because it made audible the sound of suffering. (To hear is to feel sound waves and to be affected by them.) Music was, for the enslaved, one means of meaning-making. This led to the advent of the blue note, a flatting of standard notes in a scale that expresses and evokes a particular mood. Sound is feeling; sound produces and magnifies feeling. Thus, the blue note is not simply sung or played; it is felt, embodied, performed. It resists—refusing to be contained—bubbles over, pours out. The blue note takes the standard scales that the colonizer gives and flats them to create a new, expressive sound. It is not simply an adaptation of colonial sound, but a new expression of something "otherwise"; with the new sound comes new worlds, new epistemologies and possibilities. I argue

23. Thompson and Biddle, *Sound, Music, Affect*, 9.

24. Such phrasing is part and parcel of Sara Ahmed's work, but is most directly fleshed out in Ahmed, *Cultural Politics of Emotion*.

that the development of Pentecostalism in the US cannot be divorced from the musical and theological contributions of the enslaved. Spirituals create a framework to consider sound, embodiment, and spirituality—an affective technology, as it were. Insofar as colonial music and religion seeks to master and dominate docile subjects, the spirituals alter the world by augmenting sound, rendering colonizers and enslavers' projects illegitimate, and creating otherwise possibilities.

I end this chapter by segueing to considering Pentecostalism in the US as the third vignette of how sound and affect shape bodies through sonic experiences. Having offered a few other examples, it is here, i.e., in light of the history of slavery and the spirituals, that I segue to a history of Pentecostalism. That bodies are queer comes to the fore here. Furthermore, while Pentecostalism is seen by many in the Christian tradition as illegitimate, fabricated, unpredictable and as a result, unreliable, I argue the very opposite: that because of its capricious nature, Pentecostalism exists as an example of how affect works to move bodies through affectively charged spaces. It is legitimized by a keen sense of bodily awareness. Affects are recalcitrant in that they can "kick back"[25]—pushing back against the pure categorical distinctions of Western Enlightenment and queering what is known and how that knowledge can be transmitted. Pentecostalism offers its own affective epistemologies through its queer phenomenologies. Further still, Pentecostalism produces "spirit-filled technologies of power"[26] that have the potential to reconcile and reshape worlds. Highlighting the centrality of "spirit-filled" practices underscores the various ways in which religion is embodied through a "chain of memory"; or, in affective terms, "spirit-filled" practices are attentive and attuned to the repetitive practices—and their circulative affects—which become sediment and create embodied histories in the subject.[27]

Chapter 3, "'A Queer Faith': Gender, Sexuality, and Inclusion in Pentecostalism," makes the connection between the work of the Spirit in Pentecostalism with LGBTQ+ Christians. More than nonnormative, here, I revisit William J. Seymour's precedential vision of racial reconciliation and gender equality for the Azusa Street gatherings as well as the important

25. Scheve, "Interview with Donovan Schaefer."

26. Casselberry and Pritchard, *Spirit on the Move*, 11.

27. Here I am connecting Danièle Hervieu-Léger's notion of religion as "chain of memory," quoted in Casselberry and Pritchard's *Spirit on the Move*, 5, with Schaefer's mention of "embodied histories" found in Tomkins, *Religious Affects*, 47.

contributions of queer and womanist thought as found in TFAM's gospel of radical inclusivity. A queer faith reveals a queer God who comes out and toward queer people of color. Bodies that are discounted and devalued in the modern world become a witness of and testament to God's presence.

First, I will explore Sara Ahmed's work on the affective nature of happiness. As both a script for conformity and the feeling which enforces it, happiness is often presented as synonymous with living a good life. However, peeling back the layers of the language exposes how thoughts, words, and feelings surrounding happiness are laden with modern, heteronormative dictates. Thus, it is important to expose the veneer of happiness and the affective economies which perpetuate it in order to see that a good life is not necessarily a happy one. Rather, a good life is about freedom and joy. Whereas happiness is about conformity, joy is about resistance.

Next, I move to consider how TFAM's unabashed theological claim of radical inclusivity coalesces with Marcella Althaus-Reid's "indecent theology," which focuses on bodies distanced or disqualified due to Western modern notions and norms of happiness, decency, modesty, purity, etc. Claiming indecent theology is an act of defiance and does not "center" marginalized voices as much as it renders bodies visible that have always been present. Althaus-Reid's approach, thus, embraces and reclaims the derogatory and pejorative language for its own liberative praxis. To that end, I named the chapter "A Queer Faith," which is a way of reclaiming an *LA Times* article title that attempted to criticize and discredit the Azusa Street Revival as odd, abnormal, and abhorrent.

Finally, I engage Black-queer-womanist theologizing as fertile theoretical and theological ground to think about Pentecostalism. The womanist tradition, as stemming from the work of Alice Walker, is an oral and literary tradition, which I argue is a ritual tradition. Furthermore, through the work of queer womanist theologians Pamela Lightsey and Yvette Flunder, bodies and the flesh come to the fore as the locus and site of risky theorizing and theologizing. I use the word *risky* because these approaches are not intellectual exercises but are done with great corporeal and visceral vulnerability. My hope is not to appropriate or exploit their work but honor it by showing how it is fundamental to the arguments of this project. I end the chapter by focusing on how their work brings Pentecost into the personal, embodied, political realm.

Chapter 4, "A Liberating Spirit and Political Pentecost," explores the role of the Holy Spirit in the struggle for and work of liberation within two contemporary examples: The Reverend Dr. William J. Barber II's notion of a political Pentecost and TFAM's movement as self-proclaimed Third Pentecost. Both of these ideas center Pentecost as the event by which God's Spirit becomes deeply involved in the social world, such that the work of liberation and the Holy Spirit become synonymous. Simply put, I argue that the Holy Spirit is this active force in the world.

I then turn to the politics of affect found in the work of Brian Massumi. While his work represents the Spinozian strand of affect, I find his work on microperception and re-cueing pertinent to this project. When considering political Pentecost, there is no greater example and opportunity than the present, as Donald Trump's ascendency has been effective insofar as it is affective. Trump's efficacy is a case in point for how affective economies proliferate and operate in the political realm. His ability to stir up fear through lies, misinformation, and incendiary rhetoric is uncanny. This exposes an important aspect of the politics of affect: ideas need not make sense or be true to be e/affective, which is to say, believed and espoused. While Massumi notes President Barack Obama's ability to re-cue large portions of the population toward hope, I argue Trump has done exactly the opposite. Thus, I show how affective rituals, such as protest, are praxis-oriented ways of resisting and subverting the politics of fear, racism, sexism, homophobia, xenophobia, etc.

Next, I explore the mystic-activism of Howard Thurman as a holistic spiritual praxis through the "inwardness" and "outwardness" of religion. While Thurman's witness preceded the civil rights movement as well as discourses of liberation theology in Latin America and Black liberation theology in the US, his concern for the "disinherited" and people "with their backs up against the wall" informs his theology. His work was born out of an idiom of Blackness and a deep spiritual imagination. Therefore, his writings and witness exemplify a synthesis of spiritual experience and social action.

Finally, I consider resistance through the occasions of Blackpentecost (Ashon Crawley) and enfleshing freedom. Blackpentecostal worship produces an excess that refuses to be reduced to categorical distinction, and the excess operates as the aesthetic means of possibility. Blackpentecost is inspirited by Black breath, which makes possible the practices of liberation that invoke the Spirit through worship, singing, and shouting. Invoking the Spirit, as practice, leads to fleshing out of freedom. Enfleshing freedom means constructing a theological anthropology that embraces Black bodies as the *imago Dei* and the location of God's Spirit, which necessitates new ways of being in the world. In fact, it brings about new worlds.

This dissertation is but a beginning into broader inquiries. There are issues that I will not address because the scope of the dissertation does not permit it. However, there is much to be considered and discussed about the history and future of Pentecostalism in the US and around the world. With this in mind, and in concern, I move to lay the methodological and theoretical groundwork for what follows.

CHAPTER 1

A Move of the Spirit

Exploring the Interarticulations of Affect and Ritual

Affect theory merges with LaMothe's call to begin studying religion with bodies, using our embodied practices, habits, and sensitivities to understand religious worlds.

—*DONOVAN O. SCHAEFER, RELIGIOUS AFFECTS*

Ritual is not a senseless activity but is rather one of many ways in which human beings construe and construct their world.

—*TED JENNINGS, "ON RITUAL KNOWLEDGE"*

Religion is at least as much about community as it is about the affirmation of theological propositions. And, furthermore, it often engages the body as much as it does the mind.

—*DONALD MILLER & TETSUNAO YAMAMORI, GLOBAL PENTECOSTALISM*

Introduction

WHEN I WAS TWELVE years old, my dad decided to add a Friday night worship service to our weekly meetings at the church. We would gather at 7 p.m. with no set agenda, other than the prompting to worship God however and by whatever means you were inclined. You were free to experiment with the worship experience. We did. The space looked and felt different than a typical Sunday. We would stack all of the chairs and put them on either side of the sanctuary, prompting a local preacher to remark, "What, are you going to turn the church into a dance club?" "Why not?" my dad fired back. (After all, one of his favorite sermons was to preach about how David danced out of his robe, and how his wife, Michal—for him, symbolizing the church—looked down upon the king from her window and despised David for becoming undignified. The story goes that Michal is punished with barrenness, a draconian sentence for her wrongdoing. I would watch as, every time he preached that message, my dad would end up in tears as he would say that our church would embrace dance and "bear much fruit." I knew he felt that deep inside of his being.)

During the Friday night worship services, the lights would be turned off completely, except for a few dim lights near the stage and at the entrance/exit doors in the back of the room. Rather than live worship, we would watch recordings of worship videos from Hillsong Church in Sydney, Australia, pausing it whenever someone would offer a prophetic word, prayer, vision, or word of knowledge to individuals or the group. Often, my dad would sit on the stage and cry and pray in tongues until the room began to stir. He functioned as a thermostat, affecting and regularly regulating the collective temperature of the room. Rarely, someone else would share a Scripture at the beginning to frame the night. The music, accompanied by the effervescent sounds of ecstatic praise, was the primary driving force of the night. The room itself vibrated, buzzed, reverberated with sounds of music and movement.

It was there, in the dark but warm space filled with voluminous worship music, that I first danced with God. (Maybe it is more appropriate to say that I danced "in" God?) I began by clapping suspiciously. Then I swayed subtly. Until finally—once I realized nobody was watching or judging—I jumped and spun about wildly. The mood of the room would shift as the fast-tempo praise songs transitioned to slower anthems. All the energy spent jumping around became more focused and concentrated in the body. The fast-tempo songs allow you to move through the outer courts with thanksgiving and praise; the slower songs brought about a collective reverence in the room that stilled and calmed bodies into slower movements and eventually more tranquil forms of worship. In those calmer moments, my dad would speak of this time as an opportunity to "soak" in the presence of God. People would transition from standing to kneeling and eventually to laying on their stomachs or backs. On more than one occasion I—and several others—would lie on the floor until we eventually fell asleep. To this day, I still consider it the best sleep I have ever had. I remember the sensation of a warm blanket enveloping me, as the sounds of people praying, crying, and speaking in tongues slowly faded. More than emotional outbursts and goosebumps, I felt, above all else, safe. I felt at home. And I learned that this was what it meant to feel God's presence, to know God. That presence, the feeling of emotions ebbing and flowing in the room, is what we were all pursuing.

I would wake up either when the lights were turned on, which was usually after 10 p.m., or earlier if someone started "laughing in the Holy Ghost," which was usually followed by an unpredictable amount of time where a few trickling laughs multiplying in persons and volume until most in the room would be laughing uncontrollably. These periods of laughter were contagious and often followed periods of intense worship that included sobbing and what I have come to understand as lament. I realized, even as a child, that the degree of crying and emotion often was occasioned by laughter in equal measure. When worship was over, we would head to the local greasy spoon restaurant for another one or two hours of fellowship, which was a testament to both our southern culture and Pentecostal tradition. There were many occasions when we did not leave our beloved restaurant until well after midnight. People would come in from nightclubs and drinking at a bar. My mom would joke that we were all drunk, too, but of the "new wine."

I tell this anecdote to say that Friday night worship in the sanctuary constituted a way of knowing for me—knowing God was knowing *how* to experience or encounter God. Knowing God was feeling God and vice versa. Such a dynamic is not tangential to theology but appeals to the mystic edges of Pentecostalism. Pentecostal knowing comes from personal experience. Perhaps that is why times of intense worship were described as "intimacy with God." There was a way of achieving this intimacy. I watched and learned from others. I listened to the songs and to the words of those praying and singing around me, how their voices inflected what they were saying as they talked to God and waited for God to respond. I found in music the ecstatic power of feeling all the way alive. Sundays were like Fridays in a milder manner. But I lived for those Friday nights, when, in a dark sanctuary, I would lose and find myself once again in God. This period of life was short-lived. After a church split and denominational dispute, we moved away. I did not dance much in my subsequent teenage years. The wonder and joy I experienced on those Friday nights was a thing confined to the past, memories unthought of, until I visited TFAM's biannual meeting in 2017. That was the only time I have felt those familiar feelings again. At first, I tried to resist, but eventually I gave in, even indulged.

While growing up Pentecostal instilled a sense of wonder, it also brought about a sense of skepticism. Consider the phrase "Don't make it a doctrine." Perhaps puzzling jargon to the outside observer, but for those of us *in* the community, these five words carried a caution. If Pentecostalism is considered, as Harvey Cox has argued, a protest against man-made creeds and the coldness of traditional worship, then these words serve as a careful hermeneutic for interpreting worship beyond the event. Meaning, as my mother would warn, the worship experience itself could become *like* a doctrine, and doctrines are made to be followed. When confronted with the need for doctrine in the church, she would rebut: "Someone with an experience is never at the mercy of someone with an opinion." Here, of course, opinion is synonymous with doctrine or authoritative teaching. The comment exposes her roots in the Oneness movement, a non-Trinitarian sect within Pentecostalism. Given the repetitions that occur in Pentecostal worship, I was raised to be fearful that the novelty of the Spirit, i.e., the capriciousness and capaciousness that proliferates in these Spirited-filled spaces, can be squelched if it becomes too regimented or rehearsed. Or worse, the lack of feeling could be a bigger problem like unconfessed sin or a spiritual sign that something was awry. When things would begin to feel "stale" or "dry" in the collective aura, the preacher or worship leader would cry out to God for a fresh word or outpouring and renewal. The emotional temperature of the worship experience serves as a gauge for and guide through the open-ended service. At any moment, the Spirit could take over, shifting the mood in the room even as it edits the order of worship in real time. Doctrines, as such, are not as flexible and therefore not as useful for the shifting, unpredictable dynamics of Pentecostal worship.

Another aspect of doctrine in Pentecostalism is that it tends to avoid systematic approaches to theology. There is nothing inherently wrong with doctrines, per se, but Pentecostals have a history of defending their practices, such as speaking in tongues, praying for healing, fixating on miracles, etc., against the criticisms of more reformed and formally trained theological traditions. Doctrine, like orthodoxy, has often been used to combat Pentecostals constructing piecemeal theologies through self-taught heuristic hermeneutics. Some Pentecostals established Bible colleges or institutes—usually unaccredited but affiliated with denominations or local churches—for people to seek more formal training using Pentecostal methodologies. Christopher A. Stephenson's *Types of Pentecostal Theology: Method, System, Spirit* is an important critical study of the earliest major theologians of Pentecostalism. In this work, Stephenson, assistant professor of systematic theology at Lee University (a school affiliated with the Pentecostal denomination Church of God [Cleveland, Tennessee]), explores early attempts by theologians—as early as second-generation Pentecostals—to construct and situate Pentecostalism within the field of systematic theology. While he notes the strength of nascent Pentecostal theology, informed by pneumatologically-centered experiences and biblical texts as primary sources, he also identifies five "detrimental" characteristics of it:

> First, it was rarely systematic or comprehensive. . . . Second, most early Pentecostal theologians did not have the benefits of formal academic training. . . . Third, this theology is informed largely by pre-critical interpretations of biblical texts. . . . Fourth, early Pentecostal theologians did not have the philosophical training necessary for thorough theological reflection. . . . Fifth, the theological developments in the wider Christian tradition did not extensively influence Pentecostal theology.[1]

Stephenson's comments reveal some of his presuppositions about what qualifies or legitimizes theological study. For example, Stephenson makes the claim that there is a "pre-critical interpretation" of biblical texts. "Precritical," here, means a refusal to take into account critical biblical and theological scholarship. Of course, no textual or literary scholar can fully escape bias or precritical assumptions or lenses. The detrimental characteristics of Pentecostal theology, according to Stephenson, stem from its inability to ascend to the rigors of philosophy and formal training. Pentecostalism has largely resisted philosophy and formal training, evidenced by Pentecostal theology's imperviousness to the influence of "the wider Christian tradition."

Because of the interplay between emotion, spoken word, texts, and personal reflection, Pentecostalism does not force anyone to choose between learning through embodied forms of knowledge and more philosophical processes of knowing. One does not simply study Pentecostalism, one is enveloped in its cosmology. That it is not systematic does not delegitimize it as a theology or preclude it from theological reflection, even

---

1. Stephenson, *Types of Pentecostal Theology*, 3–4.

though it does separate it from Western categorical distinctions of theology as shaped from Enlightenment understandings of the term. Whereas Western notions of doctrine have largely led to organization or systemization, Pentecostalism is a critique and reversal of the methods of Western theological thought and is usually wary of hyperintellectualized projects. Doctrine and theology are still important parts of the tradition, but there is a deeper reliance on performance; a rhythm, a *perichoresis*, a dance, constitutes a methodology for embracing Pentecostal spirituality. As my mother still contests: "I can't explain it, but I know deep down inside what is true." In this way, Pentecostalism is different in kind from theological approaches found in many other theological traditions. This project attends to this difference in ways that trace the contours of Pentecostal theologizing without reducing it or comparing it to other purportedly more "formal" traditions.

Interestingly, nowhere in Stephenson's book does he mention William Seymour. While the opening sentence names Azusa Street, none of the book considers the theological contributions of Seymour. Neither does he mention any of the sociocultural ramifications of Azusa Street, such as race, new Jerusalem, or Pentecost-as-event. It is clear that Stephenson is only interested in conversing with Pentecostal scholars that meet the threshold of what he considers to be "formal training." One can infer that the claim made by referencing "detrimental" and "negative" characteristics of Pentecostalism is that it is only legitimate insofar as it is consistent with the rigors of academic prowess, something he himself exemplifies. What does he miss with these omissions? One important contribution he misses, as an example, is William Seymour's *The Doctrines and Discipline of the Azusa Street Apostolic Faith Mission of Los Angeles, California*, a theological and ecclesiological treatise full of what the movement believed. In the opening addressed "To the Members of the Apostolic Faith Church," Seymour implores: "We must have sound doctrines in our work."[2] In what follows, Seymour lays out his doctrine with the preface that "The Apostolic Faith stands for the restoration of the faith once delivered to the saints, the old-time religion of camp meetings, revivals, missions, street mission work and Christian unity everywhere."[3] Notably, Seymour's theology had an emphasis on the baptism in the Holy Ghost, which was made evident through

2. It is important to note that Larry Martin edited the book, claiming that Seymour's grammar was so poor that he had to change the work entirely. That is to say, the integrity of the work is not fully intact, but the purported purposes of Martin were to make Seymour's thoughts more understandable. See Seymour, *Doctrines and Discipline*, 27.

3. Seymour, *Doctrines and Discipline*, 37.

such indicators as speaking in tongues and holy sanctified living (through sanctification). This distinction separated Seymour from others who believed that speaking in tongues was the initial, physical evidence of Spirit baptism. Charles Parham, evangelist and preacher who taught Seymour for a time, was another preeminent figure in the advent of Pentecostalism and made this view popular. Parham's theology was greatly hindered by his racism, which, in addition to his critique of emotional worship and caricature of Black worshipers as hypnotists, spiritualists, and animals, caused him to reject Seymour and the revival at Azusa. Returning to Seymour, his work in *The Doctrines and Discipline* cannot be understood as anything other than an attempt to organize and systematize theology with experience. While not appealing to historical Christian thinkers, most of whom were white and male, Seymour appealed instead to the exigencies of his time. As he writes, "God, Word and Spirit go together."[4] Here, we find the underpinning of Seymour's hermeneutics and methodology. The Spirit is the "person" who leads believers through this three-part interrelationship. All to say, Stephenson's exclusion of Seymour in his analysis of Pentecostal theology underrepresents the extent to which Seymour shaped the theologians—and movement—that followed and studied the tradition in more "formal" contexts.

Seymour's hermeneutics offers a unique integration of experience and reflection. Through worship and preaching, the Holy Spirit fills and sanctifies people, which shifts and shapes all aspects of social life. The ways in which bodies are in the world changes, even as their understanding of what it "means" to be in the world does. Ritual theorist Ronald Grimes suggests that religions are "little nourished by disembodied reflection, and it is a mistake to assume that dancing one's religion precludes thinking about it."[5] Grimes is alluding to what is offered in Seymour, namely, that dancing—as the choreography of the body—can produce and facilitate thought. Perhaps dancing, itself, can be thought as a form of "feeling-doing" or "doing-thinking"? Attending to Grimes's assertion, what might it mean for one to find "nourishment" in religious reflection?

An example is necessary. In the Hebrew Bible narrative, God feeds the children of Israel in the desert with manna from heaven. Manna, here, more than miraculous daily bread, is a question: "*Ma'n Hu?*," meaning "What is it?" The nourishment is found in asking the question as much as eating

---

4. Seymour, *Doctrines and Discipline*, 39.
5. Grimes, *Ritual Criticism*, 1.

or consuming the miracle bread. Partaking of the bread is the act, asking the question is the reflection. It is why in Deuteronomy the writer informs that "one does not live by bread alone; but by every word that comes from the mouth of the Lord."[6] Meals and food are a vital and ubiquitous part of social and religious life and feature as a way of connecting the daily needs of people with hunger for more, for meaning, for spiritual food. If religions find little nourishment in disembodied reflection, then Pentecostalism represents a case in point for embodied reflection—bodily-knowing-seeking-understanding, a process that begins *in* the body, informed by the needs and desires of the body, and subsequently moves to contemplation and reflection. Theology, thus, is an embodied exercise, a fleshy practice: "The Word became flesh."

This chapter builds upon what Maia Kotrosits calls "sense-making," a hyphenated phrase which demonstrates how "thinking and feeling are hopelessly interwoven experiences."[7] We may think of the hyphen as a way of bringing together things that are neither fully commensurate nor opposites. The hyphen seeks to bring together seemingly disparate things. In this way, perhaps "Pentecostal-ism" can be imagined as holding the tension of experiential knowing and theoretical, intellectualized, logocentric projects without wholesale accepting or rejecting each other. Kotrosits's notion of sense-making can be extended into the performative register; dancing suggests ecstatic possibilities of Pentecostal-ism and the interpretations of it are anchored in and performed by the body: "To say we 'make sense' of something, for instance, is to accord an intuitive, bodily, and non- or beyond- conscious force to knowing. Knowledge arrives as an 'impression.'"[8] There is a felt (sensate) or registered quality to knowing.[9] Sense-making that does not take into account performance, that does not factor in the corporeal movements, gestures, posturing that occur, is incomplete. "Dancing in the Spirit" means engaging religious experience under the assumption that it is spirit, or the Spirit, that is animating it.

---

6. Deut 8:3.

7. Kotrosits, *Rethinking Early Christian Identity*, 3.

8. Kotrosits, *Rethinking Early Christian Identity*, 4.

9. For Sara Ahmed, "impressions" highlight the contact of material forces—bodies, objects, etc.—that literally "press" upon bodies: "To form an impression might involve acts of perception and cognition as well as emotion. But forming an impression also depends on how objects impress upon us. . . . An impression can be an effect on the subject's feelings; it can be a belief; it can be an imitation or an image; it can be a mark on the surface" (Ahmed, *Cultural Politics of Emotion*, 6).

Theories of affect and ritual studies, in conversation, provide a history and open-ended, multifaceted framework for exploring this endeavor, though neither is self-sufficient for attending to the boisterous potential of Pentecostal worship. In fact, Pentecostal permutations potentially undermine the conventions and traditions of the spiritual practices of Pentecostal worship, itself. The complementarity and adjacency of theories of affect and ritual studies demonstrates the ways in which these theories coalesce, the ways that theory can bend, be inverted, and stretched beyond Cartesian anxiety that renders bodies as bifurcated halves of mind/body. Through their interarticulation, we can theorize via affect and ritual in the interstices of what remains just out of reach of cognition and language, complementing and augmenting other ongoing approaches to Pentecostalism. Some scholars reduce and relegate Pentecostalism to a historical devolution, arguing that it is a return to more primitive forms of religion. Others, especially within theological studies, dismiss it as hyper-sensationalism or superstition. Others, such as anthropologists, use fieldwork and interviews to flesh out key insights and characteristics. Still others try to inject it with philosophy in efforts to legitimize it.[10]

I propose an approach that engages Pentecostalism in all of its gestural, visceral, and corporeal potential, its paradoxical nuances, its messy ecstatic outbursts, ruptures, performances, contradictions. Embracing Pentecostal experiences means accepting that no one methodology can capture, convey, or tame it. This chapter embraces Pentecostalism as a tradition that exists within and without various fields of study, including theological traditions, and lays the scaffolding for the entire project. In what follows, I offer a brief history of the theoretical fields of affect and ritual, respectively, and suggest how each can offer insights and instances that provide a framework for conversation. Finally, I demonstrate how theory captures glimpses of the phenomenon of Pentecostal worship vis-à-vis the ecstatic singing, outbursts, and preaching which is embodied in the performative aesthetics of Blackpentecostalism, which transitions to the next chapter.

Genealogies and Theories of Affect

"Affect theory" does not exist in a singular sense. Rather, there are two main genealogies of affect; and from those two, myriad interpretations, approaches, and applications. In this section, I trace the genealogies of

10. E.g., see Smith, *Thinking in Tongues*, and Castelo, *Pentecostalism*.

affect, distinguish several of their differences, and evince how they enhance Pentecostal epistemologies. The burgeoning field of affect theories is the result of what many have considered "the affective turn," a period in the 1990s when scholars in various fields throughout the human sciences and philosophy began to consider how pre-individual, prelinguistic, and auto-nomic forces shape embodied life. This was accomplished methodologi-cally by considering how political, economic, and cultural transformations are transmuted by forces other than, or in addition to, language, reason, and ideology. However, from the outset, it is important to note there is reticence from many scholars to embrace this language of a shift because, as Ann Cvetkovich and other women scholars have pointed out, work around affect, while not always neatly defined as such, has been engaged by femi-nist, queer, and post-colonial scholars for some time. That is to say, there was work on affect being done before 1995, the year that Brian Massumi's "The Autonomy of Affect" and Eve Kosofsky Sedgwick and Adam Frank's "Shame in the Cybernetic Fold" were published, a reference recognized by many as the advent of the affective turn.

One of the first mentions of affect stems from the work of seven-teenth-century philosopher Baruch Spinoza's work on desire, passion, and emotions. Spinoza, a contemporary of Rene Descartes, was interested in naturalism and the interconnectedness of the universe, which is evident in his espoused "monism," the idea that God is concomitant and co-extensive with all that is, i.e., substance. His work in *Ethics* offers a naturalist account which stands in stark contrast to the work of his contemporary, Rene Des-cartes. In the Spinozan lexicon, affect or *affectus* connotes a body's capacity to affect and be affected. Such is the origin of the first strand of affect I outline here, the strand of affect theory developed by Gilles Deleuze and championed by Brian Massumi.[11] Ironically, the contributions and devel-opment of Spinoza's *affectus* by Deleuze and Massumi are somewhat at odds with Spinoza's own foundational understandings of monism. This departure from Spinoza's understanding is made possible by Deleuze's own reliance upon the work of Henri Bergson: "Within Deleuze's philosophy we can see a tension between relentless monism in Spinoza's work—one that posits continuity between matter and mind, the micro and the macro— and a sophisticated spectral dualism that locates affectivity in a dimension apart from the material."[12] Thus, the theory of affect Massumi propagates at

---

11. I refer to this tradition as the Deleuzian strand of theories of affect.

12. Schaefer, *Evolution of Affect Theory*, 14.

present is greatly shaped by Deleuze's reshaping and argues for a distinction between *affect* as a register of intensity and *emotions* as structured forms available to consciousness. Schaefer concludes:

> It is this register of intensity that Massumi correlates with affect, the pure zone of possibility that forms the background coordinates of experience, but that is in principle undetectable on the register of experience. Intensities—affects—leave traces as emotions as they *escape* bodies, but they can never be known or experienced in and of themselves. . . . Affects are the fully *autonomous* register of becoming.[13]

This strand of affect has currency in the humanities and French philosophy, even as its vocabulary—including the concepts intensity, becoming, excess, the event, and the virtual—are seemingly ubiquitous in contemporary scholarship. The Spinozan (or Deleuzian) tradition of affect offers a conceptual lexicon for thinking about bodies as separate from emotion.

The second broad strand of theories of affect stems from the work of philosopher and psychologist, Silvan Tomkins, who identified nine affects present from birth, the first six in pairs: interest/excitement, enjoyment/joy, surprise/startle, distress/anguish, anger/rage, and fear/terror. The other three are shame/humiliation, dissmell, and disgust.[14] Tomkins's attention to these embedded biological mechanisms emerged from his own marveling at how much information his infant son could communicate. Rather than taking the work of Freud as his point of departure, Tomkins argued that humans have a shared biological heritage with what is classified as emotion in other animals. This was a departure from Freud's notion that two drives—i.e., sex and aggression—motivate all thoughts, emotions, and behavior. Thus, Tomkins's work falls more into a Darwinian lineage than a Freudian framework. While Tomkins offers a rather rigid account of affect and emotion, it is imperative to recall Tomkins's work as foundational but not final. He provides a compelling framework upon which other scholars have elaborated.

In 1995, Eve Kosofsky Sedgwick and Adam Frank published an essay entitled "Shame in the Cybernetic Fold: Reading Silvan Tomkins." It is clear from the outset of this rather playful essay that what attracted them initially was the manner in which Tomkins's work contravenes the stubborn traces

13. Schaefer, *Evolution of Affect Theory*, 16.

14. Tomkins's work evolved over time, but for a general summary of his work with affects, see Tomkins, *Exploring Affect*.

of structuralism. Upon further reading, however, it becomes clearer that the authors are most interested in Tomkins's affect of shame as an entry point to consider bodily knowledge beyond the sedimented moniker "theory," through Tomkins's work on the autonomic nervous system. The *cybernetic fold* is a fold between postmodernist and modernist ways of hypothesizing about the brain and mind, which is to say, psychology. (One should consider the prevalence of Descartes's *cogito* in modern psychology.) Not only does Tomkins offer distinctions among affects, he also notes their irreducibility. What results is a certain queerness between cognitive and affective drives beyond the rigors of "theory." This irreducibility is represented by Sedgwick and Frank's *"finitely many (n>2) values,"* or, endless possibilities for play, freedom, affordance, meaning.[15] Sedgwick and Frank's resurfacing of Tomkins work, and the ways they attend to it in producing a queer framework through the performativity of shame, open wide the door to approach affects in novel ways.

Eve Kosofsky Sedgwick's queer reframing of Tomkins's work also makes possible more comfortable associations and connections between emotion, feeling, and cognition, especially with regard to knowledge. Her greatest contribution to that end is found in her book, *Touching Feeling: Affect, Pedagogy, and Performativity.* This book is an attempt to explore how experiences and reality are not always available in propositional form or language. Insofar as language is performative and *does* things, knowledge and affect can *do* things too. Sedgwick contends that affects can be, and are, attached to many things, including people, things, ideas, institutions, relations, and other affects. Affects attaching to affects facilitate the possibility of being surprised by hope, or disgusted by shame, etc. Further, webs of affects supplant the veneer of bodily autonomy through the compulsion of our "queer little gods." Sedgwick's chapter on the pedagogies of Buddhism is the result of her efforts to cope with her diagnosis of terminal cancer. She asks, "Is it true we can only learn when we are aware we are being taught?"[16] What drew her to Tibetan Buddhism were the "affectively-steeped pedagogical relations" that helped her come to terms with dying—deep ways of knowing she discovered beyond "an eerily thin phenomenological veil of

---

15. Tomkins and Frank are positing an irreducible quality to affect as finitely many (i.e., not unlimited) but more than two. This is to protect analyses of Tomkins's work from being subsumed into singular notions of "theory" (Sedgwick and Frank, "Shame in Cybernetic Fold").

16. Sedgwick and Frank, *Touching Feeling*, 153.

Western 'knowing.'"[17] Sedgwick confronts the epistemological deficiencies in her own life to evince how Western ways of knowing were insufficient to help her cope with the experience of death and dying. What she finds in Tibetan Buddhism is a form of felt pedagogy that is a direct challenge to the norms, assumptions, and empiricism of modern Western knowing. Sedgwick's work on the heterogeneous multiplicities of affect (*n>2, finitely many*) and queering of Tomkins, together with contributions to affect theory from Sara Ahmed and other queer and feminist scholars, have opened what Donovan Schaefer calls the phenomenological affect theory tradition to new avenues of scholarship. Schaefer's notion of phenomenological affect theory is especially based on the work of Sara Ahmed.

Sara Ahmed's work centers on how affect and emotions play out in political life through 1) the constitution of the subject and 2) a play of recursive "impressions" that shape the horizon of feeling. In other words, impressions (literally: "to press upon") shape the self and thus what can occur; they chronicle and catalog what is possible to be sensed, felt, experienced, and known. By engaging cultural constructs and exploring the emotional connections that result from them, Ahmed utilizes the field of phenomenology to substantiate her claims of how the interplay between subjects and objects leaves material traces or sediment, which simultaneously shape the subject and the object. These traces or sediment are the foundations of embedded, embodied histories, sources of subjectivity.

What exactly is the relationship between emotion, bodily sensation, and cognition? In *The Cultural Politics of Emotion*, Ahmed explores this pertinent question by considering what emotions *do*. Her analysis focuses on examples of emotional forces and textures that play a role in politics. For example, by focusing on pain, hate, fear, and love in white nationalism, she argues that bodies take the very shape that impressions make, i.e., bodies become shaped by what comes near, or that to which one comes near. Thus, it is the object of whiteness that draws white supremacists together and unites them against that which ostensibly threatens their beloved whiteness. Hate is what enables their organization with one another and maintains resistance against that which is other. Consequently, other-than-white bodies become the objects of their hate. Consulting the work on emotions by various theorists and scientists—William James, Rene Descartes, Emile Durkheim, as well as Silvan Tomkins and Charles Darwin—she argues that emotions do not simply arise and escape from the inside out, but they can

17. Sedgwick and Frank, *Touching Feeling*, 168.

move from the outside in and even circulate between bodies. The etymology of the word *emotion*, she notes, comes from the Latin *emovere*, connoting movement: "to move, to move out." Further, emotions not only move or circulate between bodies, but they are also sticky. Thus, impressions and attachments are formed by the circulation and stickiness of emotions as well as objects; bodies become stuck in webs of affect and entangled in attachments with objects that leave their traces upon bodily surfaces. The emotions, encounters, memories, and relationships between attachment and movement constitute affective economies. An affective economy is a system in which affects and emotions are the currency—or value—produced, circulated, and consumed. If emotions are the feeling of bodily change as William James argues,[18] and if they are indeed intentional in that they tend to be "about something" and/or "involve a direction or orientation toward an object,"[19] then these affects are the material sediment of feelings accumulating over time. This history and repertoire of feeling becomes a means of shaping subjectivity. No aspect of life—political, religious, or otherwise—is left unmarked by these affective/emotional networks. Bodies, like marionettes, are entangled in and environed by the sticky webs of embodied life.

Ahmed continues her work on the inter-corporeality of emotions, affective objects, and bodies in *Queer Phenomenology: Orientations, Objects, Others*. Once again, she asks a fundamental question: "What does it mean to be oriented?" In short, orientation involves turning—or being turned—toward certain objects. However, turning or being turned toward certain objects means turning or being turned away from others. At its core, her work on orientation is meant to bring queer theory in closer conversation with phenomenology in order to highlight the importance of (sedimented) histories, how they are embodied, lived out, performed:

> Why start with phenomenology? I start *here* because phenomenology makes "orientation" central in the very argument that consciousness is always directed "toward" an object, and given its

18. Here, Ahmed is referring to William James's understanding of emotions.

19. While Ahmed can be categorized as an affect theorist, it would be more appropriate to situate her work in queer and feminist studies on emotion as contributing to theories of affect. In fact, her use of affect is as much Deleuzian as it is from Tomkins. However, since Massumi's reading of Deleuze differentiates between affect and emotion, Ahmed's work on emotions and the visceral corporeality of bodies is more germane for theories of affect in the Tomkins tradition in general and Donovan Schaefer in particular (Ahmed, *Cultural Politics of Emotion*, 17).

emphasis on the lived experience of inhabiting a body, or what
Edmund Husserl calls the "living body" (*Leib*).[20]

A phenomenological model of emotions thus underscores how emotions
are directed toward objects, how bodies come into contact with objects and
others.[21] This relationship is foundational for theories of affect, especially
how power and knowledge are mapped out in and through the body. I will
return to Ahmed in chapter 2 to explore the affective contours of racism.

As previously mentioned, Donovan Schaefer brings together the work
of Sedgwick and Ahmed in what he calls "phenomenological affect theory."
With this phrase, Schaefer is appealing to embodied experiences outside
the productions of language (an aspect of his understanding of phenomenology) and the affects woven within these "textures of experience."[22] The
chief aim of Schaefer in *Religious Affects: Affect, Animality, and Power* is
to consider how religion might be more about the way things feel and the
things that bodies desire or need, rather than solely about books, belief, and
language. Taking this as a point of departure, Schaefer delves into evolutionary biology to suggest that, like moths drawn to an incandescent light,
humans are compelled and impelled by affects—shapes, textures, emotions,
moods that are compulsory and intransigent. Schaefer's newest work, *The
Evolution of Affect Theory*, more clearly establishes his contributions to the
second tradition of affect theory and argues why the first tradition, found
in the Deleuzian repackaging of Spinoza, cannot effectively account for the
concrete mechanisms of power in a Foucauldian sense.

Schaefer argues for a more casual approach to affect that, as he contends,
allows for more interchangeability between affect and emotion, as well as a
"crosscutting of registers" between the preconscious and conscious. Rather
than clear demarcation, there is nuance and vacillation. One problem with
the Deleuzian strand furthered and embellished by Brian Massumi is that,
by clearly differentiating between affect and emotion, it overdetermines
affect such that affectivity is elusive and exists only as the full register of
"becoming." Bodies, consequently, are distanced and estranged from the
felt particularities and dimensions of power and knowledge, limiting their
capacity, as it were, to be affected, which is, ironically, Spinoza's second

20. Sara Ahmed's work on Edmund Husserl's "table" as well as that of Martin Hei-
degger grounds her work in the phenomenological tradition. See Ahmed, *Queer Phenomenology*, 2.

21. Ahmed, *Cultural Politics of Emotion*, 208–9.

22. Schaefer, *Religious Affects*, 8, 28.

principle of affect. Massumi thus relies on a vernacular that downplays the embodied, visceral aspects of affect in favor of such terms as microperceptions, attunement, and becoming—terms that are liminal in meaning and of which the body is unaware. Contra Massumi, as Schaefer's work has evolved, he posits that the issue is no longer whether and how affects exist in the unconscious per se, but how affects "affect" the waterline of consciousness, itself—how it is drawn, including the ways in which it vacillates. For Schaefer, affects prompt one to consider onto-phenomenology: "how it feels to be the kinds of animals we are."[23] Or, as Schaefer asks, "What do affects do?" and "What do we do for affects?" Schaefer argues affect should be understood as the felt emotional textures structuring embodied experience as supplementing, not replacing, language. Affects are intransigent, recalcitrant, and autotelic; they stubbornly follow their own rules. Schaefer is distinctly Darwinian, evidenced in his preference for an evolutionary understanding of religion and affects. For Schaefer, evolutionary exploration and theory of bodies is impossible if affect is autonomous and simply defined as "becoming."

As part of the 2002 American Academy of Religion (AAR) presidential address, Vasudha Narayanan advocated for the decolonization of method and theory in religious studies, i.e., a shift beyond traditional European foci on texts, language, and belief: "charting paths beyond our 'text dominated academy and society where we privilege the word.'"[24] Schaefer, writing in dialogue with this address, attends to the work of feminist philosopher, dancer, and religion scholar, Kimerer L. LaMothe, who offers a set of theoretical possibilities for the intricate relationship between religion, affect, and dance. Schaefer notes:

> LaMothe writes that dance is found in almost all religious traditions and cultures but was neglected in the early years of the discipline of religious studies because it was viewed as an invalid art form that could not adequately express faith—religion was understood as a compendium of words and concepts aimed at transcendence. For LaMothe, not only must we attend to dance within religious studies, religion itself is best understood as a dance—a dynamic interplay between bodies and worlds compelled by

23. Schaefer, *Religious Affects*, 51. The issue of animality and race, especially blackness, is gaining more attention. See, e.g., Bennett, *Being Property Once Myself*; Jackson, *Becoming Human*; Boisseron, *Afro-Dog*; Kim, *Dangerous Crossings*; Chen, *Animacies*.

24. Vasudha Narayanan, "Embodied Cosmologies," 499; quoted in Schaefer, *Religious Affects*, 189.

affects. . . . Because religion, for LaMothe, is more than linguistic, it cannot always be translated into signification. Religion must be reconceived "as a kind of dance—as rhythmic bodily movement enacting a logic of bodily becoming *and* a cultural spiral of discovery and response."[25]

Studying religion, for LaMothe, means studying the body, or dancing a dance. She does not discount the linguistic components of religion; rather, she underscores how dance evidences bodily movement vis-à-vis meaning, or how dancing may be considered as meaning in motion. Dance involves movement, which, following Friedrich Nietzsche, LaMothe contends is *sui generis* a language of embodiment.

Dancing as movement taps into a specific time and place, creating a network of relationships, building attachments (Sedgwick), leaving traces and impressions (Ahmed), and sedimenting histories (Schaefer) that are embodied, which is to say, alive. Through dance, bodies interact and sensually engage with the world and find themselves and their place within it. Religion, itself, includes dance and functions like a dance, "a dynamic interplay between bodies and worlds compelled by affects." Dance is both conscious and unconscious; its movement is evasive and pervasive. It connects bodies to religious histories, practices, and affective technologies. Analogously, religions are constituted by patterns of this bodily movement. Another etymology for the word *religion* is *re-ligare*, i.e., *re* "again" and *ligare* "to connect or join," yielding "to reconnect," an interpretation made prominent by St. Augustine. Dance provides connective tissue, rejoining by virtue of its histories, practices, and affective technologies.

Dancing occasions movement that brings about an ordering; a cosmology is created. Returning to my anecdote at the beginning of this chapter, I concur with LaMothe that dance serves as an important metaphor, a vital example of what religion means and what it does, and a form of embodied and bodily knowledge. Whereas many theorists and scholars of religion have historically discounted dance as inadequate or insufficient to express religion, LaMothe uses dance to unlock the affective and ritualistic components of religion that, linguistically and cognitively, conceptually and kinesthetically, constitute an ensemble of embodied processes. One dances religion into meaning: "The dancer dances her worship in the temple, creates

25. Kimerer L. LaMothe, *Between Dancing and Writing*, 242 (emphasis added); quoted in Schaefer, *Religious Affects*, 189.

the temple within her body, and dances the temple in her performance."[26] There is a Trinitarian flow and relation to her cosmology—and the word *perichoresis* in Greek, means rotation—read: dance—and is used to describe the relationship between the three persons of the Godhead. Dance animates, rotates, and keeps moving, spinning webs of interconnectedness to the point of indistinguishableness, of indistinction, to the point where the lines between dancer, dance, and temple blur. Dance, as movement, is feeling in motion, feeling on display. It is learned and performed, even mastered. It is the subject of analysis from varying fields across the arts and humanities because it not only has meaning but is action. Something happens when one dances. It connotes more than words can convey. While theories of affect prompt one to consider forms of religion *as* dance, ritual also provides insights for how considering the connection between religion and dance and religion as dance.

Contributions from theories of affect can be applied to theological studies as much as religious studies. In a similar fashion to the way that Maia Kotrosits has argued for an affective understanding of early Christian identity through sense-making, I engage affect theories to engage the emotionally dense world of Pentecostal worship. I will largely remain within the genealogy of Tomkins, Sedgwick, Ahmed, Schaefer et al., but there are certain aspects of the Deleuzian strand that will at times prove useful. One thing that theories of affect lack, however, is a framework to think about social organization and change from symbolic and systemic perspectives. For example, affects account for emotional encounters and the shaping of bodies in particular ways, but how are social and religious processes themselves shaped by the repetition of bodily actions? Pentecostal worship is affective ritual, embodied feelings that vacillate within elastic forms. Thus, I contend that affect needs ritual in order to ponder how acts and affects have the potential to shape individual and collective life in practice, to bring about transformation and change, to dance the dance of liberation.

A History of Ritual Studies

Ritual, as a concept and field of study, is elusive; there are as many definitions and theories as contexts for them. The study of ritual spans the fields of anthropology and social sciences, as well as theology (liturgical) and

26. Narayanan, "Embodied Cosmologies," 508; quoted in Schaefer, *Religious Affects*, 192.

religion. Some ritual scholars, such as Tom Driver, argue that the difficulty defining ritual is precisely because ritual's meaning is not fixed. He notes that ritual—political, religious, social—is inevitable. Others, such as Catherine Bell, posit that ritual—as experience and analysis—is an interdisciplinary conversation. She notes that the term *ritual* was meant to replace the terms *magic* and *liturgy*, which were hierarchically deployed to distinguish between low and high forms of religion, i.e., differentiate between primitive superstition—*our* religion from *theirs*. Yet, to name ritual as a conversation perhaps does not fully capture the degree to which ritual functions as an action; it *does* rather than means, which is evidenced through learned and repeated bodily gestures, performance and observation, and the manipulation and circulation of objects. Still others, such as Ronald Grimes, whom I will focus on in this section, contend that ritual has gone through three stages: from questions of origin (early twentieth century); to questions of function—what it *does*, rather than what it *means*—in the anthropological studies of European and American anthropologists, who gathered their information (observations) from colonists, missionaries, and adventurers, typically in non-Western contexts; to a shift occasioned by the dissatisfaction with ritual theories that led toward more of a practice—and eventually performance—model.[27] Developing his work in dialogue with Victor Turner, Grimes distinguishes between rite, ritual, and ritualization and contributes sixteen different categories of rites.

We may say, provisionally, that ritual has many languages—only one of which is verbal. This does not mean that ritual rejects the conventions and interventions of language wholesale, only that it does not require spoken language for communication. Noting ritual's nonverbal dynamics highlights the embodied aspects of ritualizing, drawing attention to the body as a site of analysis. The body is ritualized through the circular production of rites whereby ritual, as practice and structure, becomes embedded in the dynamics of individual and collective bodies. The relationship between practice and structure invites individuals to participate in a larger collective, even as the collective is comprised of and constituted by individual participants. In fact, many scholars have linked ritual, or ritualization, to the sociocultural realm, including George Lakoff, Michel Foucault, Pierre Bourdieu, et al. Underscoring how ritual is an act and phenomenon rooted in the primacy of the body underscores the affective contours of ritualizing.

---

27. For more reading on the phases of ritual, including the current conversation vis-à-vis media, see Grimes, *Ritual, Media, and Conflict*.

I now turn to ritual studies as analogous and complementary to theories of affect insofar as it is interested in the ways that bodies are impelled by forces other than language and reason and organizes social and religious life.

Ronald Grimes is largely responsible for the third and most recent turn in ritual studies, from theory-based to more practice-based approaches, a shift away from disembodied theoretical inquiries toward theories of/with/in bodily practices. In *The Craft of Ritual Knowledge*, he critiques reductionist accounts of ritual vis-à-vis theory by appealing to the etymology of the word:

> Who owns the word theory? "In theory" is the opposite of "in reality . . . " In ancient Greek, *theorein* means "to look at." *Theoria* is what an audience does when it allows itself to be drawn into rapt identification with deeds transpiring onstage. *Theoria* is what happens when spectatorship is transformed into visual and emotional participation.[28]

Grimes contends that ritual and theory are "torqued" into an overdrawn dualism, whereby: "Ritualizing is collective and bodily; theorizing is individualistic and disembodied, a captive of the academic ivory tower. Ritualizing is something ordinary people do; theorizing is something the educated do, or, worse, a cover-up for doing nothing at all."[29] The proposition of "theorizing" over and against ritualizing is similar to Stephenson's tone about many Pentecostals' lack of "formal training," though the values assigned to the terms are not identical. Theory, in the context of Grimes's work on ritual, flattens-out and bifurcates and is precipitated by reduction. Knowledge is reduced to a single sense, visualism, an epistemological bias that privileges and prioritizes what is seen over other senses. Partnered with another related bias, logocentrism, i.e., word-centeredness, the reduction is strengthened. What is left out, thus, is how other senses inform experience and shape subjectivity—the embodied contours of what is and can be known. It is hardly possible for an onlooker to do more than speculate about how ritualizing affects the participant. Yet, at its inception, ritual "theory" attempted to do exactly that through ethnography and field notes, displacing its objects of study as a result. Returning to the Greek notion of *theoria*, one observes that the word connotes a transformation or drawing-deeper into the senses; spectators become invested, engaged, and find themselves participating, either emotionally or physically. It should come

28. Grimes, *Craft of Ritual Studies*, 165–66.
29. Grimes, *Craft of Ritual Studies*, 167.

as no surprise, then, that some scholars, such as Richard Schechner, Victor Turner, et al., connect ritual to the realm of theater, where mythologies and social dramas are acted out on stage. (While this is outside my interest in positioning theories of affect and ritual studies in conversation with Pentecostalism, notions of performance will feature at times in this analysis, particularly with regard to Blackpentecostal performance.)

A pressing question emerges from Grimes's work: When and how should one reflect on ritual? If, as Tom Driver has argued elsewhere, ritual is inevitable—meaning, one longs for it—then how does one think or talk or find meaning in it? Grimes suggests that "religions are little nourished by disembodied reflection, and it is a mistake to assume that dancing one's religion precludes thinking about it."[30] If dancing and thinking are not hierarchized, but rather complementary and consonant epistemological methods, how might reflections on ritual be representative of more bodily ways of knowing? First, it must be acknowledged that, "Regardless of how we imagine theory, we do not escape metaphor."[31] Metaphor comes from the Greek *metapherein*, meaning "to transfer." Thus, no matter how one thinks of ritual or one's religion, one will never cease from dancing it. Insofar as Western theories are largely constituted by words, "theorizing, especially in the arts, is an act that is implicitly metaphoric, tacitly narrative, and peculiarly imaginative."[32] Consonant with LaMothe's appeal to religion as dance and dancing as a gateway to religious knowing, metaphor connotes movement—to transfer is to carry over or move from one place to another. Ritual and metaphor, vis-à-vis Grimes, coalesce with LaMothe's invitation to consider dance as one tool of many in a theoretical toolbelt and offers a case in point for how affect and ritual interarticulate and function together as an interdisciplinary methodology.

Academic approaches to ritual have by and large privileged and wed themselves to the word through logocentrism and to sight via visualism, Grimes contends. Moving beyond these limitations of linguistic-laden approaches suggests embracing metaphor while at the same time confessing that the most rooted metaphors resist translation or reduction. Grimes offers the example of the Eucharist, which at once declares "this is my body" and "this is *not* my body." What is left is mystery, meaning that lingers but is never rigidly defined, at least not exclusively in words. The meaning

---

30. Grimes, *Ritual Criticism*, 1.

31. Grimes, *Craft of Ritual Studies*, 173.

32. Grimes, *Craft of Ritual Studies*, 176.

transcends the words "This is my body," for the one pronouncing the words of institution is doing so vicariously, i.e., metaphorically. What is experienced cannot be fully explained, only mysteriously consumed. The dance continues. What is spoken is mystery and metaphor, but no less real or true. Grimes also likens efforts to define ritual as tantamount to defining jazz. Answers to "What is jazz?" largely depend on the context and the expression of the musician. Diverging styles, preferences, and eras of jazz provide disparate answers. For example, Glenn Miller, American big band trombonist, arranger, composer, and bandleader in the swing era, notes that jazz is "something you have to feel; a sensation that can be conveyed to others." Jazz pianist Jess Stacy likens jazz to "syncopated syncopation." Pianist, vocalist, composer, and bandleader Terry Shand adds that jazz is "a synthetic cooperation of two or more instruments helping along or giving feeling to the soloist performing." Finally, Louis Armstrong notes jazz is "my idea of how a tune should go."[33] Each of these definitions makes clear that the meaning of jazz is not fixed but varies. It is something that is felt and heard, something dynamic, something improvised.

While there are structures and forms in terms of musical chord progressions and jazz standards, they are loose enough to allow elaborations and improvisations which shape the soundscape by their making. Likening ritual to jazz affirms Driver's idea that "ritualizations do not start from nothing. They are elaborations upon simpler behaviors already known."[34] Framing ritual in this way allows for unencumbered riffing and expressive interplay between individuals and collectives even as it is organized by the familiar tones and recognizable forms. It is imperative to address the historical milieu and crucible out of which jazz emerged, that is, the spirituals and slave songs. Without the contributions of African music, jazz would not exist. Neither would other forms of music influenced by jazz. Parenthetically, I will speak to the history of the spirituals and their contributions to Pentecostal worship at a later point; but for now, suffice to say that comparing ritual and jazz uncovers a shared, racialized history.

One final contribution of Grimes to ritual studies is the notion of ritual criticism. At first these two words may seem oddly paired, even paradoxical, but fidelity and criticality are not opposites. Critiquing something means holding it accountable to standards—queries intended to refine it. Criticism, literally, "to judge," does not have to carry a negative timbre.

33. Grimes, *Craft of Ritual Studies*, 186.
34. Driver, *Liberating Rites*, 19.

In fact, it can be more nuanced and neutral. Grimes aptly defines ritual criticism as "the interpretation of a rite or ritual system with a view to implicating its practice. Because ritual criticism is itself a practice, it implies a politics and an ethic, as well as an aesthetic or poetics."[35] For Grimes, the word *practice* implies not perfection, but imperfection. It implies trial and error, acknowledging that sometimes rituals "fail." Further, practice connotes a heuristic process that learns as it does and does what it learns. Practice, vis-à-vis ritual, is akin to what theologian Ted Jennings refers to as *ritual action*, which "is a means by which its participants discover who they are in the world and 'how it is' with the world."[36] Ritual action yields *ritual knowledge*, which, combined with ritual action, "alters the world or the place of the ritual participant in the world."[37] Self-reflexivity comes to the forefront of ritual criticism insofar as it causes ritual participants to become aware of themselves and their place in the world (orientation).

Another word to describe this phenomenon is *performance*. Performance, like practice, is a language that primarily *does* to create or communicate meaning. It is an action verb. Grimes notes that ritual and performance coalesce and culminate in postmodernism, a rupture and departure from modern notions of ritual that center upon narrative and disembodied, objectifying observations. This departure is characterized by sociocultural and epistemic shifts, as well as the end of humanism and anthropocentric privileging. Ritual criticism makes possible a future of theorizing beyond the constraints of the modern era toward postmodern practices rich in metaphor, criticism, practice, performance, and generative reflexivity.

With an eye toward ritual as practice and performance, I now shift the question to that of ritual outcomes. Can rituals be liberative or restrictive? Catherine Bell's work on ritual uncovers a tension, namely, the different perspectives between theological and social science approaches: 1) mystifying ritual (theological perspective) versus 2) seeing mystification as essential to what ritual *does* (social science perspective).[38] This tension is no less pronounced or present in participants than it is for observers. Does this tension propose an impasse? On the contrary, it is possible to embrace the mystic nature of ritual through performance and critique its practices

35. Grimes, *Ritual Criticism*, 13.

36. T. Jennings, "On Ritual Knowledge," 113.

37. T. Jennings, "On Ritual Knowledge," 115.

38. These examples, regarding Bell, are meant to generalize but not essentialize these approaches.

and outcomes without creating objects—or texts—out of the participants. Undoubtedly, questions of authenticity, accessibility, and authority arise; which is to say, who gets to critique and participate, and by whose authority can they do so?

Tom F. Driver's work on ritual offers a lens to consider ritual outcomes as liberative. In *Liberating Rites: Understanding the Transformative Power of Ritual*, Driver speaks to the longing for ritual, such that "our longing for ritual and our longing for freedom may come together."[39] Thus, because of the ubiquity of ritual, that it exists always and everywhere in political and religious forms, Driver contends that it is not a question of *whether* to ritualize, but when, how, where, and why. If this premise is accepted, even provisionally, then one can concur with Driver that the health or disease of rituals affects everyone. Anthropologists have for a considerable time discussed the prevalence of rituals and their inseparable relationship to social processes, including how ritual is foundational to the ways life is lived and shaped by the interaction of living creatures. It is one quotidian vehicle by which life unfolds, even as organization and processes emerge. But, of course, ritual is not exempt from epistemological prejudice: "The liberal theological world has partaken of the same Enlightenment bias, while Protestantism inherited a Puritan suspicion of rituals as pagan, idolatrous, and popish."[40] Catherine Bell has pointed out that *ritual* was meant to replace words that constituted a hierarchized binary, such as *liturgy* and *magic*; the latter is a pejorative that has been deployed since the Enlightenment and meant to distinguish between high and low forms of religious practices, i.e., high religion versus primitive superstition. Historical bias against ritual, according to Driver, has resulted in a largely ritually deficient, impoverished Western world. Yet and still, Driver argues that ritual has the power to transform, to liberate, to bring wholeness.

Is Driver's thesis that ritual has the power to transform actually liberating? If the terms of liberation and transformation are qualified, yes. It is more accurate to think of Driver's notion of liberation in terms of social change, while transformation is more of a transition or integration of individuals into community (i.e., wholeness). Driver asserts at length:

> From a purely theoretical point of view, if that [ritual assisting the dynamic of social change through ritual processes of transformation] were possible or desirable to achieve, it would be an open

39. Driver, *Liberating Rites*, 4.
40. Driver, *Liberating Rites*, 9.

question whether rituals should be thought of first as instruments of order that happen to enhance communal bonds and to facilitate various kinds of transformation; or primarily as community-making events that incidentally generate order and transform it; or first of all as techniques of transformation that help to order life and deepen communal relationships. Theory, however, is always affected by a thinker's social orientation and ideology. In my own case, although I belong to the privileged gender (male) and race (white) in North American middle class, my theory is that ritual is best understood from a vantage point created by a "preferential option for the poor." That is to say, we cannot well appreciate the power of ritual unless we see its usefulness to those in need, especially those who, having little social power and, being the victims of injustice, have a need for the social structure to be transformed.[41]

Driver casts doubt on the likelihood of theoretical certainty but offers three different modalities of how ritual—through rites—functions. Here Driver is suggesting that ritual's meaning, or, rather, what it is does and is capable of doing, depends on the context from which it is practiced; both the context of the actor or practitioner and the conditions of the practice are determining factors.

Driver's awareness of his own social location is an important determinant in the construction of his own theory of ritual, which thusly informs how he believes ritual should function (i.e., from the vantage point of the poor, marginalized, and those without social power). As a result, Driver's notion of ritual as the means of community-building and the transformation of social structures are informed out of necessity and concern for those that need it most. In conversation with Thomas Peterson, Driver reminds that the "meaning of ritual is never fixed and is always shifting because its meaning comes from its use."[42] In other words, rituals are dynamic—they grow as the ritualizer grows. The conditions are directives for how, why, when, and where rituals occur. Because rituals are always shifting, they resist the reductive tendencies of theory and accumulate meaning, power, and efficacy.

Ritual shifting, or adaptation, is part and parcel of ritual itself. In fact, the word *ritual* has evolved since first mentioned. Ritual first appears in English in 1570. As postcolonialist scholar Talal Asad has shown, the word

41. Driver, *Liberating Rites*, 166.
42. Driver, *Liberating Rites*, 187.

originally appeared in the *Encyclopaedia Britannica* and connoted a script or book to be followed in directing a worship service (i.e., the Book of Common Prayer). However, he notes that the word is not used after 1852, until it reemerges in 1910, by which time the meaning had completely changed. No longer did ritual signify a script, it was now a practice, religious or nonreligious, that relied on symbols and actions in relation to the social world. Another example, offered by Driver, is Monica Wilson's work on the Anglican Book of Common Prayer's Preface:

> It is a most invaluable part of that blessed "liberty wherewith Christ has made us free," that in his worship different forms and usages may without offense be allowed, provided the substance of the Faith be kept entire; and that, in every Church, what cannot be clearly determined to belong to the Doctrine must be referred to Discipline; and therefore, by common consent and authority, may be altered, abridged, enlarged, amended, or otherwise disposed of, as may seem most convenient for the edification of the people, 'according to the various exigencies of times and occasions.'[43]

Wilson's example underscores the relationship between scripts, prompts, and customaries and the need to change these structures due to the exigencies of time. Meaning: what someone experiences and their context may alter what one needs; and ritual is (ostensibly) a way of tending to these needs. Efforts to concretize rituals, to write or script them in efforts to make them changeless or ageless are futile; to do so, Driver suggests, is a violation of their nature. Said differently, as a form of "doing-knowledge" (T. Jennings), ritual, as both a means to transmit and a means to discover knowledge, does not remain something static but changes as it discovers new knowledge. Thus, ritual can be imagined as something rehearsed, something performed—acts by which "people confront one kind of power with another and rehearse their own future."[44] Confronting and rehearsing illustrate the performative contours of ritual and appeal to a word that buzzes and teems with controversy: magic.

I would be remiss to engage Driver's work on transformation without attending to how he employs magic in his analysis, for it is essential to what he argues ritual does. While Western intellectuals have since the Enlightenment regarded magic as superstition—and paganism for

---

43. Monica Hunter (Miller), "The Wedding Cake: A Study of Ritual Change"; quoted in Driver, *Liberating Rites*, 186.

44. T. Jennings, quoted in Driver, *Liberating Rites*, 188.

theologians—Driver teases that "one person's 'magic' is another person's 'religion.'"[45] In other words, "magic" is not a pejorative, but an integral aspect of ritual life. The binary of magic and science, for Driver, is problematized by empirical bases, such as herbal cures practiced and transmitted ritually. Therefore, it is this vision, that magic is how the world is ritually ordered, which enables transformative action. Arnold Van Gennep uses the term *magico-religious*, which is meant to highlight how religion cannot be religion without performance. Driver concludes:

> The aim of religion is not simply intellectual understanding; it is also, and primarily, transformative action, for which the principal technique is 'ceremonies, rites, and services.' Ritual-making may not be a religion's first or last word but is surely its most essential. A religion is a *praxis*, a certain way of acting or attempting to act in the world, and this is established through a certain way of acting ritually.[46]

Grimes agrees: "The force of magic lies in its use of desire as a contributing factor in causing hoped-for results."[47] Hope is not optimism, but something that has to be acted upon. Magic, or the spirit of ritual, is the currency for possibility.

Driver continues: "Religion is not about the elimination of desire but its *transformation* from lower to higher forms—the transformation of the suffering world into one more compassionate, loving, and just."[48] But is it not true that ritual also has the power (or magic) to do the opposite: to create more suffering through coercion and control? More than function versus dysfunction, transformation is not always about liberation or ascending to higher levels of care and concern. To assume so is to buy into the very Western Enlightenment bias that Driver critiques, i.e., notions of progress that are steeped in capitalistic colonial conquests and logics. Western teleology purports and asserts that society, like time, is going somewhere. However, there are many who live their lives in different ecologies and cosmologies that are governed instead by cycles and patterns. Of course, Driver's theory of ritual offers a vantage point centered on a "preferential option for the poor," but caution must be exercised when using the same tools and toolbox by which one becomes poor in the first place. We must,

---

45. Driver, *Liberating Rites*, 167.

46. Driver, *Liberating Rites*, 169.

47. Grimes, *Beginnings in Ritual Studies*, 46; quoted in Driver, *Liberating Rites*, 175.

48. Driver, *Liberating Rites*, 172.

therefore, widen our vantage point from considering "the poor" to making room for other epistemological tools and sources that are often excluded from analyses. This, I contend, would draw the circle wider, making the field more inclusive and representative of everyone, and thus be a transformation in and of itself.

Malidoma Patrice Somé offers perspective away from the Western gaze of many of the aforementioned scholars and considers how ritual plays an integral role in the balance between power, healing, and community. However, ritual has been degraded in modernity under the auspices of progress: "The hurt that a person feels in the midst of this modern culture should be taken as a language spoken by the body. . . . Our soul communicates things to us that the body translates as need, or want, or absence. So we enter ritual in order to respond to the call of the soul."[49] Social life and responsibilities are bound up with/in ritual through what Somé refers to as the "call of the soul," which is characteristic of one's deepest longings. These longings are irrevocably interconnected with the well-being of a given community. The language of the soul is emotion and sensation, insofar as they are what compel, propel, and precipitate ritual action. Thus ritual "must be constantly invoked as an opportunity for the weak to become strong and the strong to get even stronger."[50] Community is the locus whereby ritual is defined, sharpened, and performed/lived out.

Ritual, for its part, is a "spirit-based" activity performed by humans through the practice of invoking the Spirit and spirits. Many scholars of ritual speak of ritual as a process or action that transmits and receives a special kind of knowledge, but Somé's contributions are unique in that they connect ritual with the soul or spirit world. In fact, the connection to the spirit realm is what makes ritual possible. Rather than magic, Somé presents a pneumatology that imbues everyday life: "So Spirit is our channel through which every gap in life can be filled. But the spirit realm does not take care of these gaps without our conscious participation. Thus our collaboration makes us central to the actual happening of ritual."[51] The spirit realm fills the gaps of life but it cannot bring healing, wholeness, or transformation without collaboration. It seems there is mutual dependence between the community and the invocation of the spirits. Ritual is the vehicle for spiritual invocation and communal change.

49. Somé, *Ritual*, 25.

50. Driver, *Liberating Rites*, 52.

51. Driver, *Liberating Rites*, 33.

If ritual is that which binds communities together, as a sense of knowing and doing that repairs and fills in the gaps of life, then we can say that ritual is co-creative; it is future-making. For Somé it is also anti-machine, the antithesis of the rapid rhythms of industrial life. Somé is unapologetic in his critique of Western progressivism and the colonial accoutrements of corporatization and globalization. Ritual disrupts and subverts such power structures and uproots the dysfunction that they cause. To Somé, the problem with the world is the misuse of overt power, i.e., power over others: "It is the action of those in power that produces the poor, the menial worker, the man and woman in debt and the homeless."[52] The conditions occasioned by this power-over-others erases those it exploits even as it highlights the person (or persons) in power. Conversely,

> The power that is felt, entertained, nourished and kept alive from within through ritual has a much different effect on a person who may be a victim of overt power. This kind of power is what many people in the West seek avidly, and, in most cases, unsuccessfully. It is spiritual power, a power that is invisible, and yet whose presence can be felt in terms of gentleness, love and compassion.[53]

It is in the ritual space that transmission occurs, where power is felt, released, and accompanies the person wherever they go. As what Somé calls a "Presence of Power," this force is not a presence to the eye (visible), but to the psyche (invisible). That the Presence of Power is invisible does not relegate it to the domain of less real or immaterial; on the contrary, this invisible force is what shapes what is possible in the realm of the visible. Its effects become visible. This empowerment, or ritual energy, is what sanctifies lives and life through the ongoing uprootal of dysfunction and invocation of the spirit, sparking the process of intervention into community affairs. The Spirit partners with humans through ritual to bring healing to the pains and vicissitudes of life as well as balance to the life of the community.

Somé concludes: "To ritualize life, we need to learn how to invoke the spirits or things spiritual into our ceremonies. This means being able to pray out loud, alone. Invocation suggests that we accept the fact that we ourselves don't know how to make things happen the way they should. And thus we seek strength from the spirits or Spirit by recognizing and embracing our weakness."[54] Rather than the "boring" liturgical ceremonies

52. Somé, *Ritual*, 41.

53. Somé, *Ritual*, 42.

54. Somé, *Ritual*, 97.

of the West, Somé invites a return to more primordial forms of ritual life, energized by the Spirit and spirits that animate this life. There is a certain rhythm felt between ritual gatherings and daily life, similar to what mystic-poetic theologian Howard Thurman calls a "systolic/diastolic rhythm."[55] By systolic/diastolic rhythm, Thurman is speaking to a cadence of religious life constitutive of worship gatherings (systolic) and daily life (diastolic), respectively. This rhythm, he reflects, is the stimulus for social change. The spirited forces that ritualize life for Somé offer balance and rhythm—ways to navigate social relationships and responsibilities, to expose incommensurability and inequity, and to empower human agents to bring about the appropriate changes. This is the power and potential of ritual life, of ritualized life. Somé's work on ritual life offers a paradigm to imagine ritual life as a spirit-filled life, fertile ground for segueing to how Pentecostalism, itself, is a synthesis of spirit into daily life through invocation of the Spirit (worship).

Affect, Ritual, and Pentecostal Worship

"I agree with you, but where is spirit in all of this?" A most gentle and generative critique, this question was posed to me by a dear friend and interlocutor. It was a time in which I was fully submerged in the theoretical world of affect, a world that seemed to make sense by accentuating the sensory contours of religious experience. The prevalence and privileging of the head over body, i.e., Cartesian dualism, in theology as well as philosophy, was obvious, even redundant to me. I began reading to find a theoretical field that would not only include the body but give it credence as a site of analysis. I found plenty of materiality and embodiment in theories of affect; but as a theological studies student, there is not much spirit or spiritual analysis to be found. There are lots of approaches to "religion," but most approaches to Christianity have been limited to sacred texts. There is no literature about affect and worship, at least not in the traditions of Spinoza or Tomkins. Eventually, I gave up and turned to ritual as a potential conversation partner, where the brilliance of various scholars once again highlighted the felt dimensions of religious life (ritual) as it is experienced in and through the body. But yet again, ironically, there was not much spirit to be found. To be honest, many theological traditions themselves have little to say about spirit or Spirit. Historically, the Western church did not

55. Thurman, *With Head and Heart*, 144.

center the Spirit like its Eastern counterparts. The Nicene Creed relegates the Holy Spirit to the third person, descending from both the Father and the Son. And yet, the recent emergence of the "spiritual, but not religious" demographic might indicate that what people are missing in their traditions is the Spirit. It may also indicate why global Pentecostalism is the fastest growing part of Christianity. Perhaps a robust pneumatology would lift an anemic, declining tradition.

My experience at TFAM's biannual gathering was the instant that this began to make sense, and it did so deeply in my being. It was something realized beyond the head, beyond the heart, and further still. Perhaps it is a place beyond the bone and marrow of bodies, a place where only spirit is, where only spirit remains—as breath, as that which gives and sustains life. It is from this place that this project was born. While the existence of a soul or spirit cannot be proven, spirit as breath, as inspiration (literally inspire, i.e., breathe into or blow), is the foundation of all life. This breath is the breath of God and that which animates life, and spirituality is a way of seeking to be attuned to that breath. The Hebrew notion of *ruach* is embodied. It is not sufficient to theorize, to "look at" embodied experience; this section seeks to bring full synthesis by considering spirit through spirit-filled-and-spirited Pentecostal worship through theories of affect and ritual.

Theories of affect and ritual studies share something in common: they both highlight the role that the body plays in making sense of, and creating meaning from, embodied experience. Theories of affect focus on how non- and prelinguistic feelings, moods, emotions, and textures inform embodied life, while ritual studies emphasize how rites are observed, performed, and interpreted through the processes of ritualization. Yet they both also observe as part of their methodologies—watching, noting, and theorizing—like outsiders peering into the windows of others' lives. As a result, one of the challenges of each is—as it is with affect in Schaefer, so it is with ritual in Grimes—that they often rely on the same text-based theoretical projects they critique. The problem is: they cannot seem to go beyond their own intellectualized inquiries. Granted, not all projects are equal. And while Driver contends that "if we did not ritualize, we would not speak,"[56] eventually, speak we must. Perhaps this is why each scholar adeptly appeals in their own ways to the arts through forms of performance such as music and dance; that without these forms, there would be nothing to *say*. However, through their interarticulation, the complementarity of the two provides a

56. Driver, *Liberating Rites*, 13.

spacious repertoire that will be further widened in this section. Returning to my proposition for this chapter, I move to consider how theories of affect and ritual studies, joined with Pentecostal worship, form a bricolage, and more specifically, how a triptych in which "feeling, doing, thinking" all appear constitutes a whole.

The power of music and dance is evidenced in their ubiquity. The Reverend Clarence Rufus J. Rivers asserts that "music, like its other self, poetry, seems capable of doing what plain rational words cannot do: namely, to express the inexpressible, to touch hearts, to penetrate souls, create an experience of things that cannot be reasoned. That is why we sing happy birthday instead of simply reciting it. This is why our ideals are frequently expressed in rhythmic chants, e.g., at football games and political rallies or demonstrations."[57] Choreographer and dancer Martha Graham offers: "Dance is the hidden language of the soul, of the body."[58] Anyone who has been moved to tears through music, or watched dancers majestically and gracefully move in sync from bodily memory, can attest to the power of music and dance to move us, emotionally and physically. How exactly one connects the senses to the spirit—or soul—and vice versa is no easy task to document. Yet, the present undertaking, with assistance from the inter-articulation of affect theories and ritual studies, seeks to do precisely that: to give voice and interpretative legitimacy to the intrinsic, native bodily languages such as music and dance.

In *Fire from Heaven: The Rise of Pentecostal Spirituality and the Reshaping of Religion in the Twenty-First Century*, Harvey Cox traces a history of Pentecostalism in the US, as well as reflects on his experiences visiting different churches as he engrossed himself in the culture of Pentecostal churches. He names what he considers a pattern characteristic of Pentecostal churches: "high-amperage music, voluble praise, bodily movement including clapping and swaying, personal testimonies, sometimes prayers 'in the spirit,' a sermon full of stories and anecdotes, announcements, lots of humorous banter, a period of intense prayers for healing, and a parting song."[59] What he discovered was that "the imagery, mood, and tempo of a religious service were not just add-ons. They are not superfluous. Human beings are physical as well as mental creatures, and therefore these more

---

57. Rivers, *Soulful Worship*, 39.
58. Graham, "Martha Graham Reflects."
59. Cox, *Fire from Heaven*, 6.

tactile elements are part of the substance of worship."[60] The "substance of worship" speaks to an ambience, a material feeling that envelops and environs the gathered congregants in a dynamic ebb and flow of mood, tempo (rhythm), and imagery, which is to say, an affective economy. Teresa Brennan, author of *The Transmission of Affect*, references the moment a body walks into a room and "feels the atmosphere," a feeling not only observational, but transformative. In fact, what Brennan refers to as the transmission of affect (TOA) "alters the biochemistry and neurology of the subject"[61] materially, which alters and reshapes the embodied wirings of bodies. Spaces that gather bodies, such as Pentecostal sanctuaries, are shaped by what happens in the space—the repetitions, refrains, and reprises of sounds, feelings, moods, histories, and experiences. Thus, when Cox mentions "affective traces" as "feelings of joy, terror, awe, mystery, and well-being"[62] that have lingered with him long after his time attending Pentecostal churches, he is speaking to the impressions (Ahmed) left on and in his body from the experiences.

That Pentecostalism is constitutive of experiential modalities, however, does not preclude it from serious theological reflection or formation. On the contrary, in contradistinction to Fundamentalists who attach unique and total authority to "the letter of the verbally inspired Scripture" (what Cox calls "text-oriented believers"[63]), "those [beliefs] of Pentecostalism are imbedded in testimonies, ecstatic speech, and bodily movement. But it *is* a theology, a full-blown religious cosmos, an intricate system of symbols that respond to the perennial questions of human meaning and value. The difference is that, historically, Pentecostals have felt more at home singing their theology."[64] Cox's peregrinations through the Pentecostal world offer an example and validation of Pentecostal methodology as a synthesis of experience and symbol. Rather than being oriented toward texts, people, in their bodily particularities, are the "text" or locus of theological exploration and interpretation. The orientation is toward an awareness of the dynamism of bodies. The languages of bodies are not primarily those of classical theology—not of Hebrew, Greek, Latin, or German—but of song sung in melodies, dance performed through synchronized rhythms, and

---

60. Cox, *Fire from Heaven*, 11.

61. Brennan, *Transmission of Affect*, 1.

62. Cox, *Fire from Heaven*, 13.

63. Cox, *Fire from Heaven*, 15.

64. Cox, *Fire from Heaven*, 15.

spirit encountered through sensation and inspiration. These languages are different in kind from text-oriented paradigms but certainly not lesser. Interestingly, however, Cox engages "Pentecostal spirituality" from inside and outside perspectives—through participation and observation—yet somehow manages to keep emotional distance from the project while underscoring the intrinsic emotive nature of Pentecostal worship. It is neither an exposé nor an "objective" historical treatise, but *Fire from Heaven* offers important insights to consider the rise of Pentecostalism and its contributions to the religious landscape of the twentieth century.

Thinking along the lines of ritual emotion, Anthropologist Pamela Klassen attends to the authenticity of ritual emotion in her article "Ritual" in *The Oxford Handbook of Religion and Emotion*. She asks the following questions: "What is the relationship between physiology and culture in the practice of religious ritual? Does physically choreographed ritual engender universal emotional responses? What is the role of culture in the evocation as well as the ritually produced emotion?" Klassen argues for a holistic consideration of ritual that attends to "embodiment and physicality, as well as to the social, historical, and cultural networks within which ritualized emotions 'make sense.'" In other words, Klassen is suggesting that approaches to ritual attend to both physiological and cultural assemblages by which ritual action and ritual bodies are shaped. Emotions are not ephemeral. In fact, the history of discussions of the cultural phenomena of ritualized emotion is itself "enmeshed in discourses" that are "highly emotional."[65] She explains:

> Important to my arguments is the underlying claim that discussions of both ritual authenticity and the relations of cognition and culture are situated within the larger contentious terrain of the relative status of emotion with regard to reason in Western scholarship and culture. Especially in the context of religion, charges of emotionalism have been used against a variety of groups construed as less evolved or more deprived, whether women undergoing possession, indigenous and colonized peoples involved in sacrifice, or the religiously devout in the West experiencing glossolalia or transubstantiation. Keeping these uses of emotion in mind, it is no surprise that discourses of ritual authenticity and of cognition and culture have their own (often hidden) histories of emotional sedimentations.[66]

65. Klassen, "Ritual," 2.
66. Klassen, "Ritual," 2.

Klassen's contribution to the current project is to rethink ritual, seeing emotion not as something that cheapens or illegitimates ritual, but as a part of how rituals are made and how they unfold. Rather than emotion being a way of discounting ritual, what might emotion teach us about the efficacy and power of ritualizing? Emotions, as Ahmed has demonstrated, are power-ful. They are "sticky," as Ahmed puts it; they make impressions and leave traces; they leave their sediment on and in bodies.

Klassen gives an example of her emotionally charged experiences with ritual while attending a twenty-six-day retreat at a Theravada Buddhist monastery in Thailand. The retreat consisted of a rhythm of daily sitting and walking meditations in a small room and progressed in intensity as the days went on. What began as six-hour alternations of sitting, walking, and meditation culminated in "'determination,' a final three days and nights of continuous meditation in the form of one hour of sitting meditation and one hour of walking meditation, for seventy-two hours straight."[67] Each day she was asked to give a report to the abbot of the monastery. Half-way through the retreat, Klassen began experiencing "vivid and terrifying dreams." These dreams did not end with morning but began to hound her, even in her meditation practices. However, to Klassen's surprise, the abbot informed her that these dreams were not an impediment to her practices, but part of her progression. The abbot smiled and informed Klassen that her feelings were part of the rhythms of the Vipassana ritual: "My psycho-physical reactions meant I was progressing well on the way to the days and nights of determination."[68] In other words, rather than a distraction or ritual failure, emotions were a mark and method of progress, a visceral reminder of ritual potency and efficacy.

Klassen's experience underscores what I am proposing here, namely, that those engaged in ritual practices are neither ritual robots nor autono-mous beings but are enfolded in the currents of dynamic processes in which bodies are pushed and pulled through worlds via emotion as well as the historical, social, and cultural networks within which these emotions are anchored, experienced, parsed out, and interpreted. This is consistent with Victor Turner's notion that ritual is constitutive of the relationship between symbols and natural elements that evoke emotional responses, memories, and social connections—two poles being 1) ideological and 2) sensory. There is a certain fluidity between the poles that allows for vacillation

67. Klassen, "Ritual," 1.
68. Klassen, "Ritual," 2.

between them; one cannot be certain where one begins and the other ends. For Turner, this interpretation, this meaning-making, is rarely conscious or articulated. Rather, ritual symbols, not speech, "do the complex work of bringing together norms, emotions, and signifiers for a socially diverse group."[69]

To summarize: Klassen's work deepens this inquiry into ritual, highlighting the affective and emotional contours of its processes and performances that are always already embedded in social, historical, and cultural networks. Emotion, in this sense, is catalytic to and characteristic of the relationship between ritual experience and sense- and meaning-making. While conversations continue to unfold with regard to the authenticity of ritual emotion, such conversation is futile, because it presupposes and is overdetermined by rubrics tarnished by Enlightenment bias, such as hierarchized binaries between higher and lower forms of religion. Rather than asking whether and how emotion is authentic or legitimate, or by whose authority it becomes so, I suggest a more generative question: How does emotion shape and inform the ritual process and notions of subjectivity within it?

Klassen's framework is helpful to think about the relationship between ritual, emotion, and context in anthropological studies but can be extended further into religious and theological studies. For example, ritual emotion and conversations around authenticity are consonant with theological notions of worship. The emotive contours of ritual, in this way, could be thought of as the animating force of worship. This shift in vocabulary is indicative of a larger paradigm shift, i.e., that there are differences in vocabulary but similar lines of inquiry between religious and theological studies. The former represents a broader set of questions concerning religion and its practices—hence, ritual—while the latter is more interested in theologizing, of speaking of God, and thus, of sacraments and practices of Christianity in particular.

The word *liturgy* comes from the Greek and means "the work of the people." Robert McAfee Brown, in *Spirituality and Liberation: Overcoming the Great Fallacy*, observes that "liturgy" was not used originally in a strictly religious sense, but meant the work that people do *"wherever they are."*[70] Only in recent years has liturgy connoted services or forms of worship in

---

69. Here, in concert with Jonathan Z. Smith and Arnold van Gennep, Klassen is drawing on Turner's work from *The Forest of Symbols* (Klassen, "Ritual," 3).

70. Brown, *Spirituality and Liberation*, 87 (emphasis in original).

exclusively Christian terms and contexts. This differentiation is symptomatic of what Brown calls the Great Fallacy, that is, the (false) separation of life into dualisms or binaries, "two areas, two spheres, two compartments."[71] Brown then identifies thirty-four pairs of binary oppositions, the first of which is "secular versus sacred." Through the process of deconstruction and reconstruction, Brown invites readers to reconsider these divisions that have plagued and are plaguing Christian thought and life. To live in the tension between two compartments is to live a fragmented life; the gospel or good news according to Jesus, on the contrary, is more about liberation and holistic integration.

Liberation, for Brown, is the means of integration. This convergence occurs on two planes: the dissolving of dualisms, such as secular versus sacred, on the one hand, and the renewed emphasis of everyday life in liturgical theology, on the other. In 1987, Ted Jennings published an article in the *Journal of Ritual Studies* entitled "Ritual Studies and Liturgical Theology: An Invitation to Dialogue," in which he suggests that a dialogue between the two discourses sharpens one another. Highlighting the emergence of liturgical theology, Jennings observes:

> Finally, the growing awareness of liberation theologians that it is essential to bridge the apparent chasm between a theology of liberating praxis and the shared life of the worshiping community has resulted in a new appreciation of the latter as a paradigm for action outside the walls of ecclesial piety. As a consequence, attention to liturgical action requires a new degree of pertinence for broader ethical and theological reflection.[72]

Whereas previous Western Christian interest in liturgics and theology has "intersected only at the point of the definition of sacrament," this new awareness and appreciation, fueled by what Jennings calls "liturgical action," simultaneously 1) critiques the "isolation of the sacramental movement" that renders theological reflection upon liturgy abstract and barren, and 2) makes the development of liturgical theology possible.[73] The emergence of this emphasis was greatly shaped by the Second Vatican Council (Vatican II, 1962–1965), a time of renewal in both focus and function, which is to say, a more comprehensive understanding of liturgy. Father Clarence Rivers sums up the shift by referring to the *Sacrosanctum Concilium*: "Liturgy

---

71. Brown, *Spirituality and Liberation*, 25.

72. T. Jennings, "Ritual Studies," 36.

73. T. Jennings, "Ritual Studies," 37.

is the summit toward which the activity of the Church is directed; and that it is at the same time the font from which all her powers flow."[74] Rather than maintaining age-old dualisms of spiritual versus material and sacred versus secular, Vatican II shifted the grounds of theology and practice from an emphasis on partaking of the sacraments to living sacramentally.

Likewise, upholding rigid barriers between ritual and liturgical studies reveals the binary between the secular and the sacred. Considering these discourses as different but complementary methodologies and angles of inquiry broadens and richens the conversation about religion and spirituality, about how practices shape and transform subjects, about the textures that inform and structure everyday life. Whether one stands before the table of Christian worship to receive the Eucharist or stands before the altar of creation to bask in the experienced communion of God in all things, is a matter of perspective. Though one may consider ritual as part of religious or political life and only religious in instances, processes of life have so problematized the divide between secular and sacred that untangling the web would be impossible. Thus, this project is interested in interfacing, in integrating, in improvising, which occurs in, between, and throughout the interstitial openings. This is the modus operandi, and these are the rich contributions of Pentecostalism. Rather than succumbing to the rupture of what Brown calls the Great Fallacy, we are invited to be immersed into a Great Mystery.

As a theology, Pentecostalism is not subject to the standards of classical theology. It does not exist in volumes of leather-bound books encased by libraries of rich mahogany. Coherent doctrines and divides—between secular and sacred, for example—are the products of the Western tradition of theology and politics. This is McAfee's Great Fallacy. Instead, Pentecostalism has a different kind of fleshy, human origin. The meaning of Pentecostalism derives from its function and experience, its context and dynamism. Another way to evaluate the movement, as Ashon Crawley has pointed out, is to see the phenomenon of racialized history and practice of Pentecostalism. That ecstatic spiritual experiences occurred in the antebellum South among enslaved Africans is evident in telling of ring shouts and hush harbors. The flesh that was treated as chattel, beaten and discounted, becomes the locus of acts of contestation though communal inspired dance and songs. For Crawley, these practices constitute an aesthetics for "otherwise possibilities," that is, space to live different modes of existence

---

74. *Sacrosanctum Concilium*, quoted in Rivers, *Soulfull Worship*, 10.

over and against the Western gaze and norms of theological-philosophical enclosure and limitation. Crawley writes:

> I consider dancing, singing, noise making, whooping, and tongue talking as ways to resist normative modes of theological and philosophical reflection, the same sorts of thought that produce categorical differentiation-as-deficiency such as race, class, gender, slave, and so on. I argue that the aesthetic practices of Blackpentecostalism constitute a performative critique of normative theology and philosophy that precede the twentieth-century moment. The practices existed, in other words, before they were called Blackpentecostal, before a group cohered on Bonnie Rae Street for prayer in April 1906.[75]

Thus, since the making of blackness as an object was part of their projects, Crawley contends that to speak theologically or philosophically is to speak racially.

Blackpentecostalism not only contests this enclosure of the subject or need to maintain pure categorical distinctions and dualisms, but it flourishes in the practices that occasion it. Thus, returning to my original hypothesis regarding whether and how Pentecostal worship can be liberative, the answer, at least for Crawley, is yes, insofar as the terms of liberation are not (over)determined by whiteness and Western expectations of what liberation means. Blackpentecostalism, is an *a*theological-*a*philosophical practice whereby such terms and divisions are unraveled by the witness and practice of otherwise possibilities.

In this chapter, I have focused on interarticulation of theories of affect and ritual, evidencing how they, together, can offer important insights into theological inquiry in general and Pentecostal worship in particular. Theories of affect focus on bodies, how they are shaped function in everyday life, which is to say sense-making or making sense of the world. Ritual asks questions of personal and communal function, organization, structure, and meaning-making in the practices of religiosity and spirituality. Finally, I turned to consider Pentecostalism, specifically Blackpentecostalism vis-à-vis Crawley, which adds a layer of critique to these formations and may consider "dancing in the Spirit" as a triptych of "feeling, doing, thinking." I now turn to consider how sound in general and music in particular contributes to affective and ritualistic formations through three influential instances of Pentecostalism.

---

75. Crawley uses Blackpentecostal as one word to stress the inextricability of the two. (Crawley, *Blackpentecostal Breath*, 7).

CHAPTER 2

Dance-Possible Epistemologies of Sound and Space

And suddenly from heaven there came a sound like the rush of a violent wind, and it filled the entire house where they were sitting.

—*ACTS 2:2*

Such songs and sound—Blackpentecostal noise that is always grounded in joy—is a critique of such a normative world.

—*ASHON CRAWLEY, BLACKPENTECOSTAL BREATH*

Introduction

I HAVE HEARD IT countless times, the noticeable quiver in my father's preaching voice. It is the sound that sonically marks the exact moment when he is moved by his own preaching, an instance when the messenger becomes affected by how the message feels. The quiver usually is accompanied by tears, causing the message to become somewhat garbled by speech difficult to understand; but the sounds are full of feeling. His face flushes in shades of red as he tries to communicate through trembling, shaky speech. Colloquially, we would say that his words were "moving"; but really what is indicated is that something in him—ostensibly emotion—moved, swelled, changed, and inflected with the words themselves. The quaking sound signals a change in tone, in breath, in pitch. Perhaps it is a combination of what is said and the way that it is said, but it seems to be more a matter of tonality and feeling than semantics or content. In fact, in our Pentecostal tradition, this was often a moment where he would go from preaching in our shared common language to speaking in tongues. Any chance of understanding him once his speech "went into tongues" was lost, but something collectively, in the room, would begin to stir. Something is still communicated, still said, in the slide from common language to tongues. This shift was a felt transition, a "breakthrough," such that it invited others to join in without any spoken cues. Others would often start speaking in tongues; and the emotional temperature in the space would continue to rise. Those who didn't slip into speaking in tongues would just say a phrase or name over and over again: "Jesus, Jesus!" It was implicit that this prompting was the prompting of the Holy Spirit, both from within and without—a tangible presence that saturated every inch of the worship space.

Indeed, we learned how to be *in* those moments, observing and participating as we watched and sensed our way through them. The more we experienced such moments, the more comfortable we were with and in them; our shared "ritual knowledge" shaped and oriented us in the space through the sounds of preaching and crying in both unintelligible and intelligible forms. What was generally known but seldom spoken was an awareness that we were cued concurrently by something-other and something familiar. Such moments could last a few brief seconds or tarry for an hour. The duration depended on the intensity—volume in sound and participation—of the tongues. My dad and those in the room interpreted the moment together, simultaneously queued and cued. They had shared a history of such moments, which shaped them and the space of the disruptive unfolding tongues. Like the "groanings too deep for words" in Rom 8, these unintelligible sounds and their meanings were excessive, dwelling just beyond the conscious efforts of the community. Moreover, we developed a "theo-acoustic memory"[1] through the repetition of the ecstatic worship and spirited preaching that we experienced and heard. God could be felt as well as heard, in sounds, vibrations, and sensations. The collective memory of the community also served as a repertoire, an accumulation of past encounters that inform what is possible. What is it that happens when such unexpected moments occur, when emotion emerges in such a way that it breaks down the attempt to communicate "clearly"? How does sound serve as a means of knowledge distribution and organization?

On a scientific level, sound is constituted by vibrations. It is the result of constant movement, not only heard, but felt. A wave is a disturbance

1. Moss, *Blue Note Preaching*, 44.

or eruption that carries energy from one point to another. Sound waves are thus matter: the material of movement. Sound oscillates and resonates along certain frequencies, some heard within audible range, while others are inaudible. Sound is something propagated and something received, and how the differences are studied and pronounced depends upon disciplinary focus.[2] Generally speaking, audible frequency ranges vary from species to species. For example, generally humans can hear 20 to 20,000 Hz, while other animals can hear into the ultrasonic range, i.e., higher than the upper audible limits of human hearing. This chapter homes in on sound through the Pentecostal emphasis on music, breath, shouting, and preaching by focusing on the significance of how it is produced and reproduced in designated spaces or contexts, how it shapes those gathered in the space as well as the space itself, and how this shaping constitutes the horizon of what is possible—dance-possible.

Recalling Teresa Brennan's example of what it means to walk into a room and "feel the atmosphere,"[3] I explore how sound affectively organizes bodies and sanctifies spaces, giving the latter a tangible aura. For example, consider the quiet reverence of an old sanctuary or the solemnity of a burial ground as places marked as sacred, as places that cause us to approach them in certain ways. It is only by virtue of the histories of what is said or done or sung in those places that give it an aura. In what follows, I engage the a/effects of sound and space as a lens for exploring Pentecostal epistemologies and histories, tracing the tradition in three vignettes, from the upper room narrative to the introduction of the blue note in the spirituals, blues, and jazz, and finally to Azusa and Ashon Crawley's notion of the *choreosonic* to underscore how shouting, singing, and preaching in Blackpentecostal[4] tradition(s) undoes the irreducibility of movement and sound, even as it contests and resists Western subject and knowledge formation. What is thus produced is excess, that which cannot be neatly separated, organized, or even communicated. It is precisely this excess that overwhelms and problematizes the Modern privileging of rationalism, not as irrational, but as an irreducibility of the rational, transrational, and *a*rational.

First, a word of caution. In *The Sonic Episteme: Acoustic Resonance, Neoliberalism, and Biopolitics*, Robin James argues that the "sonic episteme"

---

2. E.g., the difference of how sound is studied and defined in physics versus human physiology.

3. Brennan, *Transmission of Affect*, 1.

4. Crawley, *Blackpentecostal Breath*, 28.

is the product of neoliberal, biopolitical attempts to "quantify every last bit of reality" which elevates a "special kind of math."[5] James speaks of a synthesis between music and mathematics whereby the themes of liberalism are reiterated and reinscribed—e.g., autonomous individualism, rational subjectivity—in modulated voicings. That is to say, applying mathematics to sound shifts (reduces) the focus from the domain of the social to "calculative rationality." While James's project diverges from the current project's integration of sound studies, it serves as a preliminary warning of the ways in which privileging one sense over another (here, sound) in service to rationalism can lead to a reductive, calculative biopolitics characteristic of neoliberalism,[6] which is no different from the privileging of language in logocentrism. (Parenthetically, Ronald Grimes's caution about visualism and logocentrism resurfaces, which indicates that, while the senses can supplement and enhance knowledge or theory, they also can be the means of reductive approaches.) James argues that sound studies should be considered in concert with race and material cultures, lest the frequency ratio become the "basic unit of reality."[7] My interest in sound is how it informs and shapes individuals and collectives as a form of knowing that coalesces with the interarticulations and intergesticulations of theories—affect(s) and ritual—and how it is separate but supplemental to language. This analysis accepts that all of life is always already racialized, and that it is precisely this racialization that Black experience in general and Blackpentecostalism in particular responds to, refutes, and rejects.

Affects and Feelings in Sonic Experiences

While Silvan Tomkins's work on affect derived from his observations of the communicative repertoire of infants, there has been growing interest in considering music as a universal and intrinsic form of communication, as well as a transmitter and magnifier of affect. Music's ability to evoke and provoke—with or without words—makes it an easy site for affective analysis. How does sound organize and prompt religious engagement or ritual,

5. James, *Sonic Episteme*, 1.

6. By neoliberalism, James concurs with Lester K. Spence's definition as "the general idea that society works best when people and the institutions within it are shaped to work according to market principles" (Spence, *Knocking the Hustle: Against the Neoliberal Turn in Black Politics*; quoted in James, *Sonic Episteme*, 8).

7. James, *Sonic Episteme*, 9.

such as the call to prayer in Islam, or digital media—TV, radio, internet—in various traditions? The phenomenon of sound, when amplified and distributed, carries messages and cues and orients bodies in spaces designated for ritualizing. Music, in particular, has the ability to affect bodies on a physiological level. Consider:

> Research has shown that music may influence central physiological variables like blood pressure, heart rate, respiration, EEG measurements, body temperature and galvanic skin response. Music influences immune and endocrine function. The existing research literature shows growing knowledge of how music can ameliorate pain, anxiety, nausea, fatigue and depression.[8]

While there is scientific basis for music's physiological a/effects, even medicinally, it is likely that the context in which the music is made, distributed, and listened to determines the types of effects it can have. For example, music used for meditation can evoke a sense of calm and lower heart rates and increase breathing rates, while, by contrast, other forms of music can do the opposite. A study on heavy metal music found: "Researchers have found that people who are angry and aggressive can experience more positive emotions because of the increased arousal from metal music which matches the person's physiological state. This congruence between anger/aggression and arousal from metal helps with anger regulation."[9] However, when heavy metal music was used to experiment on mice, the mice began to kill one another.[10] Animal brutality notwithstanding, the point of the study is that music, as tones and sound, can affect and inform one's body, emotional state, and orientation in terms of dissonance and resonance. A third cited study found that "energetic and rhythmic music was positively associated with using all examined forms of musical emotion regulation, suggesting this dimension of music is especially useful in modulating emotions. These results highlight the potential use of music as a tool for emotion regulation."[11] Caution should be taken when thinking of music as a "tool," as that which can be used to accomplish a desired outcome, especially in light of the historical use of music and other forms of media as tools for fascist propaganda.[12] Donovan Schaefer's extension of Foucault's

8. Myskja and Lindbaek, "How Does Music Affect."

9. Shukla, "Social Psychology."

10. Educational CyberPlayground. "Listening to Hard Rock."

11. Welker, "Music."

12. One should consider the Frankfurt School, particularly the work of Walter Benjamin and Theodor Adorno, before consulting music as a "tool."

nexus of power-knowledge to power-knowledge-affect is, perhaps, an attempt to make room for the ways in which language, reason, and art are already imbued with affects, thus cannot be reduced to the singular. While the emotional and physiological a/effects of music are well researched and documented from the social sciences to biology, the question arises: are these cultural or creaturely responses or a form of both? How does sound in general and music in particular produce a sort of felt pedagogy, a tactile way of learning and living in the world through embodied, perceptual emotions, or fields and networks of affects? Further, how do affective economies of racism become the site of production of what Ashon Crawley calls "otherwise possibilities" and epistemologies, otherwise ways of being in the world, ways not limited by the abstraction of thought or flesh but imbued with possibility? That sound provides the occasion for the coalescence of experience and expression is the notion that I attend to in my exposition of Black preaching and Black music, particularly the spirituals, the incipient sounds for blues and jazz.

Hélène Cixous asks, "Why do we love music that is without words?"[13] What is it that happens when music—as sound, as ephemeral textures heard and felt—moves us in such a way, with such intensity, that we feel a connection to and affection for it? Marie Thompson and Ian Biddle's volume, *Sound, Music, Affect: Theorizing Sonic Experience*, seeks to theorize the link between affect and sound in complementary, if not synonymous, ways by how it functions in political life. Music, in this way, is sonic affect—as emotive, dynamic textures—that mobilizes and brings together a collective, even as it provides the sonic backdrop for collective action. Writing of protests in England, Adam Harper identified the presence of music at protests as the accompanying force instilling a sense of collectivity "ten times as strong as that whipped up at the very best of raves."[14] Thompson and Biddle argue that Grime music[15] became the chosen soundtrack for sociopolitical unrest, likely because "the protagonists are those frequently demonized by the establishment: the poor, the young, and black."[16] Some

13. Quoted in Schaefer, *Evolution of Affect Theory*, 1.

14. Adam Harper, "Being Heard"; quoted in Thompson and Biddle, *Sound, Music, Affect*, 2.

15. Grime music is a blend of electronic music, more like UK garage than hip hop, dancehall, and raw sounds characteristic of Bow E3, East London in the early 2000s. Typically the music is at or around 140 BPM—a fast, preferred tempo for many producers that distinguishes the music from other genres.

16. Thompson and Biddle, *Sound, Music, Affect*, 3.

Grime track music can be described as carrying a political message; however, the political utilization and significance of it lies in the emotion (energy, tonality, voicings, tempos, rhythms) of the music to which it gives voice. Julie Adenuga is the disc jockey (DJ) for London's Beats 1 Radio and a leading voice in the Grime scene. She remarks that Grime music is "the most raw form of energy in music that we have in the UK, in that, at times it can feel aggressive."[17] In fact, the song "POW!" by Lethal Bizzle was banned by the police from being played in nightclubs on the basis that it would incite a riot. Form 696 (risk assessment) is a form that police used to target and shut down Grime parties, specifically citing "DJs or MCs performing to recorded backing tracks."[18] Backlash against Form 696 as "racist police form" has been well documented and, in November of 2017, London Mayor Sadiq Khan finally banned the form from use, advocating for a "voluntary partnership approach" instead.[19] DJ Julie Adenuga concludes by alluding to the similarities between Hip Hop and Grime:

> The lines [are] getting really blurry. But one thing that stands so strong in those two genres of music is the fact that they're lifestyles now, they're not just songs you would hear on the radio or that you can buy from iTunes. They are actually communities and lifestyles that people live.[20]

Returning to Thompson and Biddle's analysis of Grime in the political sphere, one curious component of Grime music as the soundtrack of political unrest and protest is that, while the music rarely has an explicit political message, it remains politicized. Thus, the loud, "aggressive sounds" of Grime become an auditory response and contestation of the conditions from which they emerge. The music becomes anthemic by virtue of creating a vibe, an aura, such that it organizes and facilitates resistance by providing aggressive soundtracks for collectives. By and large, "it's not about the content, it's about the energy and the aura."[21] Another way to consider aura is as affects, as shapes, moods, textures, and feelings that inform, shape, and structure embodied existence (Schaefer). Grime music is a conduit for bodies to absorb the sounds, channeling the aggressive sounds toward political resistance to use "within a particular space."

17. Vox, "Grime."
18. Vox, "Grime."
19. *BBC*, "Form 696."
20. Vox, "Grime."
21. Thompson and Biddle, *Sound, Music, Affect*, 5.

Returning to Schaefer's questions "What do affects do?" and "What do we do for affects?," a connection emerges between sound, affect, and the mobilization of bodies as a collective. This accentuates the materiality of sound as organizational, affective, and material—sound as affect and affect as sound. In other words, the sounds, the vibrations, serve as an audible reference and palpable aggressive soundtrack by which to protest. Protestors become moved by the vibrations, even as they move. The music cuts through to the physiological level. However, organization-through-sound does not happen through protest only. Anyone who has sung "Take Me Out to the Ballgame" during a seventh-inning stretch at Wrigley Field, or joined in the chant-like musical traditions of football and soccer, knows the power of voices magnified in collectives at high decibel levels in sports traditions. Volume has a way of increasing or magnifying stimulation.

Affects are not relegated to the personal or private spheres of embodied experience but spill over and vacillate between personal and private, public and collective domains. It is here, in potential, in intensity, that Spinoza's affect (*affectus*) has currency, offering new ways to think the political, the social, and the religious, not as separate spheres of life, but as an assemblage of messy, blurred, yet integrated aspects of embodied existence. Thompson and Biddle conclude that their interest in sound and music is to think of them as ways of "*manifesting* affect" such that "music is thus imagined in this volume as facilitating acoustic entry into affective fields, as offering a way to both abstract and particularize affective states and as furnishing a reflective medium for imagining affect 'itself,' if only figuratively or strategically."[22] Bringing affect in conversation with ritual, they continue: "The affective is to be felt in those processes by which the boundary rituals are instantiated, put in place, embedded, 'somatized' to use Pierre Bourdieu's term."[23] Underscoring the somatic as the means for creating felt boundaries is part and parcel of an affective sonicity that can be heard or unheard, felt or not felt, but always registered in the body. I now turn to three vignettes for considering acoustic entry into affective fields as a framework to ponder Pentecostal epistemologies of sound and space.

The Upper Room and the Outer World

It begins with a sound:

22. Thompson and Biddle, *Sound, Music, Affect*, 16.
23. Thompson and Biddle, *Sound, Music, Affect*, 17.

47

> When the day of Pentecost had come, they were all together in one place. And suddenly from heaven there came a sound like the rush of a violent wind, and it filled the entire house where they were sitting. Divided tongues, as of fire, appeared among them, and a tongue rested on each of them. All of them were filled with the Holy Spirit and began to speak in other languages, as the Spirit gave them ability.[24]

Pentecost is the fiftieth and culminating day of Easter in the Christian tradition and commemorates the impartation and incarnation of the Holy Spirit in the upper room. Unlike the Gospel of Luke's descent of the Holy Spirit on Jesus "as a dove" and in decipherable words, the Acts account describes the event with a sound "like the rush of a violent wind" accompanied by divided tongues "as of fire." Indeed, the Spirit's acoustic entrance into the upper room was a disruption, a commotion that affected bodies through the senses of hearing, touch, and sight, integrating the spiritual and physical into shared, common materiality. Tongues of fire suggests a burning sensation, reminiscent of the prophet Jeremiah's confession that the word—or message—from God is like an uncontainable "burning fire shut up in my bones";[25] or perhaps recalling Moses's encounter with the burning bush that is consumed but not destroyed.[26] Fire is an ancient motif and element, a recurring theme that speaks of God's accompanying presence by night.[27] Fire was a medium to flag messages as coming *from* God. Fire is both symbolic and literal, and there often is some slippage between the two. For example, John the Baptist declares that he baptizes with water, but the one that comes after him (Jesus) baptizes "with the Holy Spirit, and with fire."[28] Yet, in the Acts account, as it is for Moses, the Holy is not found *in* the fire per se, but in the sound that accompanies it.

The Greek word used for wind is *pneuma*. In the Hebrew Bible, *pneuma*'s counterpart is *ruach*, a force that hovers over, animates, and brings order to the waters of created chaos in the Genesis story. Sometimes *ruach* is interpreted as breath, sometimes as spirit, and other times as wind. Breath, though automatic and often unnoticed, is material, something felt and heard. It is a reminder that one is alive. Practices that call attention to

24. Acts 2:1–4.
25. Jer 20:9.
26. Exod 3:2.
27. Exod 13:21.
28. Matt 3:11.

breath, such as yoga or meditation, are ways of nurturing the connection between breath and life. Neither song nor sound is possible without breath. Breath makes possible, supports, and sustains. Wind is the animating force of gases moving through the atmosphere precipitated by changes in pressure. Wind carries birds and small seeds, shapes landforms, and provides a breeze, but it can also overwhelm in forces such as hurricanes, tornados, and gales. Nothing can control the wind or escape its touch. Like breath and fire, there is considerable biblical precedent for the significance of wind. John's gospel suggests that the wind "blows where it chooses, and you hear the sound of it, but you do not know where it comes from or where it goes. So it is with everyone who is born of the Spirit."[29] Jesus calms the sea through rebuking the wind.[30] Wind symbolizes and materializes the expansive, boundless reach of the divine and confirms divine presence in the primal elements of the cosmos.

The meaning or significance of breath and wind is made evident by what they do. How might we contemplate the question, what does spirit do? To answer that, we must first indulge the slippage between interpretations of *ruach* and *pneuma*, a familiar nuance prevalent in the Acts narrative. The author of Acts, largely recognized as Luke, a gentile, is appealing to the Hebrew tradition as he pens at the intersection of national identity, diaspora, and the universality of God's mission and message, spinning a web in which the Spirit is the silk-like material of interconnectedness. Thus, using the elements of wind and fire harkens back to the Hebrew Bible as primordial languages of theophany, i.e., God's revelation, to highlight that the same Spirit is now revealing or doing something new. The creative winds once again are blowing, and nothing is left unaffected: "It filled the entire house where they were sitting." How does one interpret the wily wind or tongues as of fire? As the wind fills the house like breath in one's lungs, and fire touches the tongues of those gathered, new languages, new ways of communicating, emerge. Acts indicates that the gathered began to speak in other "tongues" (*glossais*) or languages miraculously. Here, those familiar with the Hebrew Bible tradition are also reminded of the story of Babel, in which God introduces other languages in order to stymie human efforts to build a city that would reach the heavens. The Tower of Babel is both an origin myth about the diversity of human language and also the rebuke of the hubris of human progress.

29. John 3:8.
30. Mark 4:39–41.

New languages, in the Acts narrative, evidence the impartation of the Spirit as a universal force. Situated in the context of a people within a people, a nation within a nation, those in the upper room are waiting for the fulfillment of what was promised by Jesus, namely that he would "give the Holy Spirit" to them.[31] Here, the Spirit inspires them by overcoming language barriers and enabling the disciples to speak to foreigners in their own native tongue. Thus, the gift of tongues is an act of justice through the act of hospitality. For those far from their motherland, which is to say those living in diaspora, it is the sound of God's unfolding message to them in their mother tongue:

> And how is it that we hear, each of us, in our own native language? Parthians, Medes, Elamites, and residents of Mesopotamia, Judea and Cappadocia, Pontus and Asia, Phrygia and Pamphylia, Egypt and the parts of Libya belonging to Cyrene, and visitors from Rome, both Jews and proselytes, Cretans and Arabs—in our own languages we hear them speaking about God's deeds of power.[32]

The disciples, through the prompting of the Holy Spirit, become empowered with the ability to speak in the languages of virtually everyone around them. This miracle is not about a unity as uniformity, such it that compresses and universalizes one language or sameness; but it suggests that the Spirit is interested in the gift for all to hear God's message in the idioms of their own language, in their own culture, resting on their own tongue. One language is not superimposed, as with colonialist projects, but there is a plurality of sounds and voices. We could deduce from the story that the sound of the violent rushing wind is meant to radically reorient their social world, forging new relationships through the unique expressions and intimate sounds of one's native language. The Spirit in Acts gives the gift of tongues for the disciples to erase the limitations and borders of language, as it were. The cultural chasm is overcome by the universal and unifying Spirit of God. The spontaneous appearance of the Spirit occasions the annunciation of God's message so that all can understand. There are no longer outsiders or foreigners in the kindom of God, for all are included in God's

---

31. This account, perhaps unbeknownst to the author of Luke, is complicated by the Johannine community's inclusion of Jesus breathing the Holy Spirit into his disciples in John 20:22. Regardless of the means, however, that the promise is fulfilled in the early disciples is most important. This reference is from Luke 11:13.

32. Acts 2:8–11.

all-encompassing family. This radical reorientation demands a new world and way of living, of sharing, of giving, and of possibilities.

The people respond, amazed and perplexed: "What does this mean?"[33] The reader must consider that they are not speaking literally. The spoken word, as an event, destabilizes, making meaning excessive, irreducible, and indecipherable. Interestingly, the meaning of the Greek *logos*, like spirit, is polyvalent. While it can apply to everyday spoken language or communication, it also refers to the incarnation: the Word as, or becoming, flesh. This event is foundational to the Christian story and further demonstrates the complex relationship between language, interpretation, and meaning. The people, hearing these words in their own language, are perplexed. Since the disciples are now speaking in their native languages, they should now be able understand their words. But they do not. Spoken language is structured sound constituted by the repetition of recognizable utterances. These utterances—formed by consonants and vowels—together with references, make meaning intelligible. But spoken language and words are also reliant upon inflection and tone; they can be communicated differently depending upon affect, sound, and through intelligible and unintelligible forms. "What does this mean?" thus is a more general question about how such a miraculous event of hearing of God's deeds of power changes, deconstructs, perhaps challenges, their understanding of their sociocultural milieu. Feasibly, a more contemporary question might be "What is happening?"

In what he calls "the revolution of the intimate," Willie Jennings suggests that the miracle of Pentecost is one of language and of hospitality:

> The miracles are not merely in ears. They are also in mouths and in bodies. God, like a lead dancer, is taking hold of her partners, drawing them close and saying, "Step this way and now this direction."[34]

God's message is translated and transliterated into one's own language, idioms, and family. It is a familiar sound, in recognizable form, that opens the possibility of a commonness and togetherness. It is something experienced and translated in the syntax of shared community. Like learning a dance with God, one moves and is moved by the Spirit into new rhythms and patterns of living. However, this forging work is not as easily accomplished as its annunciation; it will cost them something:

33. Acts 2:12.
34. W. Jennings, *Acts*, 29.

But this will require bodies that reach across massive and real boundaries, cultural, religious, and ethnic. It will require a commitment born of Israel's faith, but reaching to depths of relating beyond what any devotion to Israel's God had heretofore been recognized as requiring: devotion to peoples unknown and undesired. What God has always spoken to Israel now God speaks even more loudly in the voices of the many to the many: join them! Now love of neighbor will take on pneumatological dimensions. It will be love that builds directly out of the resurrected body of Jesus.[35]

What Jennings suggests is that interpreters are not needed, but translators who will allow their lives to be translated continually. Lives become like books—open books, as it were, pages made available to be read and learned. Yet, what he does not address is how intertwined the processes of interpretation and translation are: that every translation requires interpretation and vice versa. Semantic range—call it possibilities—and biases force one to make choices. These choices, however, are informed by the context in which they are used. So, while the neat distinction of translator/interpreter is impossible to make, the mutuality of the two serves as a means of coming-together, of becoming-with, of working-out, and of finding and sharing commonality.

It is significance, not simply signification, that the Spirit orchestrates between spoken language and written text, between individual lives and collective life. Cláudio Carvalhaes notes: "The Spirit lives between orality and writing, between my ears and the *otobiography* of the people of God, between the testimonies and archives of our communities, forming a constantly multiaxial ethnography of our identities . . . by the power of the Spirit, my identity is between my brother, my sister, myself, and God!"[36] Echoing the apostle Paul's blurring of the lines of identity—"There is no longer Jew or Greek, there is no longer slave or free, there is no longer male and female; for all of you are one in Christ Jesus" (Gal 3:28)—with the sound of hearing one's story through the ears of the other, Carvalhaes makes the case for an in-between identity, which is to say, life, living, and being irreducible to the modern foci of rationalism and individualism. The Spirit draws lines of overlap, and new community emerges through the interconnectedness.

35. W. Jennings, *Acts*, 31.
36. Carvalhaes, *What's Worship*, 95.

The Acts story of Pentecost reveals essential characteristics of the Holy Spirit, namely, her uncontrollability, unpredictability, and universality. The narrative carries further Luke's inclusive theology by establishing the Holy Spirit as the material animating force of God's unifying kindom. What begins with a sound resonates within and reverberates throughout the surrounding areas. People begin to speak in new languages, new syllables, new sounds. Others hear the familiar sounds but are uncertain about what it all means. That is to say, on its own, language is never fully sufficient to interpret all that is happening. It is something to be experienced and translated in the syntax of shared communal life. Old boundaries are undone as the social circle is drawn ever wider. Sharing is a common theme in Acts, whether in language or resources, that establishes a new way of living and being in the world.

The sound at Pentecost is the sound of a revolution over and against the fractures and fragments occasioned by systemic injustices perpetrated and perpetuated by the principalities, powers, and rulers of darkness of the age. The Holy Spirit creates an alternative way of living, an otherwise epistemology, that brings about justice and liberation through sharing life together. I now turn to the spirituals, the birth of a similar sound, a disturbance of the normative sonic world, recalcitrant syncopated rhythms toward otherwise worlds and possibilities.

Hearing the Sound of Spirituals

The sound of the spirituals is born out of Black experience. Black music, like Black history, is a living reality. As James Cone confesses: "I am the blues and my life is a spiritual. Without them I cannot be."[37] Cone also contends that:

> To interpret the religious significance of that spiritual for the black community, "academic" tools are not enough. The interpreter must *feel* the Spirit; that is, one must feel one's way into the power of black music, responding both to its rhythm and the faith in experience it affirms.[38]

Is Cone admitting the limits of academic tools? Or, is his analysis, which encompasses history and experience, crashing against a particular

37. Cone, *Spirituals and the Blues*, 7.
38. Cone, *Spirituals and the Blues*, 4.

epistemology of Western academia that is interested in specific forms of knowledge formation through certain means, rigid understandings of the subject and what is acceptable as knowledge? For Cone, interpretation cannot occur without "feeling the Spirit." Feeling becomes a prerequisite for meaning-making, which means the spirituals are not captive to rationalization or reduction; rather, they overwhelm and disrupt binaries and the logics of modern thought. It is important to name reality, to feel and lament it. Cone is alluding to an embodied rhythm akin to Crawley's "otherwise" possibilities. When one *feels* the Spirit, one discovers power to make, unmake, and remake worlds. It is a contestation, a renunciation of the forces of enclosure that seek to categorize and generalize thought and knowledge. Cone asserts that if all that was known of Black history was "what whites did to blacks, there would have been no spirituals."[39] Black history chronicles Black resistance to the vicissitudes of living in an oppressed society, but this resistance is not all that Black history is. Rather, "what whites did" is secondary to Black history; the primary reality is what Black people have done to delimit the white assault on their lives, history, and culture.

Cone concludes:

> When white people enslaved Africans, their intention was to de-historicize black existence, *to foreclose the possibility of a future defined by the African heritage.* White people demeaned black people's sacred tales, ridiculing their myths and defiling sacred rites. *Their intention was to define humanity according to European definitions* so that their brutality against Africans could be characterized as civilizing the savages. But white Europeans did not succeed; and *black history is the record of their failure.*[40]

Foreclosing possibility is tantamount to seeking to create a singularity of existence, of knowledge, and of narrative. In light of this compression, without Black history, there can be no Black possibility, no future. European standards were superimposed on all aspects of life and meant to define humanity in modern terms, which is the era in which the Black subject was (de)formed. These standards create one world in their image, a singularity that Sylvia Wynter argues is the genre of the human, of Man and his overrepresentation. In this one world, *the* world, there is a particular way to be human, an only way to practice humanity. If one does not conform to these standards, then one is not—or is less—human. Wynter argues this

39. Cone, *Spirituals and the Blues*, 23.
40. Cone, *Spirituals and the Blues*, 23–24 (emphasis in original).

modern human, though normalized, is overrepresented: "The struggle of our new millennium will be one between the ongoing imperative of securing the well-being of our present ethnoclass (i.e., Western bourgeois) conception of the human, Man, which overrepresents itself as if it were the human itself, and that of securing the well-being, and therefore the full cognitive and behavioral autonomy of the human species itself/ourselves."[41] However, as Cone declares and Crawley affirms, this overrepresentation of the human, of a certain (white) Man—its standards, norms, narratives, and categories—is overcome by the force and progeny of Black expression and the living history from which it emerges. It is for this reason that the Black aesthetics movement accompanied the Black Power and liberation movements in the late 1960s and early 1970s—works of art, literature, poetry, music, and theater rooted in Black culture are co-creative acts of resistance and justice.[42]

In his work *In the Break: The Aesthetics of the Black Radical Tradition*, Fred Moten argues: "The history of blackness is testament to the fact that objects can and do resist. Blackness—the extended movement of a specific upheaval, and ongoing irruption that anarranges every line—is a stain that pressures the assumption of the equivalence of personhood and subjectivity."[43] In conversation with Frederick Douglass, he adds: "This disruption of the Enlightenment linguistic project is of fundamental importance since it allows a rearrangement of the relationship between notions of human freedom and notions of human essence."[44] Perhaps we may extend "a disruption that allows for rearrangement" as characteristic of an epistemological shift undergirding the production and function of the spirituals and otherwise performances, expressions, and possibilities. Moten's focus on Black performance indicates that it is animated by the radical materiality and syntax of Blackness, of Black history, itself.

If the sound of the spirituals is indeed born out of Black experience, how does one feel their way into it or avail ourselves to its migrations? Here, we must address the twoness found in W. E. B. Du Bois, the lowering of a veil that precipitates a "double consciousness" as "the sense of always looking at one's self through the eyes of others, of measuring one's soul through the tape of a world that looks on in amused pity and contempt. One ever

41. See Wynter, "Unsettling the Coloniality," 260.
42. Frederick, "On Black Aesthetics."
43. Moten, *In the Break*, 1.
44. Moten, *In the Break*, 7.

feels his twoness—an American a Negro, two souls, two thoughts, two un-reconciled strivings; two warring ideals in one dark body, whose dogged strength alone keeps it from being torn asunder."[45] Du Bois's dualism of being places his Blackness in binary opposition to an American, indicating that "American" here is synonymous with a particular subject, namely, anglo or white. Thus, the "color line" is a construct and governing product of the ongoing Enlightenment project meant to order and organize, with variation but nevertheless to a certain scale.

While Du Bois offers the first noteworthy interpretation of the spirituals (1903), Cone clarifies that Du Bois's work is "so rich in feeling and observation that it defies classification."[46] Once again, Cone pushes back against the grain of (Western) classification (read: epistemological frameworks) in favor of deeper means of analysis. Du Bois labels the spirituals as "sorrow songs"; however, within the songs there exists an otherwise possibility: an affirmation of life. The existential tension of double consciousness is expressed in the tension of "hope and despair, joy and sorrow, death and life,"[47] in the spirituals. These tensions are embodied—constraining, but not constrained—making possible new sounds, i.e., the production and reproduction of "inspirited materiality,"[48] the resonances of new worlds coming to be. The spirituals announce and renounce. The complex world of thought and existence of the spirituals refuses to be reduced to the singular, whether in existence or expression, as is reflected in Cone's remembrance of a particular Black women who said: "I likes 'Poor Rosy' better dan all de songs, but it can't be sung widout a *full heart and a troubled sperrit!*"[49] Finally, Cone offers a way to navigate through the tension of the spirituals in their appropriate aesthetic form:

> The spiritual is the community in rhythm, swinging to the movement of life. The best approach in interpreting the song is to *feel* one's way into the cultural and historical milieu of the people's mind and let the song speak to and *for* you. . . . The meaning of the song is not in the bare words but in the black history that created

45. Du Bois, *Souls of Black Folk*, 2.

46. Cone, *Spirituals and the Blues*, 12.

47. Cone, *Spirituals and the Blues*, 13.

48. Moten, *In the Break*, 11.

49. From Lucy McKim Garrison, "Songs of the Port Royal 'Contrabands.'" See Cone, *Spirituals and the Blues*, 27.

it. . . . Black history is an experience, a soulful event. . . . *Black history is a spiritual!*[50]

There is much to unpack in this citation. First, the community is in rhythm in a felt way of moving, organizing, being, to the movement(s) of life. Everything, it seems, is in motion. Everything is thus in flux, in process. Next, one must feel the rhythm and let the rhythm move them into culture and consciousness, or a new way of being and knowing in the world. In this new way of knowing, "meaning" does not come primarily from the words or the text but from the living history—life, culture, thought, experience, feeling—that produces it. That is how Black history is a spiritual and, as such, sings its story. The sound of the music is produced by feeling, even as the feeling of the music is pronounced by its sound. This is the reality embodied in Black experience and the inspirited materiality which birthed the spirituals.

Du Bois asks, "How does it *feel* to be a problem?" In his essay, "How Does It Feel to Be the Problem? Affect Theory and White Domination," Christopher Carter responds to Donovan Schaefer's *Religious Affects* by considering further the embodied nature of racialization and reversing Du Bois's question to "how does it feel to be *the* problem?"[51] Carter is talking about "the problem" in terms of practicing white domination as an embodied unconscious way of living in which the lines between religion, feeling right, and the forces of normativity become irreducible. He notes:

> When considered in light of colonial and settler Christianity (i.e., the type of Christianity that the majority of Christians unknowingly still practice) which misused Christian teachings to elevate whiteness over and above people of color, the distinguishing lines between the affective economies produced by white domination and those produced by this type of Christian practice are at best blurred, and at worst almost identical.[52]

The spirituals emerged over and against this type of colonial and settler Christianity, a Christian practice that seeks to produce a particular way of knowing in relation to what it means to be white, to be powerful, and to be so in the world, casting Blackness as a problem, an enclosed, foreclosed object, an aberration of the flesh, a pathology. The solution is to tend toward

50. Cone, *Spirituals and the Blues*, 31 (emphasis in original).
51. Carter, "How Does It Feel."
52. Carter, "How Does It Feel."

whiteness. Here, at this site, epistemology, phenomenology, and ontology coalesce: an embodied way of knowing and feeling and being in a racialized world. To be sure, the Black subject was made and pathologized to serve the white need for labor. Carter suggests that "affect theory helps us move past extremist positions to explore the way lived religion among whites generates economies of affect which produce bodily technologies that enable and encourage the oppression of minoritized people to continue."[53] We are reminded of Crawley's notion that to think theologically, to think philosophically, is to think racially. Schaefer's work offers a lens to consider how affects (in)form bodies in such a way that bodies are taught "this is what it *feels* like to be us," which is a particular type of knowledge and subject formation. This felt understanding of identity cuts in multiple directions: it inflicts and traumatizes those who are victims of violence, even as it justifies the violence in terms of necessity and nature for others, which masks the violence and trauma that it causes to the oppressor.

Shelly Rambo has argued how national life has been reorganized around traumatic events, especially through the cycle of "traumatic repetition," which can be seen in the histories of slavery and racism in the US.[54] Further, the personal and particularly Western European image of the individual as individual trauma victim is problematized by the multiplicitous effects of violence at communal, institutional, national, and international levels. "How it feels to be us," therefore, is an adage that seeks to cover up and obscure these histories by reifying the individualized racial constructs and categorical distinctions of modernity. What follows are the affects of racialization and the practices (effects) which are informed by them. How does it feel to be Black as an object robbed of personhood? How does it feel to be white, i.e., to be the problem yet numb to the violence of wielding a sword by the blade?

Sara Ahmed's work on emotion and race is critical to these questions. Her work in *The Cultural Politics of Emotion* explores the organization of hate and affective politics of fear as a way of uncovering the affective configurations of racism as something felt, created, and learned: a felt pedagogy. Using the Aryan Nation and white nationalism as an example, Ahmed argues that hate shapes bodies and worlds in the way it generates its object as the defense against injury or, even, as an obstacle to love. The proximity of others—as embodying a difference seen as a threat—brings close the threat

53. Carter, "How Does It Feel."

54. Rambo, *Spirit and Trauma*, 27.

of injury, the risk of taking something away, or even replacing it (the it, here, being whiteness as privileged property). Immigrants or other-than-white people become the constitutive outside and object that causes the white nation, through hate, to stick together: *"It is the emotional reading of hate that works to stick or to bind the imagined subjects and the white nation together. . . . Because we hate, we love, and this hate is what brings us together."*[55] Through a discourse of pain, people of color and immigrants are transformed into hated objects insofar as they are reduced to the feelings they ostensibly generate. Bodies are defined by their differences. Hate is the feeling that organizes and brings the group together. Love or cherishing their imagined state as protectors of their assumed race is the result. Because they hate, they love; and because they love, they hate. Affective economies are thus markets of exchange, shaping bodies and their relationships in and to the world through the circulation of affects between figures in social, material, and psychic capacities. These economies of exchange in terms of feelings shape the horizon of possibility.

Citing Audre Lorde's account of feeling as if a white woman's gaze imagined a roach sitting near her, Ahmed argues how affective economies of hate dehumanize others and consequently reshape and reorder the social world accordingly. This history is embedded and embodied as the history of the world in Wynter's genre of Man and imbues the fabric of the modern world, where, in the US, it perpetuates founding myths that praise white colonial settlers and obscures the violence and hate against the indigenous peoples of the Americas and the enslaved Africans that built the economy of the very old New World. In a sense, Donald Trump's campaign slogan, "Make America Great Again," seeks to stir feelings of hate and love—hate for those who supposedly harmed and love for those who had made it great. The genius of Trump's approach is that he has shifted the affective landscape such that any critique of the nation's history or present, more and more, is seen as antipatriotic and un-American. To question the practices of the US, therefore, is to question one's love for the nation as the imagined subject, the object of love.

But the racial implications of "Make America Great Again," coupled with his unabashed disdain for migrants—calling them animals, rapists, drug dealers—and travel bans for countries with substantial Muslim populations, reveal the racist and xenophobic underpinnings of his platform. Trump is seeking to create a particular America analogous to the ways the

---

55. Ahmed, *Cultural Politics of Emotion*, 43 (emphasis in original).

Aryan Nation operates by objectifying those who do not resonate with particular white American values that have made America "great" in the past. Mythology plays a significant role in both approaches; the stories are true, not because there is objective proof, but because they feel true. Affects teach bodies through how words and ideas feel. Words resonate within bodies and are never detached from lived reality. Ta-Nehisi Coates reminds us:

> But all our phrasing—race relations, racial chasm, racial justice, racial profiling, white privilege, even white supremacy—serves to obscure that racism is a visceral experience, that it dislodges brains, blocks airways, rips muscle, extracts organs, cracks bones, breaks teeth. You must never look away from this. You must always remember that the sociology, the history, the economics, the graphs, the charts, the regressions all land, with great violence, upon the body.[56]

The contrast between President Obama's 2008 platform of hope and Trump's 2016 and 2020 campaigns of fear could not be starker. The question remains how the public will be affected and attuned to conflicting messages—and affects—about the future of the nation.

While hate organizes and orients the social order in particular ways, and love is the idiom through which hate speaks, Ahmed suggests fear is not something that simply comes from within and then moves outward toward objects/others. Rather, it is something that circulates from within and without, which "secure[s] the relationship between those bodies; it brings them together and moves them apart through the shudders that are felt on the skin, on the surface that surfaces through the encounter."[57] Fear, in this way, moves across signs and between bodies. Consider the protests and counterprotests in Charlottesville, Virginia. As a mob of white men marched through the area around a confederate statue—an object of affective attachments of love, hate, and fear—they carried tiki torches and chanted "Blood and soil!," a Nazi slogan. The affectsphere climaxed when James Alex Fields Jr. drove his car into a crowd of protestors, killing thirty-two-year-old Heather Heyer. The videos and pictures of the attack depict bodies suspended in the air and blood smeared on the concrete. Racism is not simply an ideology that is believed or rejected; rather, racism produces and is produced by embodied, conditioned practices steeped in hate and anchored in fear.

56. Coates, *Between World and Me*, 11.
57. Coates, *Between World and Me*, 63.

Hate and fear are affective strategies to maintain a certain social ordering of the world. If Black bodies can be made into objects of hate, then they become less human, something to be feared and enveloped in fear. "Fear works to contain bodies within social space through the way it shrinks the body, or constitutes the bodily surface through an expectant withdrawal from a world that might yet present itself as dangerous."[58] Shrinking the body is to make less human, at least vis-à-vis modern man (white, rational, hetero). Out of an affective economy of fear, authority is needed to enforce the social ordering, which becomes known as the terms of order. Order, out of purported necessity, becomes the way of aligning bodies and social space; some bodies inhabit and move through public spaces while others are restricted. The uneven distribution of fear leads to uneven social relationality. Furthermore, fear becomes the founding and perpetuating force of these relations. To recognize the affective components of racism and racialization, therefore, is to acknowledge the felt conditions that justified and continue to justify the uneven, inequitable world that has been set up for profit, freedom, and privilege of some (read: white supremacy) at the expense and restriction of others. Donovan Schaefer, engaging Ahmed's work on affective economies, writes:

> Affect builds networks of power structuring social norms; fear, the pressure of a threat to *us*, "does not involve the defense of borders that already exist; rather, fear makes those borders by establishing objects from which the subject, in fearing, can stand apart, objects that become 'the not' from which the subject appears to flee."[59]

Fear creates distance from the perceived threat of the other, of difference. In doing so, fear creates borders and boundaries, which take shape in the collective life of the nation. Social norms are structured, maintained, and enforced by affective power. US institutions were built on founding myths and continue to operate, in part, because of the perpetuation of the mythic pasts maintained through the affective economies of hate and politics of fear. Whether against indigenous communities, the enslaved, or, for a contemporary issue, migrants from South America and Muslim refugees, the affective economy of fear has played a significant role in the formation of America's republic. Pushing back against the systems and institutions of discrimination and racism is, in a very real sense, seen as anti-American.

58. Coates, *Between World and Me*, 70.

59. Sara Ahmed, "Affective Economies," 128; quoted in Schaefer, *Religious Affects*, 53 (emphasis in original).

This is most starkly seen in recent efforts around the US to ban critical race theory.

Returning to the spirituals, we find a different understanding of Blackness and African history. There is no problem with Blackness; rather, there is beauty and power to be found. The spirituals produce and perform an audible sound, resonance, a vibration, that disrupts and refutes colonial myths, logics, and projects. The spirituals take the religious framework of white settler Christianity—its songs and teachings—and augments them, introducing a new sound, e.g., the blue note, which takes conventional European scales and flattens them. It is the sound of multiple worlds, not a singular one. Plural, not singular, worlds, not the world; humans, not the human; theories, not theory. Audre Lorde writes:

> The white western patriarchal ordering of things requires that we believe there is an inherent conflict between what we feel and what we think—between poetry and theory. We are easier to control when one part of our selves is split from another, fragmented, off balance. There are other configurations, however, other ways of experiencing the world, though they are often difficult to name. We can sense them and seek their articulation.[60]

The spirituals birth a sound and a feeling, a feeling-sound of suffering without falling into despair, sounds of celebration without the actualized conditions of freedom. The spirituals are a new expression, a new language, which reorder and reconfigure ways of experiencing the world in unfragmented ways—ways that do not bifurcate feeling and knowing.

The spirituals were born out of aesthetic practices, expressions, and modulations. For Zora Neale Hurston, the spirituals are "not really songs. They are unceasing variations around a theme . . . they are being made and forgotten every day."[61] Like Cone, Hurston is intimating something behind or beyond the music: a living history and embodied existence. Hurston differentiates between the spirituals, as songs sung by a group "bent on expression of feelings, and not on sound effects,"[62] and what she calls "neo-spirituals," which are the more polished presentations based on the songs and performed by glee clubs and concert singers. Essential to the spiritual are the happenings of everyday life, constituted by "harmony and

---

60. Quoted in Crawley, *Lonely Letters*, 37.
61. Hurston, *Sanctified Church*, 79.
62. Hurston, *Sanctified Church*, 80.

disharmony, the shifting keys and broken time that make up the spiritual."[63] That is why she argues that no spiritual has ever been presented for an audience. Speech and song feature heavily in Black religious services:

> The truth is, that the religious service is a conscious art expression. The artist is consciously creating—carefully choosing every syllable and every breath. The dialect breaks through only when the speaker has reached the emotional pitch where he loses all self-consciousness. In the mouth of the Negro the English language loses it stiffness, yet conveys its meaning accurately. . . . Negro singing and formal speech are breathy. The audible breathing is part of the performance and various devices are resorted to adorn the breath taking. Even the lack of breath is embellished with syllables. This is, of course, the very antithesis of white vocal art. European singing is considered when each syllable floats out on a column of air, seeming not to have any mechanics at all. Breathing must be hidden.[64]

Notice the emphasis on art expression, which makes the worshiper an artist, able to craft and create, experience and emulate. Moreover, the conscious choice of syllable and breath is a method that makes possible an emotional climax. It is a way of feeling one's way through the service. Hurston notes that the English language loses it stiffness through Black speech. That is to say, its rigidity is loosened; yet its meaning, its efficacy, remains intact. Black language, as embodied expression, bends the syllables and syntax to speak in new, but understandable, ways. The speech and song are breathy practices. Breath is the source of life; and for Hurston, it is the animating force that harnesses and heightens Black religious experience/expression. This is antithetical to white vocal art, in which breathing must be hidden ("sneak a breath where you can"). Consequently, white art does not possess the mechanics or the dynamics of Black art expression in the religious service. An example of bending the forms and norms of white art and expression is the use of heterophony, in which singers overlay versions of a melody to create a dense musical texture. Heterophony is the utilization of subtle simultaneous variations, a multiplicity of expressions of the same melody.

The spirituals emerged at the intersection of Black art expression and experience, and are the historical precursor to blues, gospel, and jazz. The

63. Hurston, *Sanctified Church*, 81.

64. Hurston, *Sanctified Church*, 83.

sounds of the music are distinguishable in terms of tones and rhythms. For example, in the context of a major scale, there are seven notes, and the intervals are: whole, whole, half, whole, whole, whole half. This is the universal pattern for a major scale. For example, if it were a C major scale, the scale would be played: C-D-E-F-G-A-B, then back to C (from E to F and from B to C are half steps). When the notes are played in form and in order, the scale has a particular (happy) sound. Any notes played that are not in the scale are departures from the pattern, which are called *accidentals*, a deviation from the norm of the scale. While accidentals are allowed, if one does not play the appropriate notes in the major scale, it can be considered out of key or wrong. These are the rules for a major scale. Yet, much music born from Black experience does not follow these rules. In fact, what is called accidental is precisely what shapes and distinguishes the tonality from other styles of music. These notes are used over and against the form of the major scale to create otherwise expressions. While jazz music is loosely organized by standards, often it refuses to be confined to one particular key.

If one takes the C major scale from above and flattens (lowers the note by a half step or tone) the third, fifth, and seventh, this creates a blues scale, with the following notes: C, Eb, F, Gb, G, Bb. The flatting of the notes (in bold) creates a noticeable change in the nature and quality of the tones. The blue note is felt as much as heard, suggesting that the meaning or value of it is just as much in the sound as sound production. Perhaps, even more so. For example, consider Frederick Douglass's assertation that those enslaved "would sing the most pathetic sentiment in the most rapturous tone, and the most rapturous sentiment in the most pathetic tone."[65] In this case, the relationship between sentiment and sound seems to be asymmetrical. Okiji addresses this discernible difference:

> The prying away of sentiment from signifiers through which it is usually understood, the calling into question of the intention or feeling behind a particular vocal gesture, releases a pool of musical and lyrical material that is mobile, malleable, even seditious. This opening-up not only enriches relational components—gaining in prospective sound-word-semantic partnerships what is lost in dependable designation and logic—it also fosters an environment where contrary sentiments can share expressive material without loss of meaning.[66]

65. Douglass, *Narrative of the Life*, 35; quoted in Okiji, *Jazz as Critique*, 78.
66. Okiji, *Jazz as Critique*, 78.

Douglass alludes to this dynamic: "The thought came up, came out—if not in the word, in the sound—and as frequently in the one as in the other. . . . They would sing, as a chorus, to words which to many would seem unmeaning jargon, but which, nevertheless, were full of meaning to themselves."[67] Okiji is interested in Douglass's mention of what she calls "extralinguistic vocalizations," i.e., growls, sighs, screams, and laughter, which frustrate simple interpretation but are paradoxically "able to pinpoint sentiment and intention (perhaps because in some cases they *are* sentiment and intention) with a degree of sensitivity that disembodied word and phrase can only hope to approach."[68]

Thinking in terms of extralinguistic vocalizations brings the affective nature of sound back into the conversation. These sounds frustrate or refuse simple interpretation, even as Black expression does so. Okiji, building on Douglass, is arguing that gestural vocals pull away from linguistic comprehension, and that Black song is informed, even structured, by a broadened appreciation of articulatable forms—otherwise possibilities. Fred Moten speaks of a place where words cannot go:

> Words don't go there: this implies a difference between words and sounds; it suggests that words are somehow constrained by their implicit reduction to the meanings they carry—meanings inadequate to or detached from the objects or states of affairs they would envelop. What's also implied is an absence of inflection; a loss of mobility, slippage, bend; a missing accent or affect; the impossibility of a slur or crack and the *excess*—rather than loss—of meaning they imply.[69]

Where do words go? Moten alludes to a realm in which only music, only sound can go. This is not a loss or deficit of meaning, but rather an excess. In Black expression in general, and the spirituals in particular, there is a wider palette of communicability whereby song-making determines and redefines what it means to speak. To speak is to breathe, is to shout, is to make audible without being confined to sedimented signifiers. To speak in this way is to bring new worlds into existence. The adroit modulations of Black expression in the spirituals are otherworldly, not merely in the sense of futurity, but in the sense that they create new worlds in the here and now. The sounds' otherwise possibilities are accompanied by otherworldly

67. Okiji, *Jazz as Critique*, 78.
68. Okiji, *Jazz as Critique*, 78.
69. Moten, *In the Break*, 42.

rhythms. I have addressed the tonality of the spirituals, as well as the sound production that unsettles and opens out communicability beyond intelligible language through extralinguistic vocalizations. I now turn to the notion of rhythm in Black music to demonstrate how sound and movement, specifically shouting and dancing, are inexorably affixed.

As mentioned in the introduction to this chapter, sound itself is a movement, a vibration. Rhythm, by definition, is the repetition of a sound. Rhythm exists as material sounds of breathing, clapping, and singing as they move in time and space. The repetition of these sounds and movements constitutes distinguishable patterns or sequences. The spirituals not only alter the (Eurocentric) sounds of hymns and folk music, but they contest and augment the time signatures, backbeats, and downbeats of European rhythms by overlaying and overlapping complex individual polyrhythms. In the same way that heterophony adds in simultaneous, subtle variations to the melody, polyrhythms create the illusion of an irregular master beat, when, in fact, they are intricacies working within the master beat.[70] For example, European music is often in a 4/4 time signature, with equal upbeats and downbeats counted as 1-and-2-and-3-and-4-and. The 4/4 time signature keeps time like a clock and as such feels mechanical, rigid, even. It is a straight rhythm. However, within the 4/4 it is possible to augment this feeling. Accented notes stress or emphasize certain sounds from others. Swing notes take the 4/4 time signature and give it a shuffle feel, like shuffling feet, a swaying within the straight time signature. Another way 4/4 time is augmented is through syncopation, "a temporary displacement of the regular metrical accent in music caused typically by stressing the weak beat."[71] Syncopation displaces the regular (normative) accent and stresses the weak beat—a rhythm characteristic of jazz and the ingenuity of other otherwise Black expressions. Swing rhythms and syncopation are both techniques and performances within 4/4 time, which is also called *common time*.

Common time is the Western norm of music, even as it is a Western norm for time itself. It is a way of ordering and organizing the musical world in even measure through even rhythms. While there are ways to diversify the tones and rhythms within it, the framework remains. In the spirituals there is a call-and-response rhythm, characteristic of West African traditions. Another variation of musical expression is through the creation of

70. Peretti, *Lift Every Voice*, 9, 11.

71. See "Syncopation" at https://www.merriam-webster.com/dictionary/syncopation.

different time signatures. 12/8 time gives twelve beats per measure and the eighth note (half the length of a quarter) gets one beat. This time signature creates a swing, a quick shuffle, a rhythm characteristic of African song and dance. The innovations and integrations of alternative, otherwise time signatures and rhythms in Black music resound with Zora Neal Hurston's claim that Black musical expressions "are one and all based on a dance-possible rhythm."[72] The movements and sounds in the spirituals, born out of Black history, are the expressions of an alternate world beyond common time—sounds and rhythms that overlay and overwhelm the master beat by stressing or emphasizing the weak beat, affirmations and performances of life and freedom amidst the daily realities of slavery, despair, and death. It is worth noting that white Pentecostal traditions have embraced some of the sounds and style of Black musical expression.[73]

The work of Walter Pitts Jr. on Afro-Baptist ritual and ritual frames is pertinent to the emergence of Black syncretized religious expressions in the antebellum South. For Pitts, *Afro-rituals* consist of two metaphoric frames, devotion and service, which are reinterpretations and extensions of African religious customs; and, by moving from frame to frame in sequence, "the ritual participant is emotionally—and spiritually—satisfied at its end."[74] Devotion is akin to a sort of preservice intercessory prayer, whereas service begins where and when devotion ends. Pitts argues that metaphor, rather than symbol, becomes the basis for ritual, and brings together "disparate entities such as speech, song, gesture," creating and controlling "desired moods over its participants."[75] The metaphoric frames are not static but are deeply connected to the emotional transformation of the ritual par-ticipants; they move "up and down an affective scale" between poles of "disparagement" and "adornment."[76] Thus, the metaphoric frames do not simply represent a bound sequence of events, but also the associated feel-ings that accompany them. In other words, the metaphoric frames become "emotional paradigms containing as fillers for such behavior as a specific

---

72. Hurston, *Sanctified Church*, 83.

73. This likely was a result from the intermingling of Black and white worshippers in camp meetings in the early nineteenth century, e.g., consider Southern Gospel music or how white Pentecostal music and preaching sometimes emulates Black expression.

74. Pitts, *Old Ship of Zion*, 8.

75. Pitts, *Old Ship of Zion*, 31.

76. Pitts, *Old Ship of Zion*, 31.

type of speech, song style, and gesture."[77] Specifically, speech and song are the emotional elements that manage and maintain the ritual in general and the metaphoric frames in particular. Once again, this African heritage is preserved and passed down through the songs and speech or preaching of Black communities.

Because the spirituals were not written down, they had to be memorized and passed down through oral tradition and embodied performance. This allowed for improvisation, that is, to give individual expression—in rhythm and tone—within a particular form. It is for this reason that modes of expression, including movement (dancing, stepping, swaying, clapping, stomping, waving, etc.) and vocals (singing, shouting, chanting, etc.) should be thought together. For Ashon Crawley, "the shout does not take place without making, taking, and breaking sound; the shout traditions are choreographic insofar as they are sonic, and are sonic insofar as they are choreographic."[78] Performance, as performance of worlds otherwise over and against the epistemology of normativity, is part and parcel of Black aesthetics. He continues: "Shouts—Afro-Arabic, Ring, and Blackpentecostal—are the itineraries for the lines of force animating an architectonics of resistance; they perform protocols for movement that always counter and intuit; they are intentionally agitational and nuanced."[79] The ring shout, in particular, in which participants ceaselessly move in a ring, or circle—feet shuffling, but never leaving the ground, a progression from singing spirituals to repeating chant-like phrases for hours, and the subsequent onset of ecstatic states—for Crawley shows that neither the choreographic nor the sonic is reducible to or privileged over one another. The ring shout, as a choreosonic encounter, as an enfleshed performance of "sociality as dissent," is a rhythmic ritual, a rotation (*perichoresis*) of self and collective catharsis, and a contestation of a world that seeks to make those enslaved socially dead subjects. Its historic emergence images the creation of otherwise social life, form, and norms in the expressive languages of the body through sighs, laughs, shouts, and other fleshy, breathy, and undeterminable utterances. Crawley concludes: "The Ring Shout as a social form of centrifugivity [i.e., simultaneously centripetal and centrifugal] carried the indeterminacy of meaning, and this indeterminacy was the condition

---

77. Pitts, *Old Ship of Zion*, 32.
78. Crawley, *Blackpentecostal Breath*, 94.
79. Crawley, *Blackpentecostal Breath*, 95.

of its possibility."[80] The Ring Shout is creation-in-motion. It is a constellation constituted by Black history, Black expression, Black possibility in an otherwise cosmos. The relationship between the song and the dance is inextricable, even as it is for the individual and the others in the ring. It is a flow of sociality, of spirituality, of relationality made and sustained by life otherwise.

Otherwise worlds are constituted through practice, performance, proclamation, and affect. The musicality of the songs (re)presents more than mere aesthetic production or entertainment; it is material, fleshy, embodied. As Alan Lomax has pointed out, "the blues have always been a state of being as well as singing."[81] Like Cone, Lomax underscores the blues as an expression of lived experience, as an embodied epistemology of existing in and navigating through the world. Such expression is an annunciation as much as a renunciation, what the Reverend Otis Moss III calls the "blues sensibilities." In *Blue Note Preaching in a Post-Soul World: Finding Hope in an Age of Despair*, Moss declares: "What is this thing called the *Blues*? It is the roux of Black speech, the backbeat of American music, and the foundation of Black preaching. Blues is the curve of the Mississippi, the ghost of the South, the hypocrisy of the North. Blues is the beauty of Bebop, the soul of Gospel, and the pain of Hip-Hop."[82] For Moss, the Blues is a way of seeing, a strategy of knowing, and a technique of empowerment. Moss's contributions to blue note sensibilities coalesce with the Holy Spirit's work in Acts and in the spirituals as the advent of a sound that "brings colors, tone, dynamics, chords, and a new time signature to the world."[83] Blue note preaching, as sound, alters the world and "delivers something external but cannot be controlled. The written word can be copyrighted, and someone can say, 'I own it.' But once a word goes out, no one can own it or grab it."[84] This word, this sound uttered, is alive and active, and it moves into bodies—becoming flesh—and begins to transform them.

For Moss, blue note preaching conjures and channels the African griot tradition, the West African people who are musicians, storytellers, custodians, and teachers of tradition through music and dance. This person embodies history and tradition and functions as a troubadour-historian.

---

80. Crawley, *Blackpentecostal Breath*, 104.

81. Robert Switzer, "Signifying the Blues," 40; quoted in Okiji, *Jazz as Critique*, 76.

82. Moss, *Blue Note Preaching*, 2.

83. Moss, *Blue Note Preaching*, 14.

84. Moss, *Blue Note Preaching*, 38.

The West African *griot* is the precedent for call-and-response in the music and communication of enslaved Africans in the antebellum South reflected in the spirituals, ring shouts, and blues sensibilities; it is the basis for the call-and-response between preacher and congregation, wherein they join together to encourage one another, bringing a new musicality to the worship experience and reaching back to old worlds and into the present and beyond to bring about otherwise and new worlds: "Here they could be spiritually reborn and emotionally uplifted, exhorting their preacher as he in turn exhorted them, both engaging in a call-and-response dialogue that went back to their ancestry."[85] In the final section, I turn to the historical happenings that led from revivals to holiness movement and, ultimately, to Azusa Street.

The Road to Azusa

The Pentecostal movement owes much of its heritage to the theology of John Wesley. As the father of Methodism, Wesley's theology of personal piety and perfection, in terms of "holiness," was accompanied by his emphasis on religious experience. Indeed, Wesley's transition from Anglicanism to Methodism was marked by a conversion "experience," a felt transition whereby his heart was "strangely warmed."[86] Wesley's conversion was followed by another experience, a "second blessing," which constituted, for him, the means (by grace) of sanctification, perfection, holiness. What Wesley meant by *heart* is uncertain. Perhaps bodily sensitivity or recognition of interior change in attitude or emotion? Regardless, the first experience, conversion (justification) is felt as change and is followed by a second experience, sanctification (perfection); this became the theological norm of Methodism, insofar as the "method" is seeking "a perfection of motives and desires."[87] While some preachers, such as George Whitefield, rejected the second blessing theory, other leaders embraced the doctrine. It was not enough to be saved (converted); one must also be sanctified, which became synonymous with receiving or being "baptized" with/in the Holy Ghost.[88]

85. Oates, *Let the Trumpet Sound*, 57; quoted in Pitts, *Old Ship of Zion*, 31.

86. This is John Wesley's famous phrase, which indicates his emphasis on emotion into religious experience; quoted in Synan, *Holiness-Pentecostal Tradition*, 4.

87. Synan, *Holiness-Pentecostal Tradition*, 7.

88. Many Pentecostals consider Holy Spirit baptism to be a "third blessing," differentiating it from sanctification.

The First Great Awakening (ca. 1730s–1740s) played a considerable role in the spread of Methodism in general and emotionally charged revivals in particular. It was an age of the import of new philosophies, ideas, and doctrines to the vanguard of Christian faith. As revivals proliferated in the eighteenth century, such rhetoric ramped up the affective temperature of religious gatherings. Vinson Synan notes:

> In *The Brief Narrative of the Revival of Religion* that [the Reverend Devereaux] Jarrett wrote describing the Virginia services of 1775, holiness religion was much in evidence. Many were "panting and groaning for pardon" while others were "entreating God, with strong cries and tears to save them from the remains of inbred sin, to sanctify them throughout . . . " At times the emotions of the sanctified Methodists would exceed the limits of control. "Some would be seized with a trembling, and in a few moments drop to the floor as if they were dead; while others were embracing each other with streaming eyes, and all were lost in wonder, love, and praise," wrote one observer. Another noted that some wept for grief while others shouted for joy "so that it was hard to distinguish one from the other." At times the congregations would raise a "great shout" that could be heard from miles around . . . as the emotional element abated "the work of conviction and conversion abated too."[89]

By the end of the eighteenth century, there was precedent for Pentecostal practices, such as being "slain in the Spirit," as well as emotional outpourings that were catalytic for the "work" of conviction and conversion. Tacitly, emotion is the means and end, the telos, of the Holy Spirit as second blessing. The theology of the First Great Awakening, including Wesley's notion of a second blessing of sanctification, shaped these emotional episodes. Some key teachings of the Great Awakening included: 1) Everyone is born a sinner; 2) Sin without salvation will send a person to hell; 3) Anyone can be saved if they confess their sins to God, seek forgiveness, and accept God's grace; 4) Anyone can have a direct and emotional connection with God; 5) Religion should not be formal and institutionalized, but rather casual and personal.[90] This is the historical backdrop for Congregationalist minister Jonathan Edward's "Sinners in the Hands of an Angry God," which so galvanized the audience through the vivid imagery of hell and biblical

---

89. Wesley Marsh Gewehr, *The Great Awakening in Virginia: 1740–1790*; quoted in Synan, *Holiness-Pentecostal Tradition*, 9.

90. Editors, "Great Awakening."

support of its existence, coupled with the imminence of God's wrath, that it precipitated audible interjections in the form of cries and groans from the people.

Charismatic preacher George Whitefield was another example of how preaching dynamically in an age of religious emotional expression was efficacious. Methodist perfectionism in America was the growth of what Wesley called "heart religion," i.e., "a swing toward warmth, feeling, experience, and morality," and away from the mechanical, permissive, de-ethicalized, and formal worship of the times.[91] And yet, based on the passage above, there is some variance between what emotions are experienced and why. On the one hand, some were lost in wonder, love, and praise. On the other, some were lost in grief and despair because of one's own wretchedness. To be sure, the affects of sanctification overwhelmed, rendering interpretive efforts futile. Nonetheless, Wesley and others stirred up a heart religion, an affective and ostensibly sensate connection with God—God as both idea and God as experiential reality—in and through the body. The work of parsing or fleshing out the excessive, irreducible meaning of religious experience, thus, is for the one with the experience. Translating or interpreting these encounters is fundamental to and characteristic of this personal heart religion.

Briefly, I want to address a question asked of me by affect scholar Donovan Schaefer, namely: "Are revivalist affects accidental or manipulative?" When he asked me this at an academic conference in 2018, my answer was and remains: yes. The "or" in his question seeks to do the impossible, that is, to know with certainty whether and how the intricate, complicated affective economies around emotive, ecstatic religious experience can be crafted, manufactured, and mastered. This is always possible, likely, even. As with ritual, feelings are ways of learning and organizing around form and symbols. Yet, there had to be a genesis, an event hitherto unexperienced and novel, that was accidental or at least unforeseen. It is here that affects' autotelic nature—Kosofsky's lurking queer little gods—become most prominent. It is clear that for Wesley, the initial heart-warming experience was novel, so much so that it became the foundational experience for his spirituality. Likewise, the revivals stirred up emotions that had recurring bodily expressions—tears, laughing, trembling, shouting—but did not have uniform meaning. The intent or desired effect of the revivalist affects, therefore, cannot be controlled or guaranteed; but it does not take much

91. Synan, *Holiness-Pentecostal Tradition*, 10.

imagination to consider how they can be used to manipulate or bring about desired effects. This is the power and liability of body-centric religious experience, authority, and legitimacy. We could speculate that the intent of revivalists in the Great Awakenings was to use their voices and the affects their words and tones stir up to produce a certain mood and effect, mainly, conviction, repentance, and conversion. However, the extent of the effect or ultimate source of it cannot be known. Inextricably entangled in the spirit of the attendees and the Spirit of God, revivalist affects are accidental as well as manipulative, cultivated as well as spontaneous. Perhaps it is this elusive mystery that gives revivals their appeal.

The spread of American Methodism, due to its circuit-riding evangelists and second blessing theology, culminated in mid-to-late eighteenth century camp meetings. Perhaps the most well-known of the outbreak of pre-Pentecostal experiences was the Cane Ridge camp meeting in Kentucky in 1801. For three summers leading up to the camp meeting, Methodist circuit riders would come to Logan County preaching revival and leading people into the sanctification experience. It was after Presbyterian pastors were sparked by the zeal of Methodist preacher John McGee that the American camp meeting was born. Just as the attendees of the Cane Ridge camp meetings lived on the frontier of the so-called new world, so too did they occupy a frontier of a religious movement. "Their 'Godly hysteria' included such phenomena as falling, jerking, barking like dogs, falling into trances, the 'holy laugh,' and such wild dances as David performed before the Ark of the Lord."[92] Rather than a pejorative, "Godly hysteria" signifies a recognition of the raised and rising emotional temperature of the camp meetings, whereby people were not only moved in emotional displays, but bodily-emotional displays—falling, jerking, barking, entrancing, laughing, and dancing. What was it that caused bodies to fall down to the ground? Was it the heaviness of sin or the weight of glory? By the early nineteenth century, it is well documented that people had begun speaking in unknown tongues, even as the camp meeting became a regular part—an attraction for some and spectacle for others—of American religious and cultural life.[93]

92. Synan, *Holiness-Pentecostal Tradition*, 12.

93. See E. Merton Coulter, *College Life in the Old South*, 194–95, for an example of a revival at the University of Georgia in which students spoke in unknown tongues (ca. 1800–1801), and Guion Griffis, "Camp Meetings in Ante-Bellum North Carolina" (*North Carolina Historical Review*), for an example of speaking in tongues at North Carolina camp meetings around the same time; both cited in Synan, *Holiness-Pentecostal Tradition*, 13.

The Great Awakening, thus, was an awakening of religious fervor, of the passionate and personal contours of religion.

John Wesley's second blessing was a catalyst for other theological developments, including baptism of the Holy Spirit as the indicator and means of the work of sanctification. It is important, here, to situate the historical developments of Wesley's work and the Great Awakenings within its proper social milieu. The eighteenth century was a time of slavocracy. The inclusion of enslaved persons into camp meetings made them interracial gatherings, a sociality at odds with everyday life: "The interracial fellowship that African Americans found in Holiness worship was different from what they encountered in everyday life. It provided respite from the racism of their surrounding communities and a platform for black itinerant preachers and laypersons to ply their ministries, often among largely white audiences."[94] And, "convinced that sanctification should bring a change in social consciousness in as well as outside the sanctuary, blacks began to form their own Holiness bodies."[95] The hope for a change in spiritual consciousness led to hope for a change in social consciousness, i.e., that the institution and practice of slavery would be seen rightly as inherently evil and anti-Christian. However, this tension would eventually bifurcate and separate the North from the South, segregating the holiness movement in the latter. The era was tainted by America's original sin, slavery, which eventually fractured the movement.

Consider the different voices of the movement: While John Wesley espoused an antislavery theology, Jonathan Edwards, a northern Congregationalist, and his ilk were decidedly pro-slavery—though Edwards argued that one could be complicit in the system without enslaving others. Edwards baptized eleven Black attendees and committed several to full membership, but he contended that, while whites and Blacks both needed salvation, the divinely imposed social order of this world would be observed in heaven through "different degrees of glory."[96] In the Second Great Awakening, Methodist George Whitefield decried harsh treatment of those enslaved but failed to condemn the institution of slavery, deeming it a necessary evil for the economy and an opportunity to evangelize enslaved communities. Despite his pro-slavery views, many Black people were converted under his preaching. We should note and remember, however, that salvation, for

94. E. Alexander, *Black Fire*, 62.
95. E. Alexander, *Black Fire*, 62.
96. E. Alexander, *Black Fire*, 65.

Black people, came reinscribed with society's racialized hierarchy, i.e., inferior, second class, and second-rate.

Estrelda Y. Alexander argues that Black people were attracted to the Second Great Awakening because its emotive style resonated with African spiritual heritage—what Hurston called *Africanisms*, in the form of jerking, dancing, rolling, and fainting—and that, because of the interracial makeup of the worship service, some revivalists agitated against slavery.[97] At the pinnacle of the American slave trade, the yearning for social inclusion to mirror spiritual inclusion poignantly proliferated. Charles G. Finney, for example, implemented the altar call as a means of bringing new converts to the front of the gathering space and also to sign them up for the abolition movement. Finney, himself, had a dramatic conversion experience that was marked by the "baptism of the Holy Spirit" and "unutterable gushings" of praise.[98] Baptism in the Holy Spirit meant entering into entire or total sanctification wherein not one part of life is left unaffected by the sanctifying presence of the Spirit. Thus, Finney's altar call was not simply an ephemeral moment of heightened spiritual experience, it was the occasion and source for social transformation. To go forward to the altar was to be empowered by the Spirit to enlist in the work of abolition. It signified a liberative event, like the afresh and anew of the Spirit in Acts 2. For Finney, worship and liberation, the spiritual and the social, were connected and integral to sanctification. As a result, Finney taught that regeneration and oppression are incompatible; through his innovative teachings, including the baptism in and subsequent fresh receptions of the Holy Spirit as the means of sanctification, Finney furthered the work of Wesley toward more Pentecostal expressions. He taught against the institution of slavery from spiritual and social perspectives; as president of Oberlin College he paved the way for higher education for Black people; he contributed to the uplift of women through promiscuous societies; and he worked with oppressed workers who dealt with addiction during Prohibition. Finney did not, however, teach full equity between white and Black people, falling short to reimagine the world beyond the act of abolition.

In the years leading up to the Civil War, Southern churches drifted from teachings on holiness. A study of Southern literature from that era scarcely mentions the word. Could it be that, because spiritual sanctification meant social change with regard to slavery, Southerners considered the

97. E. Alexander, *Black Fire*, 65.

98. E. Alexander, *Black Fire*, 14.

cost to be too much? There is hardly any other way to explain the shift from pursuing holiness to defending the institution of slavery. From 1830–1858, a time of great revival, Synan notes that Southern Methodists distanced themselves from teachings on sanctification. The relationship between social sanctification and the sin of slavery was forever changed when the first shot of the Civil War rang out at Fort Sumter in 1861. A movement that began in earnest ended in civil war. The racialized history undergirding the spread and stall of Methodism in the South must be considered as part of the road to Azusa Street. Even after the Emancipation Proclamation, Black people were hardly free and still suffered from daily life lived under post-slavery Jim Crowism. Indeed, the early twentieth century was a time of lingering racial disparities—disparities that continue to mutate and reinvent themselves. From mass incarceration (the New Jim Crow[99]) to voter suppression and income inequality, racial disparities are not a thing of the past; they pervade our present.

Yet and still, Black holiness institutions were formed by virtue of embracing religious experiences rooted in African cosmologies and practices such as dancing and singing, the ring shout, spirit possession, and shouting, and the interplay between individual and collective bodies. As Hurston remarks: "The Saints, or the Sanctified Church is a revitalizing element in Negro music and religion. It is putting back into Negro religion those elements which were brought over from Africa and grafted onto Christianity."[100] This grafting-onto is more than superimposing or overlaying one tradition over another; it is a synthesis rooted in bodily agency and performance. The Great Awakenings in general and Methodism in particular provided a Christian framework and precedent for more embodied-as-bodily-aware expressions of worship, as well as organized communities and gatherings. Against this backdrop, Black denominations and movements were born. By the late eighteenth century, three Black Methodist bodies, several Baptist, and many independent groups were formed.[101]

Notably, in 1820, after unsuccessfully voting to become a separate Black conference and constituency within the white elder-led African Methodist Episcopal Church, the African Methodist Episcopal Zion Church (AMEZ) was formed. The new denomination had a strong abolitionist bent and included members, such as Harriett Tubman, Frederick Douglass, and

99. This is the term coined by Michelle Alexander in her book of the same name, *New Jim Crow*.

100. Hurston, *Sanctified Church*, 110.

101. E. Alexander, *Black Fire*, 68.

Sojourner Truth, earning the moniker "freedom church."[102] In 1900, the Church of God (Sanctified) (COGIC), which is now the largest Blackpentecostal denomination, was formed. The turn of the century witnessed the proliferation of holiness-Pentecostal denominations, of which, several were Black. The road to Azusa is marred by racism on the one hand and marked by radical possibility on the other. We cannot consider Azusa without first considering the geography and social milieu in which it emerged. Out from the cauldron and crucible of oppression, the Azusa Street Revival evidences a new thing, chronicles something otherwise and otherworldly, something *suis generis*.

Without Azusa Street, the Pentecostal movement may have been confined to the historical burgeoning and decline of the holiness movement in the eighteenth and nineteenth centuries. However, due to the pioneering work and mission of William J. Seymour, a new movement was born. Seymour was born in 1870 in Louisiana to parents who were previously enslaved. After being baptized into the Roman Catholic Church as an infant, Seymour grew up in a Baptist tradition in Texas. While much of his childhood is unknown, we do know that he moved to Indianapolis in 1895, joined the Black Methodist Episcopal Church, and came into contact with the holiness movement. From 1900 to 1902, Seymour attended classes at Martin Well Knapp's "God's Bible School," where he deepened his understanding of holiness theology.[103] Most notably, he joined the Church of God Reformation movement, headquartered in Anderson, Indiana. Also known as the Evening Night Saints, this church was known for its radical openness to people of all races. Alexander details Seymour's experience there:

> While with the Saints, Seymour claimed the experience of sanctification and was exposed to a level of racial inclusiveness unlike any he had witnessed. The Saints saw interracial worship as a sign of the true church, and people of both races worshiped and ministered regularly in their services. More importantly, they gave racial prejudice a theological critique. Instead of testifying that they were "saved, sanctified, and filled with the Holy Ghost," Saints asserted that they were "saved, sanctified, and prejudice removed." Their radical criticism of racism extended beyond the church to American society.[104]

102. E. Alexander, *Black Fire*, 70.

103. Nelson, "For Such a Time," 9–54.

104. Scott B. Lewis, "William J. Seymour: Follower of the 'Evening Light,'" 171; quoted in E. Alexander, *Black Fire*, 113.

The theological influence of the Saints on Seymour's theology and experience cannot therefore be understated. The Saints connected sanctification with a holiness of social, in addition to spiritual, implications. This theology bespeaks a totality or entirety of sanctification—something that Seymour would model and later try to recreate at Azusa Street. With the Saints, Seymour experienced an acceptance and affirmation of his Blackness beyond the "sting of segregation"[105] that would shape his theology of holiness and ecclesiology of racial equity. It was also during Seymour's time with the Saints that he had a miraculous experience. In 1902, after a battle with smallpox, Seymour lost the vision in his left eye. Blaming his physical ailment on his reticence to follow God's call, Seymour was propelled into the next phase of his ministry.

Insofar as the Saints offer an example of how Seymour was affirmed and empowered as a Black leader in the holiness movement, his subsequent time under the direction of Charles F. Parham serves as an example to the contrary. Through a mutual friend, Pastor Lucy Farrow, Seymour met Parham and came under his instruction in early 1906. Because of Texas state law, Seymour and other Black students were not permitted legally to be full students; they were forced to listen in from the hallway. Furthermore, while Parham's racist sensibilities have been obscured from some historical accounts of Pentecostalism, it is important to note his alignment with an Anglo-Israel ideology that perpetuated the myth that Anglo-Saxons were a superior race who descended from the ten tribes of Israel.[106] For Parham, creation established two distinct types of humans: one superior and one inferior. His theology eventually added a third category, which was hierarchized as follows: "Hindus, Japanese, high Germans, Danes, Scandinavians and Anglo-Saxons, as descendants of Abraham, who 'retained experiential salvation and deeper truths.' Russians, Greeks, Italians, and low Germans, French, Spaniards and their descendants were the Gentiles 'who scarce ever obtain the knowledge of truth.' And black, brown, red, and yellow races were heathens whom he was unsure were redeemable."[107] What is striking here is that while the first two categories are organized around distinct cultural and geographical markers, the third category, to which Seymour belonged, is reduced to color, which is to say, without heritage, *acultural*. This racist theology is tantamount to pro-slavery theology and ideology.

105. E. Alexander, *Black Fire*, 113.

106. See "The Ten Tribes of Israel," in C. Parham, *Sermons*, 105–8.

107. C. Parham, *Sermons*, 107; quoted in E. Alexander, *Black Fire*, 115.

Yet, Seymour continued to listen to the instruction from Parham and attended the multiracial evening worship services. By the winter of 1906, however, Seymour had moved to Los Angeles.

It is important to consider the racial backdrop and implications of Seymour's background to fully appreciate the audacity and subsequent scandal of the Azusa Street Revival. It was not merely another holiness revival or instance of the camp meeting genre. Rather, it was a revolutionary, unprecedented event occasioned by the synchronization of the Holy Spirit and racial justice, the advent of a new Pentecost in which the color line (Du Bois) was "washed away in the blood [of Jesus]."[108] The events at 312 Azusa Street were preceded by a Bible study at 214 Bonnie Brae Street. It was there that a group of mostly Black women comprised of household workers gathered, seeking a new experience of the Spirit. Seymour, himself, had yet to have such an experience. Eventually, there, in the Asberry's home, surrounded by Black women, Seymour had his Pentecostal experience. Within days, the meetings filled the house and overflowed onto the porch, and then into the street in front of the house.

What distinguished Seymour's prophetic vision from others within the holiness movement was how it created the space and terms for racial justice, forging a burgeoning egalitarian movement. In the worship services, racism that structured and permeated everyday life was held at bay, or in abeyance, even if for brief moments:

> A prominent feature of the meetings was their radically egalitarian nature. Though most worshipers were from the lower and working classes, there was not stratification either by class, race, gender, or age in involvement or leadership in the services. Men and women, adults and children, black, white, yellow, and red freely worshiped God and admonished each other to holiness of life through speaking tongues and interpretation, prophecy, testimony, song, prayer, miraculous signs and preaching. Each one, in order, as they felt directed by the Holy Spirit, gave vent to the fire that was shut deep within their bones and glorified God for their newfound freedom and empowerment. Women and men freely participated as they felt God leading them. Even children who felt inspired by God had a voice in the worship and received Pentecostal Holy Spirit baptism.[109]

---

108. Bartleman, *How Pentecost Came*, 54.

109. E. Alexander, *Black Fire*, 121.

Walter Hollenweger notes that even Southern white pastors were eager to go to Los Angeles to worship with Black people and receive an impartation of the Spirit. Hearing the retelling of the worship services harkens back to Acts 2. Once again, the Spirit, through sound and movement, through sound *as* movement, manifests, bringing gifts, but these gifts are not only for the recipient; they are for the entire community and for social flourishing and spiritual nourishment in equal measure. The gifts are the means of a new way of living, an otherwise way to order worlds based on the possibilities in/of the Spirit, not the hierarchized distinctions of the world as it was at the time. Race, gender, class, etc. was not effaced by sameness, but all was brought into unity and equality by the liberating power of the Spirit. These phenomena are what set Azusa apart, what drew attention to the movement as spectacle and scandal, and what led to the announcement that the day of Pentecost had come once again.

While the mission of Azusa Street was to bring together all people in Jesus's name and in accordance with the Spirit, it offended the racial sensibilities of the time in LA and drew the ire of local media. For example, one headline in the *Los Angeles Times* dissented and chided the services as "a weird babel of tongues."[110] The sights and sounds of Azusa, for some observers, transgressed acceptable boundaries and social norms, proving that the community vision embodied on Azusa Street was too radical and progressive for the times, even in Los Angeles. Another offense that critics decried was what was considered inappropriate contact between genders, which was exacerbated by the mixing of races.[111] Seymour's attempt to construct a Pentecostal theological framework in which the Holy Spirit was the force of racial inclusivity and gender equality was rejected, not only by media and secular observers, but also by other holiness leaders. The goings-on at Azusa were labeled by some as satanic acts, by others as the production of Sodomites. Charles Parham's initial support of Seymour and the movement soured as he eventually dissented and condemned the movement: "all the chattering, jabbering, wind sucking, holy-dancing-rollerism," which he asserted was "the result of hypnotic, spiritualistic and fleshy controls."[112] This was but the beginning of Parham's nationwide campaign to discredit Seymour and the revival, speaking of "animalisms," "overemotive worship," even "spook-driven."

---

110. *Los Angeles Times*, "Weird Babel of Tongues."

111. *Los Angeles Times*, "Women with Men Embrace."

112. C. Parham, *Everlasting Gospel*, 54; cited in E. Alexander, *Black Fire*, 138.

Criticism of the movement came from within and without, which quickly digressed into more marked forms of harassment. Surrounding neighbors did not appreciate the "hideous" sounds or the race and gender mixing. Police were called on multiple occasions to manage the complaints. One such complaint was made to police because of the "manner" Black male elders had of "laying on of hands [on young white women]."[113] The interracial gatherings gave way to racism, and Seymour's vision proved to be unattainable in early-twentieth-century Los Angeles, as well as around the country. Parham's betrayal and subsequent campaign to discredit Seymour, by deploying racial epithets and racist stereotypes, took its toll on the mission. It appears that Pentecost had come to a people by and large unwilling to accept its potential for egalitarianism. For three years the movement thrived; however, in the subsequent four years, the movement stymied and deteriorated. What began as an interracial gathering seeking equity among races and genders could not, in fact, wash away the color line. Du Bois's words continued to ring true. After several controversies, riffs, and departures, Azusa eventually settled as a small Black congregation, its influence largely confined to the past.

The Azusa Street Mission, while short lived and full of controversy, became the birthplace of a movement, an occasion, that sparked the formation of hosts of global Pentecostal denominations, some of which are emphatic about the radical and liberative nature of holiness or sanctification through the Holy Spirit. As Ashon Crawley remarks, "The day of Pentecost has fully come. But Blackpentecost, however, has and is yet and still to come."[114] It is to the notion of Blackpentecost that I now turn. Specifically, I explore Bishop Yvette Flunder's assertion that the Fellowship of Affirming Ministries (TFAM), the queer, Blackpentecostal movement that she has pioneered, is a "third Pentecost." It is Pentecost for those still on the margins, estranged by the traditions of their upbringing, and for the purposes of radical inclusivity and community:

> It is The Fellowship's goal to create a place where all may feel free to worship, serve, and grow spiritually—without regard to race, ethnicity, social class, age, gender/gender identity, or affectional orientation. We will create a safe place for all persons to flourish— especially women, same-gender-loving individuals and their allies,

113. *Los Angeles Times*, "Rolling and Diving 'Fanatics'"; cited in E. Alexander, *Black Fire*, 142.

114. Crawley, *Blackpentecostal Breath*, 134.

transgendered persons, persons in recovery, the recently incarcerated, the economically disenfranchised, and persons infected and affected by HIV/AIDS. *We will seek to proclaim the same message proclaimed on the day of Pentecost: that God continues to pour out God's spirit upon all persons.*[115]

The sounds of such proclamation announce a liberation, a radical and inclusive message of welcome—the Spirit has come once again, but this time, it is poured out on *all* flesh. These are the terms of what it means to be free and to flourish, which is to say, ways of reclaiming and reimagining a world otherwise, a world of dance-possibilities.

115. TFAM, "About Us" (emphasis added).

CHAPTER 3

"A Queer Faith"

Gender, Sexuality, and Inclusion in Pentecostalism

Freedom in Christ is freedom in life—all are welcome at the table.
—*YVETTE FLUNDER, WHERE THE EDGE GATHERS*

"I can't breathe" as both the announcement of a particular moment and rupture in the world of the Garners, and "I can't breathe" as a rupture, a disruption, an ethical plea regarding the ethical crisis that has been the grounds for producing this moment, our time, this modern world.
—*ASHON CRAWLEY, BLACKPENTECOSTAL BREATH*

Introduction

I AM STILL PROCESSING my worship experiences at TFAM's 2017 annual conference, where decades of experiences, ranging from childhood Sunday worship to youth camps and time spent abroad, coalesced and manifested in my body. For years, I have attested that I was moved by the preaching and singing, by something within and outside of me; yet I have been unable to articulate much beyond generalities. Why was I crying and shaking so fiercely? Was it merely a biological response or familiar stimuli that I can trace back to my earliest childhood memories? (I wonder if neuroscience, perhaps, could make a compelling argument?) Recently, a spirited exchange I had with my friend and current TFAM pastor, Tim Wolfe, came to mind. As we clapped and swayed during worship at the conference, often our eyes would meet and we would smile casually, as if we were admitting without having to say the obvious: the feel and sound of our Pentecostal upbringing was happening all around us and we were caught by it. On that occasion in 2017, however, something was different. Pentecost was coming again for me, to me. It was a returning. Despite my efforts to distance myself and my self-avowed agnosticism toward all of it, I was fighting familiar feelings and losing the battle. What exactly was it that I was resisting? Perhaps it was the recognition that these feelings—the ecstatic, bodily worship that inculcated me—led to a dead-end faith and untenable, lifeless religion. I still carry the scars from all of the rigid legalism, the stains of abstinence and purity culture, the blemishes from polemic, "prophetic" decrees about either being set apart from the world or damned along with it.

I viscerally remember how shame could be weaponized, the guilt that was readily distributed to those that could not live up to the standards. I have seen the violence—often self-inflicted—that it precipitated. God was used as the means of conformity. My parents used exorcisms as a way of dealing with what they considered evil spirits: homosexuality, sexual addictions like pornography, mental illness, and poverty. They believed that these issues were a physical manifestation of a spiritual problem. It did not make sense to me back then, but the exorcisms insisted that other spirits—demonic in nature—were indeed embodied in people, and these spirits were contagious. My parents taught that we are all in need of deliverance; but once we were delivered from the spirits which cause us to live "in the flesh," we can live by the Spirit. Not wanting to disappoint them, least of all disappoint or anger God, I suffered in silence. I refused to be the apostate in the family. Questions meant doubting and doubting meant unbelief. And unbelief would bring shame on our household—on my parents, yes, but it would land most heavily on me. I could not talk to anyone, least of all God. There seemed to be an ocean between the God of love and me. I was not sure I believed in God, but I knew because of my sin, God could not believe in me. I experienced the fear of the Lord, not as the beginning of wisdom, but as an alienating force that separated me from my family. I have cried at the altar and been singed by the imminent fires of hell, which I was taught is a place of eternal torment and separation from your loved ones, your friends, and God.

I remember the sting of what my father said to me when he found my first pornographic magazine, and what my mother said when she found the box of condoms in my closet: "Why couldn't you stay pure?" Waiting until marriage to have sex was instilled in us from an early age. "Nobody wants damaged goods!" Their disappointment was great, but not as great as my own. I had let them down, yes; but more importantly, I knew God was disappointed and disgusted. Lust, I was told, would lead me to perversion, and perversion leads to the destruction of the body. I have carried these words around with me in my body, perhaps unknowingly. Years of trauma and feelings of worthlessness that I have hidden like embarrassing scars are inextricably bound up with my experiences of Pentecostalism. Worship and endless freedom on the one shoulder and sin, judgment, and a wrathful God on the other. Life was a daily struggle, a game of tug of war in which I knew, I felt, my soul was on the line. Even after my family stopped believing in hell as a place of eternal torment, the threat of missing out or disappointing God (or them) was the fear out of which I lived. I felt estranged, isolated, and alone. I was miserable, and I carried this misery around with me.

Perhaps my upbringing in and melancholic experiences with Pentecostalism can account for my resistance to the experience and flood of emotions at TFAM. Though futile in the end, I was trying to protect myself. Vulnerability meant being susceptible to opening up or reinjuring old wounds—the site for the return of festering foes. It would be like summoning old spirits that had greatly wounded me. Yet, to my surprise, this moment was markedly different. As if sensing my restraint, Tim reached over and put his arm around my shoulders. As his head leaned over to my ear, he shouted over the loudness of the worship: "What's so beautiful about this is that so many of the people [shouting and worshiping] cannot fully be themselves and are not welcome at their home churches. But they are here." He immediately returned to clapping and singing, hardly missing a beat. But what he said broke something loose inside of me; I could no longer contain the tears, nor did I feel the need to fight them. What he named, that I could not, was that Pentecostal worship experience is not owned by the people who use it to exclude others or as a means of manipulation. Rather, Pentecostal experience can be about freedom, about unmitigated connection to God and others, and about otherwise possibilities.

I watched as people, out from the closets of shame and guilt, worshiped unabashedly. They were and are free—flesh and bodies touching and interacting, being overcome by and in the Spirit of life. I felt an invitation to participate, to encounter God in a familiar way, not for the sake of appeasement, but freedom. Tears of joy washed over me. Tim, who, on my first day of the doctorate program had said, "You've got to get your tongues back!," had once again spoken a word from God to me. I do not have to be ashamed; I do not have to be afraid or alone; I can reclaim my Pentecostal heritage and also be critical of that which has shaped me and that which I love. Love and critique are not opposites, but two poles that create a healthy tension. I did need to get my tongues back. Most importantly, I started to believe again that there could be a place for me, a home, in which I am loved and accepted exactly as I am, regardless of what I believe or how I encounter the divine. The prodigal son can return, because the prodigal God runs out to meet and embrace him. This, in part, explains the tears, the feelings of relief, and the unshakable knowing that has come from them. The tears are gone. A lingering remains and continues to stir. What I thought was dead is very much alive. It has been three years, and I continue to live the nourishing questions that have remained.

On one level, watching members of TFAM—mostly Black and queer—realize and actualize freedom in God through Pentecostal expression meant that I too could experience true freedom. While I do not presume to know what it is like to be Black or queer, I can testify to how insidious Pentecostal—or any other—theology can be. It can be a language of limitation and constraint; as Crawley has suggested, it seeks to enclose, to closet. In this way, theological language, in terms of purity and categorical distinction, can become a way of serving the interests of the heteronormative world. Instead, TFAM is a way of knowing when your body is on the line, refusing to conform to the norms of this world. My intent for this chapter is to sit with what my friend Katie Kinnison calls the "affect of amazement" and reflect upon how gender and sexuality, through the gospel of radical inclusivity, constitutes a framework for liberative Pentecostal theology and life. *Queer*, in this sense, is more than crossing boundaries of normativity; it connotes a fleshiness and embodiment; it represents risk and vulnerability; it occasions revelation born out of experience and reflection.

I begin with Sara Ahmed's work on the affective imperative of happiness vis-à-vis heteronormativity. For Ahmed, positive psychology has made happiness a means to an end, as well as the end of the means; and happiness is promoted by certain ways of living.[1] In this way, happiness is a sort of world making, whereby "happiness makes the world cohere around, as it were, the right people."[2] How one feels about happiness means how one feels about what is desired or good. Thus, it also evidences how feelings can make some things good and others not. Rather than focusing on happiness

1. Ahmed, *Promise of Happiness*, 10–11.
2. Ahmed, *Promise of Happiness*, 13.

as good, as something to be desired, Ahmed instead considers those "who are banished from it, or who enter this history only as troublemakers, dissenters, and killers of joy," whom she refers to as "killjoys."[3] Killjoys murder the happiness the norm has built through critique. Furthermore, happiness creates happy objects, that is, things to which feelings of happiness (as good and desired) are attached. The more happy objects circulate, the more affective value they accumulate. And happy affects are contagious. According to Anna Gibbs:

> Bodies can catch feelings as easily as catch fire: affects leap from one body to another, evoking tenderness, inciting shame, igniting rage, exciting fear—in short communicable affect can inflame nerves and muscles in a conflagration of every conceivable kind of passion.[4]

Just as happiness can create happiness in others, in turn, shame can produce shame in others. Affects proliferate in proximity. Affects accumulate around objects, which are the location of good—or, depending on the object, bad—feelings. What happens when bad feelings accumulate around objects? How are bodies treated that bear the promise of happiness more than others?

One of Ahmed's examples for a happy object is the family: "The happy family is both a myth of happiness, of where and how happiness takes place. The happy family is both a myth of happiness, of where and how happiness takes place, and a powerful legislative device, a way of distributing time, energy, and resources."[5] The happy family is maintained as a happy object by the work necessary to do so: families "stick" together. In short, if we want to be happy and to keep the family as happy object, we must follow a repetition, a script that will ensure happiness. But what happens when one deviates from the path or script of happiness? What if the objects to which one is oriented toward, for example, the family, do not bring about happiness? That person becomes an "affect alien," which is "one who converts good feelings into bad, who as it were 'kills' the joy of the family."[6] Happiness, for Ahmed, is an affective mechanism for producing or cohering around certain values and practices. I want to suggest that the heteronormative values of "traditional" marriages and family are outcomes of these strategies.

3. Ahmed, *Promise of Happiness*, 17.
4. Anna Gibbs, "Contagious Feelings"; quoted in Ahmed, *Promise of Happiness*, 39.
5. Ahmed, *Promise of Happiness* 45.
6. Ahmed, *Promise of Happiness* 49.

Rather than being necessary for a good life for all, being directed toward happiness appears to be more in service to the preservation and propagation of heteronormative values and objects. "The queer child fails to inherit the family by reproducing its line. This failure is affective; you become an unhappiness-cause. . . . They [the family] are unhappy with you for not being what they want you to be."[7] Unhappiness, or a rejection of traditional happiness in terms of the script that has been inherited, can be an indictment against injustice and a claim for justice.

In what follows, I write in consideration of affect aliens who, like me, have rejected the objects of happiness in order to find acceptance, purpose, and new joy; those who have embraced "bad objects" to find other kin, other tables, and other families; those who, because they have felt out of place and homeless, need a safe place in which to belong and breathe. Therein lie, not only other objects, but otherwise possibilities.

A Queer Faith

Because of gender and sexuality, some bodies are distanced from the promise or possibility of happiness. In *Indecent Theology: Theological Perversions in Sex, Gender, and Politics*, Marcella Althaus-Reid tells of the lemon street vendors in Argentina, *coya* women, who sell their lemons without wearing any underwear because they cannot take breaks and must urinate in the streets. The image it induces—the blending of fragrances of lemons and sex, the raw citrus and fleshy femininity—offers an occasion for doing liberation theology at the intersection of economics and sexuality. At the same time, due to the patriarchal and heteronormative values of Latin American theological projects, it also offers a lens, a praxis, to do theology in a subversive manner in and with the body:

> Yet, an Argentinian theologian may want to do, precisely, that. Her task may be to deconstruct a moral order which is based on a heterosexual construction of reality, which organizes not only categories of approved social and divine interactions but of economic ones too. The Argentinian theologian would like then to remove her underwear to write theology with feminist honesty, not forgetting what it is to be a woman when dealing with theological and political categories.[8]

7. Ahmed, *Promise of Happiness* 95.
8. Althaus-Reid, *Indecent Theology*, 2.

Removing underwear, as that which covers up or restricts, as that which holds back and seeks to conceal, is an important metaphor and praxis for indecent theology. For Althaus-Reid, because liberation theology claims to begin in the everyday lives of people and at the contextual level, there can be no exceptions or exclusions: all theology is therefore sexual theology. And if liberation theology is a permanent process of recontextualization, then as a method it must become indecent in order to subvert sexually hegemonic epistemologies. The indecency constitutes a methodology and praxis; it allows for one to embrace the various smells, tastes, performances, and expressions of sexuality in liberative, not legalistic, ways, which opens up a new world replete with otherwise configurations and possibilities: "A living metaphor for God, sexuality and the struggle in the streets of Buenos Aires comes from the images of lemon vendors. A materialist-based theology finds in them a starting point from which ideology, theology and sexuality can be rewritten from the margins of society, the church and systemic theology."[9] Such an approach scandalizes attempts at modesty or morality in service to modern Western sexual practices and norms. This project, through affective analyses, aspires to indulge in the indecencies and disrupt happy objects.

As previously mentioned, media—critical onlookers, skeptics, and journalists—were especially unkind to and skeptical of the Pentecostal movement from its beginning. Speaking in tongues, falling out, and interracial mixing and contact between different races and genders offended the normative sensibilities of the culture. We might say these happenings were seen as offensive, even indecent. As I perused through the archives, one particular headline from a 1902 *Topeka Capital* article struck me: "A Queer Faith, Strange Acts. Strange Actions of the Apostolic Believers."[10] Perhaps this is precisely the lens to apply to explore Pentecostalism: the movement is a queer faith in both the political and theological sense. It is non(hetero)normative and thus offends, even subverts or undoes, Western categories, distinctions, and norms. It exposes the harmful creations of Western theology and subsequent theo-politics, idols fashioned in the image of what Christena Cleveland calls "whitemalegod,"[11] or what bell

9. Althaus-Reid, *Indecent Theology*, 4.

10. *Topeka Times*, "A Queer Faith, Strange Actions of the Apostolic Believers," quoted in S. Parham, *Life*, 70.

11. Cleveland, *Christ Our Black Mother*.

hooks names as "imperialist, white supremacist, capitalist patriarchy."[12] For Cleveland, whitemalegod is an egocentric god drunk with *his* own power, a demigod whose will cannot be questioned. Any question is seen as "insubordination" to a patriarchal, authoritarian God.[13] Whitemalegod produces "theobrogians [theo-BRO-gians], who are the preaching, theologizing, and publishing arm of whitemalegod."[14] This God sees with a colonial gaze. This God and his theobrogians represent the standard and wield the most power in their world.

What happened at Azusa so deeply differed from and violated the theological and political norms of the early twentieth century of white America that, rather than explain it, at best the dominant white, male culture could only dismiss it and describe it as "queer." Of course, queer at this time connoted a sense of abnormality. It was only later that the word would be a pejorative and used against the LGBTQ community. Yet, in the 1980s this word went through a process from pejorative to neutral and eventually was reclaimed as a self-identifier of LGBTQ persons.[15] Because of this reclamation, the word has been widely used, including as a methodology, and reorients the tasks of doing theology.

Bishop Yvette Flunder's theological work with TFAM focuses upon creating and cultivating a radically inclusive community through queering theology as a means of liberation: "A liberating theology of acceptance must be embodied in the atmosphere of a liberating Christian community."[16] From the outset, theology is a community project. Interpretation and practice occur in community. For this work to be established, Flunder contends that, first, one must overcome oppressive theologies—theologies of the enslaver, of the whitemalegod, that taught: "Sin and evil are black; goodness and virtue were white."[17] Because of this history of deep rooted and embodied oppression, the Black community, especially Black women, must be liberated from the worlds created and curated by white and (some) Black people. As Paulo Freire has noted elsewhere: "The oppressor is housed *within* the people [the oppressed]";[18] meaning, the oppressive ideologies—

12. hooks, *Feminist Theory*, xiv.

13. Cleveland, *Christ Our Black Mother*, 31.

14. Cleveland, *Christ Our Black Mother*, 42.

15. For more on this history, see Rand, *Reclaiming Queer*.

16. Flunder, *Where the Edge Gathers*, 2.

17. Flunder, *Where the Edge Gathers*, 3.

18. Freire, *Pedagogy of the Oppressed*, 163–64.

through norms and practices—give an identity to the oppressed. Building a radically inclusive community thus means first breaking the cycle of oppression and liberating the people to be their truest selves and most authentically so in community:

> True community—true church—comes when marginalized people take back the right to fully "be." A people must be encouraged to celebrate not in spite of who they are, but because of who their Creator has made them. The balm that heals oppression sickness is the creation of accountable, responsible, visible, celebrating communities on the margin of mainline church and dominant society.[19]

To fully "be" is to belong. Truth is faithfulness. Flunder's theological vision of liberation is found and flourishes in community. For TFAM churches, this community is predominately Black and LGBTQ; it comes from the heritage of the Black church but moves beyond the homophobic oppressive theologies that have infiltrated the COGIC and some Black Baptist traditions out of which many in the community come. TFAM is a refuge, offering a place to return, be restored, and made whole.

At the center of Flunder's work are important hermeneutical emphases, namely: 1) an emphasis on an intimate relationship with God and 2) a reclamation of cultural expressions and ways of embodying worship practices and visions of community. Emphasizing intimacy with God provides an assurance of loving relationship to God, regardless of whom one is or loves, which in turn provides security for one to interpret their experiences in light of Scriptures and traditions away from alienation toward a liberation. Flunder explains that her position is summed by an unnamed former enslaved woman who, when she was told the Bible said she was to be a slave, simply answered: "Not my Bible; I tore dat page out!"[20] An intimate relationship with God establishes love and acceptance as the starting point, making it the means as well as the end, the telos of possibility. It is love, not doctrine, that is the ultimate source of interpretation. A relationship with God reveals the Spirit of God working for liberation within human flesh. Any interpretation of Scripture that does not build upon this love, that does not confirm or affirm this God and one's personhood, must be reconsidered or disregarded. Thus, as we see, race, gender, and sexuality are important intersections that determine the conditions by which one

19. Flunder, *Where the Edge Gathers*, xiv.
20. Flunder, *Where the Edge Gathers*, 9.

experiences and understands God. Yet, relationship with God is prior to and encompassing of all of these.

Reclaiming cultural identity also is necessary for overcoming oppression sickness and building a radically inclusive community. Of course, Gal 3:28 comes to mind: "There is no longer Jew or Greek, there is no longer slave or free, there is no longer male and female; for all of you are one in Christ Jesus." This verse historically has been used to produce sameness or conformity, particularly in evangelical circles in the US. However, the writer is alluding to a unity that is deeper or stronger than how one is identified. Being a slave, for example, is something that one is forced to be; there is no choice. While unity or oneness in Christ is a spiritual reality, it must be realized in the flesh. Producing color-blind Christians only reinforces the racial distinctions and hierarchies purported and propagated by the modern Western world. In other words, it is a way of effacing differences and defaulting to the norm of whiteness and white supremacist culture. African worship and the notion of the African village have been demonized and dismissed by the colonial projects of theology and philosophy: "If we dispel that [oppressive] defeatist thinking, will we retain atmosphere, style, sound, and feel of the church as we know it?"[21]

Flunder continues:

> In my experience, I have found it is quite possible to have the sound, style, and feel of the Metho-Bapti-Costal church without the oppression perpetuated by some in these traditions. The preaching, the song, and the dance are media through which the Spirit moves; *they are ours*, and they should remain. . . . Church can be effervescent and joyful while simultaneously being theologically liberating, justice oriented, culturally appropriate, and inclusive.[22]

Speaking to the theological trappings and affective nature of religious experience, Flunder refuses an either/or binary and advocates for the creation of a liberative theology centered upon the amalgam of identity and authentic expression—or, otherwise possibilities. Those who seek to express their worship in culturally authentic ways and in inclusive environments no longer have to be subjected to oppressive theologies. Rather, there is a place they belong, a place they can encounter a God who liberates and welcomes all to the table and the family of God. Tacit in this epistemological shift

21. Flunder, *Where the Edge Gathers*, 11.
22. Flunder, *Where the Edge Gathers*, 11.

is the commitment that liberation is co-creative work; it is reclamation of resonant feelings; it is authenticity and generosity in expression, lived out and interpreted in community.

Radical inclusivity is the founding, guiding principle for TFAM. It establishes an open and affirming environment in the church as well as creates the framework for queer sexual ethics and liberative theologizing beyond the shame-laden, body-phobic theologies prevalent in parts—not all—of the Black church. Radical inclusivity makes possible a church in which those who have been discarded as the last and the least in society become enveloped in full acceptance, liberative love, and genuine community. Inclusivity is radical and revolutionary insofar as it provides a template "for a 'new Reformation,' whereby people, whether Christian or not, will see the error of exclusionary practices and biases based on sex, race, gender, and other factors, and seek to open themselves to all kinds of people."[23] To see an error, that is, admit wrongdoing, precedes opening up to all kinds of people. There can be no restorative justice without repentance. Radical inclusivity invites a new Reformation insofar as it takes other Black traditions, liberates them from the categories and doctrinal purity of white, modern visions of Christianity and the world, preserves the feel of worship practices and African cultural expressions, and reforms or recreates a world of religious and political possibilities not based on exclusion but inclusion. Relationships are reformed and restored, people are healed, and wholeness becomes the driving force and goal of the community. TFAM provides a prophetic vision that is not confined to spiritual experience but a holistic integration of spiritual and social, as was one aim of Azusa Street. Realizing that cultures are built around beliefs and that, as beliefs change, cultures shift, Flunder asserts that Christians also must shift, change, and evolve with the unveiling understanding of God and of oneself, of God within oneself, i.e., one's body. Embracing change as a constant, these shifts affect how Scripture, tradition, and experience are interpreted within and by the community, which changes the norms without changing the values of the becoming-beloved community. The commitment to love and to inclusivity will not change, but understandings of bodies, worlds, customs, and rituals may.

A queer faith exists on the fringes, from the underside of normative modern history as written and told by the victors, the conquerors, and the enslavers. And because liberation theology places that God on the side of

23. Lewin, *Filled with the Spirit*, 49.

the poor, the marginalized, and the oppressed, a queer faith reveals a queer God—male and female and neither—who is concerned with and active in personal, spiritual, and social transformation. A queer God is a God beyond the categorical distinction and coherence of patriarchal, heteronormative, and orthodox theology or God-talk. This God "comes out" and comes toward creation "in drag" in the form of the Trinity;[24] this God comes near and walks with creation in the cool of the evening; this God is neither male nor female nor human at all; this God is beyond being and description. Marcella Althaus-Reid writes of a queer God, arguing for the need of an "indecent theology" of/for liberation that disrupts the norms undergirded by puritanical theological projects. Indecent theology is scandalous, making space for a multifaceted unshaping/reshaping methodology "where sexuality and loving relationships are not only important theological issues but experiences which un-shape Totalitarian Theology while re-shaping the theologians."[25] Althaus-Reid's work exposes the exclusion of LGBTQ persons in the ongoing work of liberation theologies and offers a way to queer theology and God—an important step to disrupt—while not disregarding Christian tradition altogether:

> Queering theology, the theological task and God is all part of a coming out of the closet for Christianity, which is no longer simply one option among others, nor is it a sidetrack outside what has been regarded as the highroad of classical theology. Queering theology is the path of God's own liberation, apart from ours, and as such it constitutes a critique to what Heterosexual Theology has done with God by closeting the divine.[26]

Due to the appropriation and exploitation of God by imperialist, white supremacist, capitalist patriarchal theology and the creation of a god in its image, God has been closeted and is in need of coming out, of liberation. Queer theology, thus, offers the other-side to theology and to God beyond hegemonic sexual systems perpetuated by theology. This other-side is not from the margins, per se, but is constituted by visible centers that have been rendered invisible. This is the scandal of what T-Theology (totalitarian theology) has avoided:

24. Althaus-Reid, *Queer God*, 3.
25. Althaus-Reid, *Queer God*, 8.
26. Althaus-Reid, *Queer God*, 4.

God amongst the Queer, and the Queer God present in Godself; God, as found in the complexity of the unruly sexualities and relationships of people; God as present in the *via rupta* [broken way/path/road or way/path/road of brokenness] of previously un-recognized paths of praxis, that is, paths carved with machetes in jungles, as the paths of experience (and of people at the margins) usually are. The theological scandal is that bodies speak, and God speaks through them.[27]

Queer approaches ask: how can a project such as liberation theology, ostensibly concerned with the liberation of all persons, not liberate sex workers, gay, lesbian, and trans people? A queer God is concerned with those who have been passed over by liberation theological projects, those whose lives remain invisible and excluded from the good news of freedom in the fleshy reality of the kindom of God. The queer God who comes out always comes toward the poor, the oppressed, the last, and the least. There is no outside to God's love; likewise, there should be no boundaries or borders to the kindom. Pamela Lightsey's *Our Lives Matter* is exemplary and emerges at the intersectional history of the Black womanist tradition and the work of constructive queer theology. Lightsey applies a theological methodology she calls "queering," which she defines as:

a deconstruction and reevaluation of gender perspectives that uses as its framework queer theory and as its resources, scripture, reason, tradition, and experience. Some have seen its challenge to heteronormativity as a challenge to the Church universal. Howev-er, queer theologians must be comfortable with the Church being challenged. We come from a long history of the Church's doctrine and dogma being challenged. It has become better and its theol-ogy much healthier when it . . . explores its conceptualizations of Christ as its head and the people who are its members. Queer the-ology is the Church's *pièce de résistance* of the twenty-first century in that it offers an opportunity to include rather than exclude more voices within our various communities.[28]

27. Althaus-Reid, *Queer God*, 33–34.
28. Lightsey, *Our Lives Matter*, 27.

Black-Queer-Womanist Theologizing

Since all theologizing is contextual, exploring TFAM as a movement necessitates considering Bishop Flunder's social location and tradition as a Black queer womanist theologian with a background in the Church of God in Christ (COGIC). It is from her experience as a lesbian woman in a non-affirming tradition that she created the otherwise possibilities espoused by the fellowship. Liberation is creative work. Because her tradition could not make space for her sexuality nor affirm her full personhood, Flunder supplemented and created a movement where people like her—i.e., those who cannot and will not conform to the heteronormative values found in many Christian traditions—find a safe and welcoming home through honoring personal experience. Queer, womanist, and Methodist scholar Pamela Lightsey reminds us that "womanists have always reserved the right to make claims about their experience and ways of knowing."[29] Personal agency serves as a methodology that shapes how and what one comes to know.

Historically speaking, Black women have had to endure the compounding violence and vicissitudes of living in a racist, capitalist, and sexist society—what Katie Cannon calls "triple oppression" as Black, worker, and female.[30] The term *womanism* comes from Alice Walker's seminal book, *In Search of Our Mothers' Gardens*, in which Walker defines womanist, from *womanish*, in four ways: "1) A black feminist or feminist of color . . . ; 2) A woman who loves other women, sexually and/or nonsexually . . . ; 3) Loves music. Loves dance. Loves the moon. *Loves* the Spirit. Loves love and food and roundness. Loves struggle. *Loves* the Folk. Loves herself. *Regardless*; 4) Womanist is to feminist as purple to lavender."[31] All of these definitions (read: possibilities) are at work in various ways in the personal life and pastoral leadership of Bishop Flunder. They constitute the underpinnings of the gospel of radical inclusivity as an annunciation of the good news that, whoever you are, wherever you are from, and whoever you choose to love, you are welcome and cherished exactly as you are. Radical inclusivity invites Christians to "draw the circle wide, draw it wider still," as the hymn

29. Lightsey, *Our Lives Matter*, 1.

30. Lightsey, *Our Lives Matter*, 4.

31. Walker, *In Search*, xi–xii.

sings.[32] To love "regardless," not in spite of, means an unchanging, unwavering, and unconditional commitment to love.

In *Black Womanist Ethics*, Katie Cannon demonstrates how Black women "live out a moral wisdom in their real-lived context that does not appeal to the fixed rules or absolute principles of the white-oriented, male structured society."[33] In other words, Black womanist ethics represent ways of knowing and living otherwise, ways enlivened and informed by experience that are not based on respectability or holding on to socially-constructed power. While American society has historically and disproportionately diminished Black women, Cannon's work attends to the power of Black womanist ethics as cultivated acts of survival and crafted ways of flourishing through the literary tradition, as that which "documents the 'living space' carved out of the intricate web of racism, sexism, and poverty."[34] The literary tradition parallels Black history and "conveys the assumed values in the Black oral tradition,"[35] ritualizing readers and writers in participating communities. Black womanist ethics are not exclusively nonliterary in terms of oral and nonliterary devices, but, in fact, are constituted by an amalgam of otherwise literary and nonliterary traditions: song, dance, oral and written narrative, etc., rooted in Black history and experience. Important to Cannon's work is the life and work of Zora Neale Hurston, which serves as an example of "how to live on Black terms—how to resist, to oppose, and to endure the immediate struggles over and against terrifying circumstances."[36] I want to consider the Black womanist literary tradition as a framework for ritualization.

If we accept ritual theorist Ronald Grimes's definition of rites as "specific enactments located in concrete times and places" within the general framework of ritual, then we may think of the Black literary and oral traditions within the scope of "ritualizing" as "the activity of deliberately cultivating rites."[37] The stories and histories, both written and passed down orally, create matrices of meaning, frameworks to engage and reference, as well as forming the conditions of possibility. Rites speak and arouse something within bodies, resonating within them and inviting them into

32. Light, "Draw the Circle Wide."

33. Cannon, *Black Womanist Ethics*, 4.

34. Cannon, *Black Womanist Ethics*, 7.

35. Cannon, *Black Womanist Ethics*, 7.

36. Cannon, *Black Womanist Ethics*, 13.

37. Grimes, *Ritual Criticism*, 7.

deeper ways of knowing and living. Thus, when Cannon invokes woman-ism vis-à-vis Walker, or references the work of Hurston, she is cultivating processes of ritualization, even as she is philosophizing and theorizing otherwise. Walker's work on womanism provides a repertoire for repetition out of experience. Hurston's anthropological work on Black culture, for Cannon, constitutes a tradition. Like Scripture, it is a source that offers history and wisdom that is passed down through the ancestors to be learned, embodied, and practiced. What makes all of this ritual, I contend, is that this ritualizing occurs at the intersection of context, lived experience, and meaning. The literary tradition is not contained by the written or spoken word; it is a source of wisdom, of power, and of knowing.

Cannon's specific creation of Black womanist ethics thus utilizes the Black literary tradition as a canon by which to engage history and herstory, making possible a moral way of living in opposition to the harmful norms of the present. As Grimes points out, the shift from modern to postmodern is not merely sociocultural but epistemic also. Rather than one fixed meaning, postmodern reading techniques and criticisms destabilize singularity in terms of alterity, parody, etc. In other words, the postmodern world demands more, demands something different, of religion and from ritual. The performance of ritual, in this way, invokes the Spirit and spirits, as well as makes present or recalls the history and life force of Black culture. Tom Driver writes: "Ritual is neither a detached contemplation of the world nor a passive symbolization of it but is the performance of an act in which people confront one kind of power with another and rehearse their own future."[38] For example, confronting or opposing the oppressive powers that be and rehearsing a different future and new world encapsulate how the Black literary tradition functions as a foundation for Black ritualizing and ritualization. In fact, the Black literary tradition represents acts of remembrance analogous to a liturgy as "work of the people" and the Eucharist insofar as it is commemorated, consecrated, and consumed. The presence of the ancestors, of those that have gone on before, like clouds of witnesses, are present in the invocation of the Spirit and spirits.

Reading and quoting Hurston, thus, is not simply citing her work; it is gleaning from her life and letting her testimony, her words, speak afresh and anew, even as her presence accompanies and consubstantiates the ritual. Hurston's life allowed her to cultivate wisdom and pass it down through her work. In this way, the Black literary tradition, culminating in womanist

38. Driver, *Liberating Rites*, 188.

traditions, ritualizes subsequent generations, passing the mantle of a sort of apostolic succession of writers, artists, and leaders. This tradition, however, is always unfolding; new histories are being written. In order to draw the circle of justice and liberation wider, i.e., to announce the gospel of radical inclusion and the imminent kindom of God, however, we must first acknowledge and interrogate the historic exclusions, omissions, and limitations of justice perpetuated by Christian theology in the name of God.

Given the intersectional[39] nature of oppression and injustice, issues of racism can be complicated by classism; issues of sexism can be compounded by racism; issues of homophobia can exacerbate issues of sexism and racism, etc. Given that issues are neither neatly defined nor experienced, the intersectionality of various -isms must be considered in justice work. The fellowship in general, and Bishop Flunder in particular, serves as a harbinger of hope for this ongoing work, because the work of justice in terms of radical inclusion makes room for those who have sometimes been excluded by portions of the Black church: queer persons.

As a method, womanist queer theology is constructive. The sources, norms, and values come from experience in tension with tradition, so as not to give too much weight to the latter. Wesley's quadrilateral (reason, experience, Scripture, tradition) plays an important role in Lightsey's methodology, which speaks to her Methodist affiliation. One could say the same for Flunder, who, having come from the COGIC tradition—which is, itself, a blend of traditions—calls herself a "Metho-Bapti-Costal." Nevertheless, John Wesley's quadrilateral, particularly with an emphasis on experience, is certainly at work in Flunder's constructive theological work with a healthy suspicion toward reason, experience, Scripture, and tradition. In the same way that we must consider the intersectionality of oppression and injustice, we must likewise consider the intersectionality of identities and contexts that constitutes the locus and focus of resistance, subversion, and justice work: Black queer bodies.

LGBTQ bodies belong to the body of Christ and claim the body of Christ as queer. Lightsey continues:

---

39. *Intersectionality* is a term and concept developed by Kimberlé Crenshaw as "a lens through which you can see where power comes and collides, where it interlocks and intersects. It's not simply that there's a race problem here, a gender problem here, and a class or LBGTQ problem there" (Columbia Law School, "Kimberlé Crenshaw on Intersectionality"). Crenshaw uses the term in a legal context, originally argued in her 1989 article "Demarginalizing the Intersection of Race and Sex: A Black Feminist Critique of Antidiscrimination Doctrine, Feminist Theory and Antiracist Politics."

> The bodies of Black LBTQ women are all part of the body of Jesus Christ, who, according to [M. Shawn] Copeland, "embraces *all* bodies passionately, revalorizes them as embodied mystery, and reorients sexual desire toward God's desire for us in and through our sexuality." This is no puritanical argument. It is inclusive and affirming of Black LBTQ women and reminds the church of the queer nature of Christ's body.[40]

To think of Christ's body as queer requires relinquishing androcentric images and metaphors for God along with the sexual hetero-norms attached to them. There is a tendency in Christian theology, as it was in philosophy for some time, to make male language universal, e.g., mankind. What results is a completely masculine Trinity: God the Father, Jesus the Son, and the Holy Spirit, who is often referred to as "he." Mary Daly, among many others, has pointed out the danger of using only male language as the standard by which to represent God.[41] However, historically this is not the only language used for God. For example, consider mystic Julian of Norwich's "Mother Jesus." In *Divine Revelations of Love*, Julian writes: "So Jesus Christ who sets good against evil is our real Mother. We owe our being to him—and this is the essence of motherhood!—and all the delightful, loving protection which ever follows. God is as really our Mother as he is our Father."[42] Jesus, in this depiction, is both mother and him, male in sex but female in gender. Further, God is both mother and father. Her imaging of Jesus as mother means that, through the open wounds of his side, he brings people to the nurturing suckling of his breast. The image of Jesus breastfeeding Julian reminds of *El Shaddai*, which is interpreted by some as a feminine representation of God that can be translated as the "breasted one."[43] God also speaks of God's womb, which gives birth to Israel. All to say, considering the different language—metaphors, images—used for God, in both the Scriptures and tradition, understandings of God's body do not conform to the hetero-norms of gender or sex. Christ's body is queer, and queer bodies make up part of this body. The body of Christ is constituted by many genders, sexualities, orientations, and ethnicities. It is an embodied

---

40. Copeland, *Enfleshing Freedom*; quoted in Lightsey, *Our Lives Matter*, 10. I will be exploring Copeland's work in depth in ch. 4.

41. Daly writes: "If God is male, then the male is God" (Daly, *Beyond God the Father*, 19).

42. Julian of Norwich, *Revelations of Divine Love*, ch. 59.

43. Biale, "God with Breasts."

mystery, as Copeland argues. All bodies have value and are embraced in the radically inclusive gospel of queer womanist constructive theologizing.

The apostle Paul writes in his Second Letter to the Corinthians that there is one body with many members, that everyone baptized into Christ is made to drink of one Spirit, and that no part of the body can say to another that they do not belong. Yet, declaring what does or does not belong has been the standard practice (exclusivity) since the early church began to form doctrines and creeds to respond to heresies under the auspices of unity (ca. 325 CE). Paul exhorts the church at Corinth to make sure there is no dissension, to take care of one another, and to make sure that what the collective body experiences, it experiences together: "If one member suffers, all suffer together; if one member is honored, all rejoice with it."[44] The Enlightenment focus on rationalism and individualism have effaced efforts to build communities that seek to live and move and have being, guided and governed by collective wisdom and the common good. Indeed, such visions are often dismissed as utopic or confined to communes and monastic life. However, returning to Lightsey's queering of the body of Christ, the apostle Paul's instruction to the church at Corinth is helpful to consider the repercussions of what it means to be one body made of many members.

Reclaiming the sacred worth of bodies—*all* bodies—means cultivating a community in which everyone is not only welcomed or affirmed, but flourishes. This means one must value one's own body as having inherent worth. How else can one follow the Great Commandment(s) to "love God . . . and our neighbors *as ourselves*"[45] if one does not practice self-love? And foundational to self-love is the *imago Dei*, the notion that God created humans—as one of many earth creatures—in divine image and likeness. Even in our differences, humans bear God's image and likeness. Furthermore, when Jesus comes and incarnates the divine, the *imago Dei* is reversed, or completed: God takes on human image and likeness. The *imago Dei* does not mean only white, male, heterosexual bodies. To degrade human images and likenesses, in their diverse and myriad expressions and features, is to degrade God and devalue God's creation. Any theology of *imago Dei* that does not cultivate and nurture healthy self-love, Lightsey contends, must be disregarded. More specifically, given that Black women's bodies historically have been scapegoats for ambivalence toward Black bodies in general, "we

---

44. 2 Cor 12:26.

45. Mark 12:30–31 (emphasis added).

must turn the tables, declare our bodies to be good, and encourage healthy self-love."[46]

Bodies, like race, are historically constructed categories with hierarchized power dynamics. To reclaim Black bodies as inherently good and beautiful (as *imago Dei*) and affirm Black queer bodies as divinely made and worthy of self-love is to contest and renounce the images the world has made and valued in the likeness in varying degrees between divinity and white, male, heterosexual bodies. The closer one can appear to be white, male, and heterosexual, the higher they can be (or climb, assimilate) in a caste-like system. It is no coincidence that images of God are often white men—Christena Cleveland's whitemalegod. Images of God create images of humans, and images of humans have created a world where bodies are the site of social and political difference. Rather than one body as Paul teaches, or one Christ who we find in the gospels, there are many bodies and Christs. Reclaiming Black queer bodies means reclaiming God and God's Christ from those who have appropriated them for their own self-idolatry.

Kelly Brown Douglas's work *The Black Christ* is an important contribution to critiquing the white Christ as an antichrist who made slavery and slavocracy possible and justifiable. The white Christ is the Christ of empire, of the enslaver, representing the powerful, and bringing about peace (order) only through violence and the tools of empire. The Black Christ, conversely, is an important icon for the Black community—God's liberating Spirit as was revealed in and through the liberating life and witness of Jesus of Nazareth. The Black Christ is the reminder that God is involved in and with the liberation of peoples, as God was with Moses and the children of Israel, Jesus, and whoever is involved in the ongoing efforts that promote dignity and work toward freedom. Yet, the Black Christ has been overrepresented—and, perhaps, overdetermined—by male images. This problem must be dealt with in light of the historical exclusion, oppression, and erasure of Black people, women, and LGBTQ+ persons.

Douglas explores a womanist understanding of the Black Christ through Black women's stories of struggle through sociopolitical and religio-cultural analyses as ways to wholeness. Wherever and however Black women are involved in furthering justice toward wholeness, the Black Christ is there also. In both analytical lenses, there is a prophetic edge that must address the oppression that exists and is perpetuated in the Black community, namely, heterosexism. For example, for Douglas, some womanists'

46. Lightsey, *Our Lives Matter*, 83.

silence on issues of homophobia can be construed as holding on to hetero-sexual privilege, which fails to fully take into account Alice Walker's defini-tion of womanism as "a woman who loves other women, sexually and/or non-sexually." Furthermore, according to sociologist Patricia Hill Collins, remaining silent about homophobia "shields women from becoming the 'ultimate other' in relation to the heterosexual, white, male norm. . . . If womanist theologians continue to maintain silence concerning the oppres-sion of our lesbian sisters, not only do we perpetuate their oppression, but we fall far short of our own vision for wholeness."[47] While Douglas attends to the need for womanists to speak out unabashedly against homophobia in the Black church and community, she does so within the gender binary of male/female. And though she extends Jacquelyn Grant's notion of dis-avowing "the centrality of Jesus' maleness in determining what it meant for him to be Christ"[48] to how Christ's presence is not restricted, but rather found wherever Black people seek to bring the entire Black community into wholeness, neither is Christ's presence restricted to men and women. Such language can become a liability insofar as it reinscribes heterosexist norms. It must be extended to include nonbinary, transgender, and queer persons. The work of wholeness and justice, of wholeness as justice, is evolving, on-going, and unfolding.

A few questions emerge from Douglas's work. First, what does it mean that Jesus, historically confessed as "very God of very God, begotten, not made,"[49] of one substance with God, had a queer body, living between hu-man materiality and divine presence? How, then, is Mary's body under-stood? Church tradition later makes her a virgin, because the container must be clean and untarnished, which reveals both the puritanical prac-tices and policing of bodies in general and of women's bodies in particular. Second, what does it mean—in terms of sociopolitical and religio-cultural implications—to have this God-presence in queer Black bodies? Is this not the wholeness that Douglas is nudging the reader toward? In what ways does the Black Christ need to become the Black queer womanist Christ? Only when a person is wholly affirmed and represented can there be talk of wholeness. The task at hand, therefore, is seeing Christ in those who are unseen, devalued, and excluded. It means acknowledging Christ's pres-ence in Black queer bodies living closeted and ashamed; Black queer bodies

47. Lightsey, *Our Lives Matter*, 119.
48. Lightsey, *Our Lives Matter*, 128.
49. Britannica, "Nicene Creed."

rejected by communities of faith and family; Black trans bodies that are murdered at disproportionate rates without justice. However, there are multiple, complex issues at work with regard to seeing Christ as queer and Black. Rather than tying them all together, I am interested in how they challenge the homogeneity of the body of Christ, which seeks to produce homogeneity of bodies (sameness) under the auspices of unity.

Queer womanist theologizing is always practiced, always considered in terms of the wholeness of the community—"loves the Folk," as Alice Walker writes—and practices self-love. As Jesus asked Peter, "Do you love me?," to answer yes is to put love into practice by feeding the sheep. Womanism is a capacious tradition of making room for the wholeness and nourishment of all people, as well as cultivating lived wisdom and an ethics of resistance in a world governed by unjust policies, systems, and structures. Leaning into the queerness of womanism keeps the tradition from claiming heterosexual privilege and thus creates solidarity and affirms all bodies to flourish. The *imago Dei* reminds us that God is queer, that Christ, in Jesus, is queer, and therefore, that the body of Christ is queer. Yvette Flunder's vision of radical inclusivity serves as a model and a gospel, i.e., good news, to queer persons who, because of their sexual orientation or gender identity, have been estranged from their faith traditions. Flunder's vision is that of a beloved community in which all are welcome as they are. There is no pretense. God is a God for the invisible and forgotten ones, working to bring the good news of radical inclusion to those who need to hear and believe it.

As a new way of living and being, radical inclusivity and communion with God and with others is found in Jesus's words: "This is my body. Do this [eat, fellowship] in remembrance of me." The Eucharist celebrates and commemorates the body of Christ in its vast diversity. It offers a pattern of living-with and becoming-with community. It is a spiritual practice of sharing and offering of bodies for the nourishment of the community. It is a radical reordering and rehearsing of how the world should be. The invitation is to remember, to be re-membered and put back in one's rightful place: surrounded at the table by friends and new kin. All are included in the kindom of God and welcome at God's table to sup and dine with God and the community as they remember Jesus the queer Christ and radically reimagine, reorder, and rehearse the world as it should be. What is the response to this good news? It must be experienced and proclaimed for all to hear that the last shall be first and the first shall be last; that they are the head and not the tail. It is an invitation to come, hear, see, and believe. It is high time to get your tongues back, because Pentecost has come once again.

I want to end this chapter by naming that I am a cisgendered heterosexual white man engaging womanist theory and practice. This may seem suspect, and rightfully so. I hope that by embracing it, learning from it, and sharing it, I do not simply enhance the privileges I have, or appropriate other's work for my own purposes, but show how the insidiousness of whiteness works, even in me. As a white man, I am more the problem than the solution. However, I hope that the voices and witness of Walker, hooks, Cannon, Lightsey, Douglas, Cleveland, and Flunder are magnified in this chapter, because their voices expose the sins of white supremacy. I believe their work is vital for embodied theologies and practices of liberation. I use their work aware of how their bodies are not theoretical in their work, but on the line. I seek to honor their example by practicing allyship and putting my body in the way of injustice.

CHAPTER 4

A Liberating Spirit and Political Pentecost

The white fathers told us: I think, therefore, I am.
The black goddess within each of us—the poet—whispers in our dreams:
I feel, therefore, I can be free.

—*AUDRE LORD, SISTER OUTSIDER*

Praying for freedom never did me any good 'til I started
praying with my feet.

—*FREDERICK DOUGLASS, NARRATIVE OF THE LIFE
OF FREDERICK DOUGLASS*

"Here," she said, "in this here place,
we flesh; flesh that weeps, laughs,
flesh that dances on bare feet in grass.
Love it. Love it hard."

—*ALICE WALKER, THE COLOR PURPLE*

Introduction

WHEN I BEGAN THIS CHAPTER, I did so with news on in the background. Protests and riots were flooding the streets of cities around the US, including my own, in response to the brutal murder of George Floyd. Cell phone video captured Floyd's last minutes as he cried out, "I can't breathe," while one officer, Derek Chauvin, refused to remove his knee from George's neck. In total, four Minneapolis Police Department officers held George down under their weight. After nearly nine minutes of pleading, George died. Later, President Trump stood in front of St. John's Episcopal Church in Washington, DC, and, first having driven out peaceful protestors with tear gas, posed for a photo-op as he waved around a Bible—which did not belong to him—as he mouthed the words "Law and order." Threatening to invoke the Insurrection Act, Trump spoke not of unity, but rather of domination, by declaring he would deploy the military to end the protests around the country—an exercise of First Amendment rights.

This public display is not unprecedented or unimaginable from Trump, but his overtly fascist tendencies are symptomatic of a particular performance of power. When I speak of the history of ideas—theological and philosophical—that constructs a particular subjectivity and subject-hood, I am speaking of the foundation and basis for the construction of race and racism, of white supremacy. The continual assault on Black life—from police brutality to implicit bias to other insidious systems and structures of racism—is a performance, a demonstration of whiteness, which is a practice of authority rooted in and propped up by modern philosophical and theological projects. Black life, Black breath, or *pneuma*, is constantly restricted, choked, at the hands of state-sponsored injustice and violence. This is not one instance of a breakdown of American governance, but the way things have been set up, from the beginning, an authority through leadership that Cedric Robinson traces as the "terms of order."[1] Liberation cannot occur without a change in direction, a fresh wind of the Spirit that blows and brings with it the powerful means of change.

As I discussed in the previous chapter, Pentecost came to the US at Azusa Street, but it proved to be premature for its social milieu. While Azusa was the beginning of and source for many Pentecostal denominations, disparate movements fractured along the color line. The racial rupture is evidenced by the demographics of the two largest Pentecostal denominations: the mostly white Assemblies of God and the mostly Black Church of God in Christ (COGIC).

At the same time, near the turn of the century, Black Americans were dealing with the political chaos after emancipation—failed Reconstruction, Jim Crow laws, and segregation. Emancipation did not guarantee freedom. Without opportunity, a job, or property, there could be no equality. This exposes a hard truth: there has never been a united or unified America. The American idea, founding myth, and "dream" are not commensurate

1. Robinson, *Terms of Order*.

with America's actual, painful history of genocide, slavery, and civil war. Much of what makes the American experiment exceptional is based more so on myth than history. Just as Du Bois declared a twoness of being, there are certainly (at least) two Americas. The reason that Donald Trump can hold a Bible and mouth "Law and order," which is little more than dog-whistling to his base, is because the historical connection between the Bible and brutality has been strongly established in his America, the America in which "great" and "white" are synonymous. Appealing to the use of force to dominate people into docility is, in fact, very American.

Azusa Street transgressed both political and ecclesial norms and order of the early twentieth century. For example, Vinson Synan notes the absence of racial discrimination, evidenced by how Black, white, Chinese, and even Jewish persons attended the services to hear William Seymour preach.[2] Azusa Street dared to present an alternative vision of the world in which racism was overcome by the power of the Holy Spirit. The notion of a new Jerusalem played an important role in the lead-up to Azusa. The city of God would bring a new world and society in which all injustices would be made right. As Frank Bartleman wrote in *The Way of Faith* in light of the happenings at Azusa Street: "Pentecost has come to Los Angeles, the American Jerusalem."[3] However, the American Jerusalem was met with immediate resistance. Critic Nettie Harwood visited the mission and claimed that different sexes and races were kissing, and she was incensed when she witnessed a Black woman with her arms around a white man's neck. Charles Parham, Seymour's former teacher and mentor, became his greatest critic. Among the many polemical attacks Parham brought against Azusa, including the racially charged characterizations of the worship, he contended that the worship had gone "beyond the bounds of common sense and reason."[4] Azusa Street's renunciation of the order and norms of society was ultimately what caused many people—religious leaders as well as journalists and other skeptics—to turn against the movement.

It is imperative to understand the histories of the US to comprehend how audacious—and thus, controversial—Seymour's egalitarian vision was at Azusa Street. Bringing together races and genders to erase the color and gender lines was a bold political statement and offered a theo-political vision that pushed America to an uncomfortable place. The US has been

2. Synan, *Holiness-Pentecostal Tradition*, 99.

3. *The Way of Faith*; quoted in Bartleman, *How Pentecost Came*, 63.

4. Synan, *Holiness-Pentecostal Tradition*, 102.

established by and on the supremacy of whiteness, which is the standard and source of power and exceptionalism. Here are conflicting views of America, as well as conflicting views of new Jerusalem and Pentecost. Will Pentecost visit the least of these in American society to set the captives free?

This chapter explores the notion of a political Pentecost in the flesh that is informed and shaped by Pentecostal spirituality. Whereas liberation theologies have tended to draw upon a cadre of theological and political tools (such as Marxist thought), my interest is in how enfleshing freedom, as the praxis of liberation, is affective and embodied. Further, rather than a theology formed only from Western sources, norms, and practices, as well as the privileged and powerful within them, I explore how the Spirit informs the work of liberation in the lives of the oppressed. In order to do so, however, I must address how power operates and how specifically bodies are embedded in networks of power. How we arrive at knowledge affects the type of world we create. Thus, as I have argued, the Enlightenment brought about modernity, which brought about scientific revolution, leading to projects of classification and categorical distinction. Ideas promulgated by white, male, Eurocentric scientists and thinkers became the example par excellence of knowledge. A standard emerged for what could be known and the terms upon which it could be known. This is the world that I argue is undone in a Pentecostal spiritual vision for how the Spirit moves and operates. The Spirit is the felt a/effect of the anointed one and the anointed. Where the Spirit is, freedom rules. In a Pentecostal understanding of the indwelling of the Holy Spirit, therefore, bodies become the locus of this freedom. However, the tension between the social world and religious world is stark. It is into and out of this tension that Pentecost comes and comes again. When Pentecost arrives, it disorients and reorders the world, making possible new configurations of knowledge, power, and relations, as well as new enfleshed spiritualities that cut against the grain of conventional and traditional forms, norms, and logics.

A Liberating Spirit

In *On Earth as in Heaven: A Liberation Spirituality of Sharing*, Dorothee Söelle writes:

> These are great words: *Spirit, pneuma, life, freedom, eleutheria* . . .
> The question to all great nouns is the question the great Polish philosopher Stanislaus Lec raised: "Liberty, equality, fraternity—very

beautiful! But how do we get to the verbs? How can we move from nouns to deeds, to action?"[5]

How do we get to the verbs, that is, to the action? How is freedom enfleshed, such that it is practiced and realized, not just reserved to the theoretical. Of course, it is important to theorize—which can strengthen and undergird practice—but, what Söelle is inviting the reader to do is move beyond the written word and static meaning toward a dynamism that is always action-oriented. Words alone will not suffice; they will not bring about change until they are translated and transformed into verbal form, i.e., action. Just as "the Word became flesh and blood, and moved into the neighborhood,"[6] Pentecostal spiritualities that focus on the indwelling of the Spirit toward freedom, joy, and agency animate and move bodies into otherwise configurations of social and spiritual life that are based upon a vision of total freedom. This does not preclude the propagation of legalism under the auspices of freedom. On the contrary, legalism is often about conformity to certain social norms by utilizing spiritual means, methods, and terminologies.

While the language of liberation has become associated with Marxist thought, I contend that freedom and liberation are synonymous and interchangeable: freedom is liberation and liberation is freedom. Thus, where the Spirit is, there is God's liberating action in the world and processes of liberation. The connection that must be reestablished, and what I hope to do in what follows, is to demonstrate how the social is inextricably tied to the spiritual—there is no neat separation between them. Liberation cannot be reduced to the fate of the soul but must address the fate of the body in everyday life. If a Spirit-filled liberating theology has nothing to say to the exigencies of the age, e.g., Althaus-Reid's lemon vendors who work with no underwear so they can urinate in the streets to continue work without taking breaks, it is not truly liberating. Many Christian traditions have reduced and flattened the notion of salvation, relegating it to a spiritual-only status as the fate of the soul. It is this dangerous tendency that Söelle cautions against; as soon as freedom congeals into the suffix -*dom*, it can stiffen into

5. *Eleutheria* is the ancient Greek term for, and personification of, liberty (Söelle, *On Earth*, 90 [emphasis in original]).

6. This is how John 1:14 reads in the Message translation, which is a loosely paraphrased version. While I acknowledge the problematic and often inaccurate nature of paraphrased versions, this particular interpretation of the Word-become-flesh is relevant for this chapter.

an ideology.[7] And when such stiffening occurs, it is time, once again, for an in-breaking, for new languages, for Pentecost.

The Reverend Dr. William Barber II declares: "Prophetic and liberationist Pentecostals in America recall it [Pentecost] with special devotion because it is central to our understanding of how the Spirit interrupts this world's systems to offer us a new way forward in times of crisis."[8] Beyond the Sunday that is celebrated in the church calendar, Pentecost represents an occasion to respond to crises and challenges; it is the action verb that shakes out the stiffness of nominal and normative life; it is the interruption and eruption of the world as it is known, opening up new worlds of possibility. Given that Barber's work with the Poor People's Campaign focuses on the intersectionality of race, class, gender, and sexuality as the locus of the Spirit's work as liberating action, he invites Spirit-filled Christians to move beyond the languages of the day, in the syntaxes of racism, sexism, homophobia, and classism, toward a new language, vision, and world that the Spirit makes possible: "We need tongues and we need fire. But if we're going to have a political Pentecost, we also need fresh wind. We need a moral fusion movement blowing in every community across this land."[9] What is needed, therefore, is to hear the Spirit speak in new ways through Spirit-centered movements that usher in political Pentecost—total freedom, equality, and equity for all—in the US. As Söelle prophetically declares: "Where the Spirit is, there grows liberation."[10] Barber's political Pentecost parallels what Yvette Flunder calls "third Pentecost." The Azusa Street revival shows what can happen when a liberating Spirit is accosted by the social norms and boundaries of the day. It is for precisely this reason that I move to consider the Spirit's constant presence, a prominent theme in Pentecostalism, as a liberative response to the injustices and unjust practices of society. The Spirit awakens and invites believers to social action. What begins in an encounter with God leads to renewed engagement with others.

In her sermon "The Third Pentecost," Flunder suggests that the disciples in the upper room were working within a particular and limited worldview. They were experiencing something new, and it required a sort of sense-making in the moment that drew upon repertoires of what was

7. Söelle, *On Earth*, 96.

8. Barber, "Rev. Barber."

9. Barber, "Rev. Barber."

10. Söelle, *On Earth*, 97.

previously known. Reaching back to the prophet Joel, "this is that" is all they could say; it was the only association they could make at the time. However, in the same way that the Holy Spirit stirred a movement in and beyond Jerusalem and in and beyond Azusa, Flunder contends that "we are embarking on a third Pentecost. Beyond Jerusalem (Pentecost 1), beyond Azusa (Pentecost 2) . . . We are the third generation of the Pentecostal movement. . . . I'm not talking about a denomination . . . I'm talking about a fresh upper room. This [the church, the moment] is an upper room where God is speaking something that Joel didn't know anything about. . . . What is God saying?" she asks. "You are an epistle to be seen and read by humankind. Who you are is impossible to those who say it is impossible, but you are here. . . . We are becoming, and when you're becoming, you have to be people of Spirit . . . the Spirit moves too quickly for the Law."[11] For Flunder, the people of God are living pastoral letters to the world. God's Spirit indwells believers. What God has to say is written upon and within bodies. Revelation is tied to fleshy experience, and fleshy experience to revelation. Like the Spirit's movement throughout the Scriptures, there is a "fresh wind" that can be felt but only seen and recorded in retrospect.

The church was born of Spirit, in a locked room of fearful followers; but it has become overly institutionalized, which Flunder asserts has been the unfortunate plight of the church. The overly institutionalized church seeks to keep a "dead Jesus in his place" and subsequently seeks to superimpose order on the social and theological world. But, "the wind is calling, and we are becoming people of the Spirit again. . . . The letter killeth, but the Spirit makes alive."[12] She continues:

> I fear the sin of biblioidolatry. Why? Because there are people that worship the letter more than they worship the Spirit. . . . God intended for you not to worship the book, but for you to be the book. . . . I am against biblioidolatry because Jesus never wrote anything. . . . People say, "Jesus said!" I say, "How do you know that?" . . . When you know Jesus, you're able to go back to the book and tell what Jesus said and what Jesus didn't say. When you know Jesus, there are things you can hear people say if Jesus said them. . . . Your spirit will be a corrective. The Spirit in you will be in disagreement. The Spirit of God in you speaks from the home of where Jesus is. I think this is why he didn't write anything: because God is Spirit and they that worship must worship in spirit and

11. Flunder, "Bishop Yvette Flunder."
12. Flunder, "Bishop Yvette Flunder."

truth. . . . Tell someone that I know that I know that I know who I
am and whose I am. . . . All we really need is a fresh wind, a fresh
Pentecost. Because when the Pentecost comes, the Spirit of God
will set all things straight. . . . *The ones who are most abused and
misunderstood and sidelined by religion are the ones that will break
the spells of religion.*[13]

There's a wind coming; it is God's weather pattern for Pentecost. Pressure
brings change. Bodies are affective barometers. As Spirit-filled and spirited
people, stirred and changed by a fresh wind, the Fellowship of Affirming
Ministries (TFAM) is a like a new upper room through which a third Pentecost is being birthed. God's Spirit is poured out on those who are "sick of
religion" but hungry for relationship.

Something happens when words are written down: they become crys-
talized, sedimented, and over time, distanced from the context in which
they were originally written. The Gospels themselves were first an oral
tradition before they were written down, edited, and eventually canonized.
No original texts survived antiquity. All that remain are copies. Thus, the
notion of tradition and authority is at stake in Flunder's sermon, as Flunder pushes back against oppressive Christian norms and theology formed
by and with support from the Scriptures. In turn she offers new ways of
knowing and interpreting Scripture and tradition, not simply through the
literal letter-as-law, but through experience informed by the indwelling of
the Spirit. The "authority of Scripture," a phrase used in evangelical sects
of Christianity, does not come from the words themselves, but rather from
how the words are translated, interpreted, and most importantly, how people have chosen and choose to give the Scriptures authority in their lives.
In a word, Scripture's role in the life of the believer is a matter of consent.
When Flunder prophetically problematizes the notion of "biblioidolatry,"
she is alluding to doctrine—and its intellectual projects of theology and
orthodoxy—as that which can cast a spell, as that which can stymie and
even kill the Spirit. It is a body-and-spirit awareness of how one's religion
is experienced, understood, and parsed out as one is guided by the Spirit
and within the context of community. While it may appear, at first glance,
a reductive approach, upon further consideration, it becomes clear that
Flunder's destabilization of oppressive theological norms and values is an
invitation to live life by, in, and with the Spirit, who makes new and other

13. Flunder, "Bishop Yvette Flunder" (emphasis added).

worlds possible. Her work is not a subtraction but a holistic hermeneutical integration of self, community, and Spirit.

Walter J. Hollenweger writes that "*Pentecostalism is revolutionary* because it offers alternatives to 'literary' theology and defrosts the 'frozen thinking' within literary forms of worship and committee-debate."[14] Hardly unbiased, Hollenweger equates dogged doctrine with frozen, or set in place, thinking. "It [Pentecostalism] gives the same chance to all, including the 'oral' people. It allows for the democratization of language by dismantling the privileges of abstract, rational, and propositional systems."[15] Pentecostalism, in this way, is approachable for and belongs to all, not just those who have the educational rigor to theologize and philosophize from ivory towers. Educational rigor and academic acumen are not precluded, but Pentecostalism remains accessible to everyone. It is a spirituality of and for the people; hearing the words and telling the stories will suffice.

Hollenweger's work on the connection between Pentecostalism and Black Power is seminal, not only to ongoing studies of Pentecostalism, but specifically to my argument here that Pentecostalism was and is greatly influenced and shaped by Black expression—hence, Ashon Crawley's fusion of the two into Blackpentecostalism. Merging oral tradition and experience, Blackpentecostalism provides alternatives to literary theology, such that it overcomes and overwhelms the privileging of rationalism and abstract language over the Spirit as the domain of the nonliterary. That which cannot be rationalized and neatly organized or categorized, as I argued throughout this project, must be diminished, demeaned, and disqualified in modern theological and philosophical projects. Rather than enclosure, Blackpentecostalism evidences an openness and opening that occasions possibility.

The excess of meaning and proliferation of possibilities found in these alternatives is different in kind but not lesser in degree; in fact, they are fully attuned to the body and generate a way of vulnerable, authentic knowing and expression. Blackpentecostalism appeals to and intervenes in the relationship between "the logic of the guts" and "the logic of the brain," asking: "How does the dance speak to us and how does the word move us? How does the guitar talk and how does the thesis provide a variation on a theme?"[16] Nonliterary aspects and expressions of worship take on new roles and characteristics: dance speaks, words move, and guitars

---

14. Hollenweger, "Pentecostalism and Black Power," 234 (emphasis in original).

15. Hollenweger, "Pentecostalism and Black Power," 234.

16. Hollenweger, "Pentecostalism and Black Power," 237.

talk. Blackpentecostalism represents a synthesis, a fusion, which provides a means for people to embrace various methods available to them, problematize inherited ideologies, and create new political and spiritual possibilities: "The Black Pentecostal approach forms a new unity between prayer and politics, social action and song."[17] Rather than living as abject and abstract beings, severed and segregated from the world created by whiteness, Blackpentecostalism is a way of evidencing how prayer and politics, the spiritual and the social are indistinguishable.

The ongoingness of embodied life is a process of becoming-with, such that the spiritual and the social coalesce to affect the total life of the person and community. In fact, Cheryl Bridges Johns points out that Hollenweger's understanding of Pentecostalism "gives a voice to those who have been reduced to silence by intellectual concepts and racial prejudices."[18] Once reduced to silence and relegated to lower status, Blackpentecostalism rejects categorical coherence and neat and defined doctrine, preferring shared experience and community instead. That Pentecostalism integrates "oral-affective dimensions"[19] as part of its method evidences the ways in which theologizing is embodied, performed, and passed down from generation to generation through the ritual retelling of history and the affective histories embedded and embodied in bodies. God is not only involved in history generally but is involved in the history of people always and everywhere fighting for liberation and freedom as promised in the ministry and announced good news of Jesus. But Christians must discern the spirits by evaluating the fruit: if the Spirit invoked does not bring wholeness, goodness, love, patience, kindness, etc., then is it really the Holy Spirit? Pentecostals often boast of the gifts of the Spirit, but rarely appeal to the fruits of the Spirit. I now turn to consider the affective dynamics of political and religious experience and practice as an example of how the social and spiritual function together.

Exploring Political Affects

Political Pentecost necessitates reorientation. But bodies, through webs and networks of affects and their attachments, tend to get stuck. The intransigence of affects makes change difficult, particularly through the

17. Hollenweger, "Pentecostalism and Black Power," 230.

18. Johns, *Pentecostal Formation*, 19.

19. Johns, *Pentecostal Formation*, 22.

stubbornness of how ideas, people, and things are accustomed to feeling. To change how one thinks or acts necessitates changing how one feels. Disorientation, then, becomes a necessary first step in the process, as bodies unlearn and learn again through felt pedagogical mechanisms. As Eve Kosofsky Sedgwick argues, pedagogy is about circulation—opening up the possibility of repetition, reiteration, mutation, and transformation as the horizon of experience and possibility.[20] Pedagogy transforms how the world feels, as well as our place in—and with—the world. This is very similar to what Ted Jennings calls ritual knowledge. Of course, this felt pedagogy can bring about good or ill in the world. Thus, we see again the complementarity of affect and ritual, which is the lens through which I engage how political affects shape bodies, tending them toward or in certain directions/orientations, and how religious practices, such as ritual, are important in resisting or reifying the political.

In *Politics of Affect*, Brian Massumi discusses the connection between affect and the political within the tradition of Spinozan affect theory. In the chapter "Of Microperception and Micropolitics," Massumi extrapolates Baruch Spinoza's definition of affect in two parts. The first part is rudimentary: affect is an ability to affect or be affected. The second part is more complex: "a power to affect and be affected governs a transition, where a body passes from one state of capacitation to a diminished or augmented state of capacitation."[21] Furthermore, this transition—from one state to another—is a felt transition. Because affectation occurs in an in-between state, a transition is necessary in three parts: 1) the felt quality of the experience; 2) the felt transition leaves a trace, constituting a memory; and 3) the capacitation of the body is completely bound up with the lived past of the body.[22] Massumi's use of Spinozan affect highlights how traces are felt, cached, and embedded in the history of bodies. Affect, in this way, creates the conditions for what is possible through past encounters, i.e., the lived past. Affect accumulates through *microperceptions*, which are not smaller perceptions, but perceptions "felt without registering cognitively,"[23] within bodies. Affects, through their attachments, resonate even as they make

---

20. See ch. 5, "Pedagogy of Buddhism," in Sedgwick and Frank, *Touching Feeling*.

21. Massumi, *Politics of Affect*, 4. Parts of this section previously appeared in Watts, "Ritualizing Bodies."

22. Massumi, *Politics of Affect*, 49.

23. Massumi, *Politics of Affect*, 53.

impressions and orient bodies toward certain ideas, people, and words, and away from others.[24]

The political sphere produces political rituals. Trump's presidential campaigns made clear that affects proliferate in the gathering of crowds. The former president's ability to communicate power through his pointed rhetoric is an example of how affect attaches to language. The truth, told by Trump, is true not because it is provable or demonstrable (indeed, it is often demonstrably false), but because it *feels* true and resonates with/in bodies. The historical accuracy is inconsequential. In 2016, "Make America Great Again" registered in bodies as an appeal to a certain reading of history in which America, because of President Obama and liberal politics, had lost its way. Voters expressed their disapproval with politics as usual in Washington and decried the purported plight of the nation. Of course, what is not said but is implied is that the election was a form of white backlash ("whitelash"). This is nothing new, but an appeal to a way of ordering and governing society, i.e., white supremacy. Chants of "Lock her up!" were used to paint Hillary Clinton as antithetical to this vision. Trump made no efforts to conceal his sexism. Overt racism spilled out into the open. Despite a pandemic, the worst economic recession since the Great Depression, ecological crises, and mass protests calling for racial justice and police reform, Trump's 2020 campaign ran on the slogan "Keep America Great." Any critique of America has been painted by the Trump administration as unpatriotic and un-American.

It is unknown whether Trump's rhetoric resonates within the people who are shaped by this mythic narrative or if they shape this narrative with their own beliefs, feelings, and values. However, the resistance to these ideas demonstrates how different affects attach to objects, ideas, words, and people in varying ways. Defeating Trump in November of 2020 would have been easier by re-cueing individuals and masses away from affective attachments that are fear-based toward a hope-centered vision of the future. Hope and fear are directions in which affect can compel and propel bodies. Affect, in this way, is neutral. But what affect makes bodies do is never

24. I use *affect* and *affects* interchangeably to speak in the general and particular. For Massumi's strand of affect, affect is more singular, as the register of becoming. In that way, it floats downstream from the particulars of bodies and embodied emotions, which are dealt with in a more satisfying way by the contributions of Ahmed and Schaefer. I use both strands of affect theory to blur the lines of how affect/affects have currency in different ways depending upon their use. There is no singular approach but only theories of affect.

neutral. Said differently, microperceptions register in different ways. While fear is strong and can grip the body, hope can heal and recue bodies in different directions. Joe Biden framed his campaign as a "fight for the soul of the nation." However, the 2020 election fundamentally was about two views of and visions for America, both of which generated great emotional, affective temperatures in the body politic.

On another level, what was at stake in the election is symptomatic of the modern world. The memories and traumatic traces of modernity are affectively cached in bodies. Hundreds of years of its ideas, strategies, and practices—white supremacy, slavery, sexism, war, categorical distinction, hierarchical ideas of the human etc.—have been embedded and embodied in the flesh. Black bodies bear the scars and the trauma of living with the legacy of slavery, failed Reconstruction, Jim Crow laws, and ongoing systemic and structural racism. White bodies also have scars and trauma from the legacy of slavery, stemming from their inhumane and cruel practices against Black and Indigenous people, but these wounds often go unattended or unacknowledged. To shift this praxis, i.e., to name the pain and transgressions that remain, would begin to unsettle the affective attachments that have been sedimented.

The affective economy around Trump's campaigns represents these interests, which serve to conserve modern understandings of how the world is—and always should be—ordered. It is uncertain how aware Trump is of this. What is certain, however, is how his performance of power is used to further his avarice and self-preservation, even as it unleashes chaos and fury toward those that dare speak against him. Regardless of intent, Trump's actions have aided and abetted the micro- and macro-aggressions of racism, sexism, homophobia, ableism, and xenophobia. For example, when he referred to Mexicans as animals, he was using a modern technique, alluding to a sliding scale of what it means to be human. When he called Hillary Clinton weak and ineffective, he was signaling that women's bodies are not as strong as men's bodies. When he tried to ban people on the basis of their religion in response to terrorism, he was making the connection between Islam and violence. When he mocked a reporter with a congenital joint condition called arthrogryposis, he perpetuated the stigma toward people who are differently abled. All of this is effective and affective language, because it communicates by what is felt but unsaid. It is a technique to maintain the power dynamics of a white-supremacist-cis-hetero-patriarchal-capitalist world, and Trump's ability to stir up affects through

A LIBERATING SPIRIT AND POLITICAL PENTECOST

his rhetoric is his most effective strategy. Coupled with constantly lying and misleading the public, he is able to construct a narrative of nonsense that is not only believed by large portions of the population but mirrored and parroted by his sycophants in affectively-charged ways.

Given Trump's adept ability to tap into the fears and anxieties of millions of people, how can religious practices bring about political Pentecost in response? First, political Pentecost means reclaiming the synchronization of the spiritual and social spheres. Any social movement without the Spirit is unsustainable, because to whom or what one appeals or invokes reveals the sense of one's ultimate concern. What is the inner foundation from which one works? Resistance requires stamina. Conversely, any Spirit-led movement without the social is meaningless. What is needed, therefore, is synchronization: Spirit-led social action. Since spiritual experience can open up bodies in material ways, could we think of microperceptions as a framework for Spirit-awareness? Moreover, how might we think of affective re-cueing as the work of the Spirit? For example, spiritual experiences that cultivate empathy rather than judgment, love rather than hate, and hope rather than fear.

What I am suggesting is that liberating social action, born of affective, spirit-led attachments to hope, love, and justice, must be enfleshed. These practices are no less a/effective than Trump's, but they do require a different relation and orientation to the objects in question. Trump's antics affectively register with people but resonate deeply. Sustained resistance comes from deeper, inward work. There is a mystical purgation evident in many struggles for justice that flows from introspection. As the psalmist writes: "Create in me a clean heart in me, O God, and put a new and right spirit within me" (Ps 51:10).

Politics is not simply about ideology, language, or feeling, but a combination of the three. In other words, we must be reoriented away from fear toward love, toward hope, and toward justice. The Spirit changes our hearts, our attitudes, our emotions by changing our relationship to others. Is this not what Jesus is suggesting with neighbor and enemy love? Is this not what the Spirit performs and makes possible at Pentecost? Fear is not absent in the upper room, but the people are re-cued and reoriented toward, not away from, others by the Spirit. Thus, the Spirit's liberating work leads to reconciliation, healing, and peacemaking, but never at the expense of justice. The Spirit makes it possible to change how we feel when we encounter others, including reshaping the impressions (Ahmed) that are and can be made. However, this requires bodies to come into proximity with one another, rather than succumbing to disembodied prejudices so easily maintained in isolation.

If bodies are shaped by the histories of their encounters with others, they can be reshaped through new encounters. There have been countless examples of white supremacists and nationalists changing their position (heart/mind) because of experiencing and encountering others. Conversely, others can be radicalized. Returning to Ahmed's work, bodies are shaped both by the impressions that objects make on them and by the formed histories that these encounters/impressions constitute.[25] Through a process of ritualization, objects are oriented toward certain objects/other bodies and away from others. Perhaps this is most obvious with regard to protests. Bodies come together and are oriented toward the same ideals, which is demonstrated by walking together, participating in chants and songs, and, when necessary, interrupting social life. At the same time, often counterprotesters gather. The affective temperature rises, too often boils over, and violence ensues. While bodies contain the sediment of these histories of encounters, there are always opportunities for elaboration, improvisation, and even change. Pedagogy is about learning through how the world feels,[26] which is always subject to change vis-à-vis one's position in, or in relation to, it. When people become proximate to others' pain, it can change how we feel, thus changing what we value. Justice work requires empathy.

Another example is needed. Ritual theorist Ronald L. Grimes critically engages the work of Pierre Bourdieu, who believed that, by placing bodies in prescribed postures, their associated feelings and states of mind are reevoked.[27] Ritualizing bodies, through protest, perform—that is, act out—the way the world should be. It is a prophetic performance. The #BlackLivesMatter movement, which was formed in the aftermath of Michael Brown's killing by Ferguson police officer Darren Wilson, imagines and images a just society where Black lives are valued and cherished, a society in which police officers and others who inflict violence upon Black people are brought to justice, a society where Black people do not live in fear of being killed by police for any host of reasons. Protest brings together acts of individual and collective solidarity. Being proximate to the event (protest) intensifies the affective potency of the event, such that bodies

25. Ahmed, *Queer Phenomenology*, 54–60.

26. Schaefer, *Religious Affects*, 67.

27. For more on *habitus*, see Bourdieu, *Outline*; cited in Grimes, *Craft of Ritual*, 245.

become attuned to and enveloped in the affective elements of the event: chanting, singing, marching, signaling, and gesturing. Consider the chant of "Hands up, don't shoot!"[28] This rite reenacts the story of Michael Brown's execution as an act of remembrance. In the retelling, bodies are affectively attuned to the event (protest) through the affective currency that is generated. It is a rite of the flesh.

Christopher Carter argues that "for white people, solidarity ought to begin with *amamnesis*, the intentional remembering of the exploited, marginalized, and minoritized victims of their historical legacy of oppression."[29] This intentional remembering is a sacred act that opens the door to not only empathy, but also repentance. Bodies move in a concerted effort to interrupt normal life, for example, in die-ins, where bodies obstruct the flow of traffic. By halting the flow of traffic, this ritual forces people to become observers or participants—there is no choice, no middle ground. Consider also the words of Assata Shakur in a chant led in a liturgical manner—call-and-response:

> It is our duty to fight for our freedom.
> (*It is our duty to fight for our freedom.*)
> It is our duty to win.
> (*It is our duty to win.*)
> We must love each other and support each other.
> (*We must love each other and support each other.*)
> We have nothing to lose but our chains.
> (*We have nothing to lose but our chains.*)[30]

In creating an emphatic call-and-response, the chant unites the gathered community. The words exude affectively from the leader and are echoed by the crowd, amplifying the sounds of struggle and vibrations of freedom. To join the chant is to lend one's voice to those ends. Repeating the chant, like the stanzas of a hymn, allows more voices to join. In this way, the chant not only unites and organizes the voices of the gathered, but it also reimagines reality toward the responsibility (duty) of fighting for freedom. Carter adds: "Through the praxis of solidarity one apprehends and is moved by the suffering of another—you feel their suffering as though it is your own."[31] Protest brings together bodily histories with collective memories and histories,

28. *Fox 2*, "Hands Up Don't Shoot."
29. Carter, "Blood in the Soil," 59.
30. Shakur, *Assata*, 52. Italics represent the repeated line by the crowd.
31. Carter, "Blood in the Soil," 59.

which is an important and vulnerable place to address violence, fear, and injustice. The aim is to recue bodies toward solidarity and justice.

Protest, in this way, is a liturgy, a work of people that moves and teaches bodies how to feel and thus how to act. It is the embodied manifestation and call-to-action of that which is hoped-for in society—an announcement of political Pentecost. The open-ended and affective nature of the event always points to the future, a "to-come" in which things do not have to be as they are now. As the civil rights movement taught the world, marching and interrupting social life in service to a cause of justice provokes and agitates the status quo, even as it grabs the attention of media. Cell phones and the use of social media to livestream, record, and archive acts of violence are showing this generation that much work is yet to be done. Protests invite others to be affected by the pains of injustice and to be reoriented in the direction of a more just, beloved community. And until that day comes, it is important to organize, rehearse, and model a better world. Ahmed argues that "orientations point us to the future, to what we are moving toward, then they also keep open the possibility of changing directions and of finding other paths."[32] For protest, these other paths are marked by hope, freedom, and justice. However, as I stated earlier in this chapter, political Pentecost is about a synthesis of social and spiritual life guided by the Spirit. The two are bound in tension, and freedom hangs in the balance. Charles Péguy writes: "Everything begins in mysticism and ends in politics."[33] There is a source deeper than the surface from which resistance arises and is nourished.

Learning from Howard Thurman's Mystic-Activism

To consider a synthesis between spiritual—or mystical—and political experience, I can think of no greater example than the work and life of Howard Thurman. While his works are not as well known as other Black theologians, his influence on thinkers such as Martin Luther King Jr. and James Cone cannot be overstated. While not a Pentecostal theologian, Thurman's work embodies attunement to an abiding presence of the Spirit that informs and shapes his thought. The first time I read Thurman, I found in him a synthesis, a balance, of personal experience and communal life; what is disclosed to the individual in religious experience, for Thurman, is defined and interpreted in community. His mystic edge kept him always sharply

32. Ahmed, *Queer Phenomenology*, 178.

33. "Tout commence en mystique et finit en politique" (Péguy, *Notre Jeunesse*, 548).

attuned to whether and how Christianity was up to the task of responding to those with their "backs against the wall."[34] Thurman's understanding of authentic religious experience is never isolated from human suffering; to the contrary, his understanding of religious experience is that it affects the totality of the person, what he calls "the inwardness and outwardness of religion."[35] "The dichotomy that exists between professional and private life, formal and informal life, inner and outer life, must be reduced steadily to the vanishing point."[36] The vanishing point speaks to an integration, a synthesis, transcending and including all aspects of life.

Alton Pollard builds upon Thurman's holistic understanding of the inwardness and outwardness of religion through his reading of Thurman's work as "mystic-activism," which is "a praxis-orientation to the world which relies but in part—albeit considerable part—on the political and intellectual arguments and dictates of society; the more demanding motive is located in the obligation engendered by spiritual experience."[37] Spiritual experience—an encounter with the Holy—informs social action; it is the experience that makes all other experiences possible. Rather than being concerned primarily with the transformation of social structures, Thurman's work of social regeneration focused on the transformation of individuals as the means of transforming others and society. Social regeneration was an ethical program that had three levels: 1) intra-individual (personal), 2) inter-individual (communal), and 3) inter-group (societal).[38] Social regeneration begins locally and grows outward, reminiscent of Jesus's instructions for how the disciples would be his witnesses "in Jerusalem, in all Judea and Samaria, and to the ends of the earth."[39] Likewise, Thurman's vision and witness has grown and spread considerably over time, and his influence and thought continues to challenge his readers.

Thurman's grandmother, Nancy Ambrose, who was previously enslaved, greatly influenced his understanding of religious experience and Christianity. One of the axioms he inherited from Nancy was that religion must begin with the affirmation of the individual's dignity and significance. Because of the ramifications of race and racism, Thurman's work grew out

---

34. Thurman, *Jesus and the Disinherited*, 11.

35. These themes are fleshed out in Thurman, *Creative Encounter*.

36. Thurman, *Creative Encounter*, 146.

37. Pollard, *Mysticism and Social Change*, 1.

38. Pollard, *Mysticism and Social Change*, 7–8.

39. Acts 1:8b.

of the idiom of blackness as he contended that religion must speak to the existential needs of people.[40] With an emphasis on spiritual experience in tension with the social order and the vicissitudes of the oppressed, Thurman's work is a Spirit-filled praxis, akin to some Pentecostal approaches, which seeks to integrate all aspects of life with the aim to flesh out freedom in everyday life. In the God-encounter, one is affirmed and finds their ultimate worth and significance to God, which, in turn, removes barriers from experiencing God and communing with others. This is the beginning of how the mystical affects and saturates every aspect of life.

Thurman's insights continue to challenge the mechanics of modern religion. The God encounter is "creative" in the sense that it promotes new ways of living in the world: "The religious experience as I have known it seems to swing wide the door, not merely into Life but into lives."[41] Being wide open to the Spirit of God is being open to God's liberating action. Thus, Thurman's contribution to the connection between spirituality and social action is that the two are entwined and relational; one informs the other. However, it is through religious experience that an awakening happens, and that is what makes social transformation possible. This is yet another analog to Pentecostalism. Personal experience of the divine is the primary driver of life. He believed that the answer to these injustices was found in religious experience, which began in the inner workings of the personal and emanated out to communal and societal domains.

Thurman gives an example from his time as pastor at the Fellowship of All Peoples in San Francisco. One day, he walked by a storefront and saw a depiction of a racist mammy caricature in a shop window. This deeply troubled him. He mentioned it that Sunday in his sermon. By Monday, the following day, he walked past the storefront again and the racist caricature was gone. The story illustrates Thurman's understanding of how religious experience affects people through the process of removing that which keeps one from the presence of God and communion with others. Racism is a sin that distorts the image of God in others and breaks the bonds of communion. Justice is the response to that sin by removing that which caused others pain. Justice, in this way, flows naturally. Thurman's reflections on his time at the fellowship, which Pollard calls the transmission of his societal vision, offer remembrances of worship times that overwhelmed him and the congregation and instilled in the people—individuals from diverse

---

40. Pollard, *Mysticism and Social Change*, 28–29.
41. Thurman, *Luminous Darkness*, 111.

backgrounds—a sense of being united. In this example, the congregation embodied the transmission of his vision for how religious experience affects the totality of the person and binds together a community.

Spiritual disciplines play an integral role in Thurman's understanding of religious experience. In his work, he identifies five disciplines: commitment, growth, suffering, prayer, and reconciliation.[42] These are the means for removing that which keeps one from living totally in the presence of God. 1) Commitment is an awareness that life is alive and dynamic. It is a seeking to be nourished and committing to something of ultimate concern. 2) Growth is defined as development, in terms of awareness. 3) Suffering, like religious experience itself, is personal and private. However, pain also opens one up to the communal. 4) Prayer is the meaning of existence. In the same way that Jesus found that God breathed through all that is, through prayer one finds that God breathes in/through all living things. Prayer makes us aware of God's presence as the Spirit of life. 5) Finally, there is reconciliation. Simply put, reconciliation is a concern for wholeness he contends everyone longs for. God reconciles, reassembles, brings back together, and heals. These five disciplines function as a way, not only of working for social justice, but of removing the things that keep people from experiencing God in their inner places, their innermost self. The only response is to let that God-encounter rewire and reorient people toward a unified and unifying vision of humankind.

Thurman offers a Spirit-filled vision in what he describes as a systolic and diastolic rhythm, which is constituted by an examined daily life and moments of worship. Together, they form a mystic flow of life in, or by, the Spirit. These God-encounters formed affective bonds within the congregation:

> The door between their [i.e., the congregation] questing spirits and my own became a swinging door. At times I would lose my way in the full tide of emotions as a sense of the love of God overwhelmed me. At such moments we became one in the presence of God. . . . The congregation and the participants were fused in a single moment of spiritual transcendence. I discovered, again through worship, that an experience of unity among peoples can be more compelling than all that separates and divides.[43]

---

42. Thurman, *Disciplines of the Spirit*.

43. Thurman, *With Head and Heart*, 73, 95.

Worship, for Thurman, is the central and most significant act of existence. Notice in the quote above it is not only the Holy Spirit that is circulating between Thurman and the congregation but the human spirit—the moment when the presence of God appeared "in the head, heart, and soul of the worshipper."[44] The congregation collectively modeled the inwardness and outwardness of religion through moments of worship and togetherness that translated into societal transmission of their espoused values. Most importantly, it was their shared encounters with God in worship that created the conditions for otherwise possibilities in daily life, demonstrating how religious or mystical experience is profoundly relational. It is lived experience and the interaction between God, people, and society that reorients and empowers people for the struggle for social change and liberation. Thurman's mystic sensibilities push the conversation, once again, to the brink of perpetual Pentecost.

Experiencing Blackpentecost and Enfleshing Freedom

James Cone names white supremacy as America's central *theological* problem.[45] It is no less a problem in Pentecostal circles. In fact, methods to avoid painful histories, such as language of "oneness in the Spirit" and color-blind Christians, are often deployed. These terms and ideas fall short of racial justice because they do not actively oppose or dismantle racist ideas and practices; they are not anti-racist. But it does not have to be this way. Pentecostalism is an open-ended framework that anticipates the in-breaking of the Spirit to interrupt the ongoingness of life, including injustices of society (racism, sexism, homophobia, xenophobia, etc.). This is Seymour's legacy at Azusa as well as the Spirit's *modus operandi*. When deployed toward justice, the framework can be helpful to see and name the Spirit's work as the liberating force and impetus found in life: That wherever the Spirit is, there is the work of liberation, and wherever the work of liberation is, there is the Spirit. Pentecost, thus, is always coming, always being announced, and always being birthed into the world.

Ashon Crawley writes: "The day of Pentecost has fully come. Blackpentecost, however, has and is yet and still to come."[46] Perhaps what he is suggesting is that, while there have been movements and responses to

44. Thurman, *With Head and Heart*, 159.
45. Cone, "Theology's Great Sin."
46. Crawley, *Blackpentecostal Breath*, 134.

Pentecost, there has not been a Blackpentecost because the movements and responses, e.g., the Great Awakening revivals, were aversive to Blackness. This aversion is in tension, in contradiction, with God's presence and identification with the oppressed, which is confirmed in God's presence in Jesus's social location as a peasant minority who was executed by the state. Jesus is the prototype for incarnation. By that, I mean God's presence is with, among, and in those who are victimized, oppressed, and marginalized. For this reason, Jesus teaches that how we treat "the least of these" is how we treat God.[47] The passage reminds that Christians are responsible, not only for what is done, but what is left undone. The solidarity of Jesus with the oppressed makes possible the praxis of solidarity with the oppressed in every age and society even as it locates God's presence there. Thus, my emphasis in this section focuses on the Spirit and work of liberation in Blackpentecostal traditions.

Blackpentecostal worship, as proximate practice, as an aesthetic practice of being together in one place, is an occasion for Ashon Crawley's notion of choreosonics, which is the irreducibility of sound and movement through shouting and announcing otherwise possibilities. The result of Blackpentecost is a creative act—an opening-up to possibilities and an explication of Blackness. Shouting is the aesthetic practice par excellence that Crawley explores:

> In this choreosonic shout tradition, vitality transferred, a way to create a social form was carried to and then dwelt within this particular way of life. What sorts of injunctions existed against certain modes of social life and how were the aesthetic dances of Blackpentecostalism in response to such injunctions? Is Blackpentecostal shouting but one other example of "stealing away" to produce an old form otherwise? Possibly. Exhaustedly? Certainly. To steal away is the topical thrust, the undergrounded verve of black performance; it is the unceasing theme around which black performance varies. It is a different relation to time and space, the grounds for, without being educated into, modernity. The shout tradition is an ethical demand to vary and antagonize, to be restless and restive against the dominant political economy and its ordering of the world.[48]

47. Matt 25:31–46.
48. Crawley, *Blackpentecostal Breath*, 134.

Shouting informs and inculcates social life and spiritual experience. It is a response to a particular ordering of the world through "stealing away"; in this sense, it radically reorders and overwhelms the singular world, leading to places and possibilities that are not the result of some afterlife fantasy, but life in the here and now. Shouting as a creative act is exemplified in Charles Mason's performance of shouting, leaving behind one world—its constraints of time and space—and through empowering the people, the congregation, goes further and deeper into experiences of the divine. As Crawley suggests, this inculcation "presented the possibility of repetition as a means to having this 'Pentecostal experience.'"[49] The phrase "possibility of repetition" can be imagined as a ritualistic form or frame (Pitts Jr.) intrinsic to Pentecostalism in general and Blackpentecostalism in particular.

For example, consider the "Yes, Lord!" praise break originally attributed to Bishop Charles Harrison Mason of the Church of God in Christ (COGIC). The song is considered a prayer and chant, an interruption in time and space during the worship service, that invites the congregation, pastor, and musicians to tarry together. Often, it precedes an altar call or moment of invitation/invocation. One such occasion is recorded at Pentecostal Temple COGIC in Memphis, Tennessee.[50] In the video, Bishop James Oglethorpe Patterson Jr. stands with both arms lifted and leads the congregation in singing yes, as the organ follows and fills in the interstices—the breaks—in the music. The congregation begins to shout, hands clapping, such that the sonic sounds of shouting/singing become indistinguishable; it is not clear where one starts or ends. Bishop Patterson removes the microphone from the pulpit and begins walking among the people, waving his hand as he begins to exhort them. The music provides for him a dynamic accompaniment, a call-and-response rhythm that ebbs and flows and accents notes and syllables through rhythm. Much of what is said is unintelligible, audibly mixed in with the music; but the affective temperature of the room continues to rise. Something is stirring.

When Patterson says "Praise him!" the band immediately launches into a two-step praise break—what is often called "cutting a step," which involves complex, coordinated footwork while shouting and dancing simultaneously. The video pans to the congregation, mostly women dressed in white, and depicts hands clapping, bodies swaying, and people dancing as they shout, shouting as they dance. The praise break lasts approximately

49. Crawley, *Blackpentecostal Breath*, 135.

50. Simply Tomas, "'Yes Lord' Praise."

four minutes and ends with unutterable sounds and audible sighs—joy unspeakable—and the congregation sits back down in their pews. As the moment settles and the music quiets, Patterson addresses them once again from the pulpit.

The dynamic flow of "Yes, Lord!" evidences Crawley's insistence on the irreducibility of sound and movement—choreosonics. For Crawley, "worship, even in the context of congregational gatherings, is a deeply intimate practice. The clapping of hands, the shouting, these are all grounded in the fact of the flesh. They're a sort of publicly intimate practice, communal but deeply stylistic for the individual, they unmake the desired subject of western thought through a releasement into practice, through a relinquishment of the hoped-for individual."[51] The song's structure is simple: six intervals ascending and descending melodically through melismatic singing of the word *yes*. Because of the simple form there is much room to improvise within it; voices soar, overlapping and adding artistic verve to the sound of a congregational choir. Yes is an affirmation of and to God; but, conversely, it is also a refutation. Hence why it is sung as both "Yes" or "Yes, Lord!" We are not sure to whom or to what the first is responding. The yes can be sung as a response to the nos of modernity, the nos of white supremacy, and even the world. It is a yes and amen to otherwise possibilities, dreams, hopes, and worlds; it is a new hallelujah, a nevertheless praise; it is the announcement of a Pentecost, a visitation and enfleshment of the Spirit that brings about the freedom that has been promised but by and large not actualized.

I have been arguing that Black worship expression and experience represent a certain excess that refuses to be reduced, and this excess constitutes the conditions for otherwise possibilities, otherwise epistemologies, otherwise ontologies. Indeed, Black worship expression and experience refute the categories by which the World is ostensibly ordered. But not this world. Rooted in the politico-spiritual hush harbors, where secrecy meets subversion, the world is radically reordered in the ongoing and unfolding annunciation of Blackpentecost, which creates the conditions of possibility and offers other ways of knowing and being. In *Sketches of Slave Life*, Peter Randolph describes one of the secret meetings:

> They [the enslaved] first ask each other how they feel, the state of their minds etc. . . . then praying and singing all around, until they generally feel quite happy. The speaker usually commences by calling himself unworthy, and talks very slowly, *until feeling*

51. Crawley, *Lonely Letters*, 65.

the Spirit, he grows excited, and in a short time, there fall to the ground twenty or thirty men and women under its influence. . . . As they separate, they sing a parting hymn of praise.[52]

These words were written by the firsthand account of Peter Randolph, who was born into slavery but freed upon the death of his enslaver, Carter H. Edloe. Randolph converted to Christianity as a young child and began preaching at the age of ten.[53] Later, he would become an abolitionist, minister, and member of the antislavery society. In this passage from his collection of accounts and stories of the lives of enslaved people, we see an affective flow at work, particularly in how the Spirit visits and excites the preacher, who, with twenty or thirty others, falls to the ground under the Spirit's influence. Bodies are affected and moved, literally, because of the onset of feeling and emotion.

Here, the Western African world of spirit possession and trance coalesces with Christian practice, serving as an antecedent for ecstatic worship in Black church traditions. Following the rituals of Western Africa through singing and dancing, the singers/dancers would fall into a trance and often transmit a message of and from the divine. Thus, there is a connection to and participation between spirit and power; the Spirit participates with the soul and empowers the participants. Randolph notes that while visitors would smile and laugh from amusement, "the worshipers, perspiring at every pore, were never more serious."[54] These rituals were amusing to visitors, even as Black shouting and dancing was nonsensical—even "primitive"—to whites. White theology had no way to bring coherence to the excess that comes from singing and dancing, shouting and breathing, but these are the practices that organically emerge from Blackpentecost.

Unbeknownst to whites was that their inability to make these acts intelligible had no bearing on the power that flowed in and through the ritualizing; in fact, the grounds of emancipation were vibrating underneath their feet. While whites try to force Christianity on the enslaved to perpetuate slavocracy and the status quo, the enslaved found in Christianity a way to subvert, resist, and dismantle the system through affective economies of spirited worship. As freedwoman Millie Anne Smith revealed, "We hummed our religious songs in the field while we was working. It was our

---

52. Randolph, *Sketches of Slave Life,* 68; quoted in Pitts, *Old Ship of Zion,* 38 (emphasis added).

53. Williamson, "Review."

54. Randolph, *Sketches of Slave Life,* 106.

way of praying for freedom, but the white folks didn't know it."[55] Humming, as resonance, as unintelligible vibration but through distinguishable melody, was the sound of prayer, of ritualizing, toward the goal of liberation. It was an instance of choreosonics, as bodies vibrated audibly. The sound of Blackpentecost was oscillating and stirring; it was being announced even as it was done so unbeknownst to the oppressor.

From whence comes the source of this resistance? Blackpentecost is inspirited—given life—by and through Black *pneuma*—breath, spirit— which is the contestation of a world that seeks to asphyxiate Black bodies to death. "I can't breathe" is a reminder of how the world, through systems and structures of violent and demonstrative power, seeks to take away breath, to knock the breath out of people, to extinguish Black light and eliminate Black lives. However, while Black *pneuma* contests and reorders the world, it does so on the same terms or means that oppositional power does: "Violence is not the grounds of our justice; oppression and social death are not the grounds for our resistance. Rather, the breath—black breath, blackpentecostal breath—is why we live and move and have our *breathing*. It is a conundrum of possibility, black life irrepressible. . . . Our breath is Black."[56] Adkins, here, echoes both the concern of womanism to "love the folk," *all* the folk, and highlights Crawley's reliance upon breath, Black breath, which exhales possibilities rooted in love, joy, generosity, and communal sociality. Breath, unrestricted, enables speech and annunciation.

Looking at the Pentecost account, it is just as acceptable to interpret the upper room as being filled with the sound of a violent (or strong) breath, analogous to *Elohim* breathing life/breath/spirit into the nostrils of *haAdam* to animate the earthling. Breathing is constitutive of two movements: breathing in and breathing out through the lungs. It involves taking in what is in the atmosphere, embodying it, letting it fill the capacity of the lungs, and pushing out the air, the waste, the excess of CO_2. Blackpentecostalism, therefore, is not simply only about Black breath, but about the capacity to breathe in what is needed—through Black pulmonic capacity—and breathe out the harmful chemicals of the atmosphere, that which is not needed for life. Blackpentecostalism through the lungs, in terms of communal breath and collective shouting, teaches how to breathe deeply, diaphragmatic breathing beyond shallow breathing that plagues society; it teaches how to filter the air and remove the harmful chemical agents in it,

55. Campbell, *Empire for Slavery*, 175; quoted in Pitts, *Old Ship of Zion*, 57.
56. Adkins, "Symposium Introduction."

so as not to suffocate; it reminds that the Spirit is life, wind, and breath—
Spirit is all around, within, and anywhere teeming with life.

Blackpentecost is announced by the exhalation of Black breath. It is at
the place of proclamation that Crawley's Blackpentecost and Bishop Flunder's third Pentecost coalesce toward political Pentecost (social change).
The good news (gospel) has always been about annunciation. The response
to good news is sharing it with others. In fact, the Gospel writers used and
subverted an imperial method of the transmission of Pax Romana, a peace
achieved through military exploits and victories or divine decrees and
mandates, to share about the now-but-coming rule of God through the Pax
Christi, achieved only through justice, peace, and goodwill. The Pax Christi
is good news proclaimed in Mary's song, in which the proud are scattered,
the powerful are brought down from their thrones, the lowly are lifted, the
hungry are filled with good things, and the rich are sent away empty.[57] The
prophetic imagination of Pax Christi is also confirmed in Peter's assertion
that "This is that" regarding Joel's vision of an age when all voices (all flesh)
are represented, including those so often silenced—women, children, the
enslaved. Flunder states:

> We have a prophetic responsibility. We are Acts 2. The new book
> of Acts. We are the ones responsible now to do some of the things
> that couldn't happen in the first century AD. We are the new Pen-
> tecost. We are the fresh revelation. The change is coming through
> us. We who once were the tail are the head. We who once were the
> gum on somebody's shoe are now the prophetic voice of God in
> the earth. And that's why God uses like God uses us.[58]

What does it mean to be, to embody, Acts 2? Both as the early prophetic church and as the people through which a fresh revelation (divine
message) is announced? Flunder asserts "This is that," meaning TFAM is a
prophetic and spirit-filled tradition, the people responsible for announcing,
sharing, and spreading the Spirit's message of radical inclusivity and God's
liberating good news. "We," here, represents those who have historically
been excluded from the "we" of imperialist white supremacist capitalist
heteropatriarchy. "We," here, represents the other, the last, and the least.
Yet, marginalized communities are precisely the people who bring God's
message into the world. Because of this profound and subversive mystery, it

57. Luke 1:46–55.

58. Quoted in Lewin, *Filled with the Spirit*, 149.

is no wonder that the Scriptures so often mention that the good news seems to be folly and confounds conventional wisdom of every age.

The Spirit falling upon "all flesh" is crucial, considering the political construct of race along lines of melanin, which is to say, the flesh. Like the ancestors who were brought over and enslaved against their will but gathered in the swamps and wooded areas to worship and exhort one another, Flunder is invoking the Spirit and spirit, both of the African ancestors—a cloud of witnesses, as it were—and of daily life, of daily breath. The Spirit falls upon Black queer bodies, invalidating attempts to stigmatize queer flesh, and affirming the Godness—the *imago Dei* and indwelling of the Spirit—in their bodies. The change Flunder speaks of happens first to liberate the hearer of the good news, which, in turn, is announced to and shared with others. Otherwise worlds operate uninhibited by the world, akin to mystic modes of spirituality, whereby the Spirit leads and is the unpredictable force of life. The Spirit makes free.

How can freedom be fleshed out, or enfleshed? M. Shawn Copeland argues that it necessitates refuting and redefining theological anthropology. She writes: "To privilege suffering bodies in theological anthropology uncovers the suffering body at the heart of Christian belief. Reflection on these bodies, the body of Jesus Christ and the bodies of black women, lays bare both the human capacity for inhumanity and the divine capacity for love."[59] Because the Black body is the most vivid reminder and remainder of slavery, it is also the site for divine revelation, i.e., a human sacrament, for the Spirit's work of liberation. Copeland grounds this work in the fact of the flesh, arguing that bodies—individual and social—are simultaneously the locus of theological reflection and social action.

Reclaiming and redefining theological anthropology is about "seek[ing] a new way of being in world,"[60] otherwise possibilities, which accept and affirm the beauty and inherent worth of the flesh, of Black bodies.[61] Whereas slavery defiled and distorted theological anthropology by adhering to a hierarchized category of the human, in which the white male was the apex, enfleshing freedom rejects this privileging and in turn embraces the *imago Dei* and redeems Black bodies from the evil constraints of the paradigm. Copeland notes that since enslaved people were forbidden to worship, i.e., invoke the Spirit, freedom was something that seemed

59. Copeland, *Enfleshing Freedom*, 1.

60. Copeland, *Enfleshing Freedom*, 22.

61. Copeland is interested specifically in Black women's bodies as sacrament.

unattainable; yet, as she quotes another source: "I've heard [the enslaved] pray for freedom. I thought it was foolishness, then, but the old-time folks always felt they was to be free. It must have been something [re]'vealed unto 'em."[62] What does it mean to feel or exercise freedom in the face, the reality of its unattainability?

Freedom must be "fleshed out":

> Inasmuch as the body becomes the medium through which the human spirit incarnates and exercises freedom in time and space, enslaved women *fleshed* out the words of the Spiritual: *Oh Freedom! Oh, Freedom! Oh Freedom, I love thee! And before I'll be a slave, I'll be buried in my grave. And go home to my Lord and be free.* Literally and metaphorically, black women reclaimed their bodies and the bodies of their loved ones from bondage. . . . Literally and metaphorically, black women chose struggle and death for the sake of life, for the cause of freedom in this life and the next.[63]

We return again to the notion of the spirituals as embodied praxis done with/in the body. The words, the sounds, the melodies, represent affective resonances of resistance and reclamation. Whereas the Enlightenment era's "turn to the subject" precipitated particular dynamics of domination,[64] Copeland redefines the theological anthropological "subject" as female bodies of color, who, like Jesus, are despised and exploited. Such a turn reorients bodies and dis- and reorders the world, showing God's solidarity with and among bodies that are not white or male, neither entirely autonomous, individualistic, or isolated: "Solidarity presents a discernable structure with cognitive, affective, effective, constitutive, and communicative dimensions" and "sets the dynamics of love against the dynamics of domination."[65]

In Copeland's work, therefore, there is an inward change that alters outward life. By reclaiming the sacramentality of bodies and identifying, aligning, and participating with Jesus's broken body as the locus of God's liberative presence in the world, she invites us into the practice of *anamnesis*, which at once invokes the Spirit as the connective tissue of the mystical

62. Jamie T. Phelps, O.P., "Providence and Histories: African American Perspectives with Emphasis on the Perspectives of Black Liberation Theology," 14; quoted in Copeland, *Enfleshing Freedom*, 39.

63. Copeland, *Enfleshing Freedom*, 39 (emphasis in original).

64. Copeland, *Enfleshing Freedom*, 88.

65. Copeland, *Enfleshing Freedom*, 94.

union of the body of Christ and summons the dangerous memory of the broken body of God in Jesus, the force of love and freedom that death could not kill. Jesus's message of love transforms and transfigures the bodies of those deemed "other," a subversion of norms and values across millennia.

What then, can be done to flesh out freedom in the present age? Since the 1960s, theologies of liberation have been engaging this question, using a plethora of methods, sources, and practices. As I close, I want to offer a few possibilities for what invoking a liberating Spirit may look like. I use the term "liberating Spirit" to show the slippage, or perhaps the blurred line, between human and divine spirit. Like the mystery in Jesus, I believe created creatures are containers of the Holy Spirit. How God indwells created life is a holy mystery. The first possibility may be obvious at this point, but it is worthy of being said again: to invoke the Spirit in the cause of freedom means changing one's heart and mind from one way of thinking/being in the world (Enlightenment worldview) to a kindom worldview that runs counter, subverts, and reorders the sociopolitical world, including which bodies matter and have value. In the Christian vernacular, we can use the word *metanoia* to describe this process. It is a "turning," which is always a turning-toward one another and God. It is a rendering of the "other" as part of the body of Christ, seeing the inherent worth of all of God's children. This turn is, simply put, a change of heart, a new way of feeling that can affectively shape the horizon of what is possible.

Second, to invoke the Spirit in the cause of freedom means engaging in spiritual praxis, especially rites of remembrance. Just as Jesus is remembered and made known in the breaking of bread, the Christian imaginary should also think of all bodies that have been broken, crucified, lynched, and oppressed. It is remembering that some bodies have been devalued, disfigured, and distorted while others have benefitted from, perpetuated, or performed these acts of violence. The cross lives on in the lynching tree, through the violence inflicted by police or military states against bodies of color, in genocide, religious wars, and white supremacist terrorism. Engaging in purposeful acts of memory brings all to the table. While the table is open to all, people are invited first to repent as they are confronted by the harms they inflicted on others.[66] Only once people are reconciled can they boldly approach:

> At the table Jesus prepares, *all* assemble: in his body we are made
> anew, a community of faith—the living and the dead. In our

66. Matt 5:23–24.

presence, the Son of Man gathers up the remnants of our memories, the broken fragments of our histories, and judges, blesses,
and transforms them. His Eucharistic banquet re-orders us, re-
members us, restores us, and makes us one.[67]

Thus, the songs and preaching should be imbued with these memories,
which permeate the present with pain, but also possibilities. Ritual, as
worship, is the empowering energy of Christian spirituality, especially in
Pentecostal circles for which it is the climax of religious life. Worship has
the power to shape and reshape lives. At the table, there is room for all,
oppressor and oppressed.

Third, to invoke the Spirit in the cause of freedom means engaging
in practices of proximity—allyship, solidarity, protest, and self-sacrifice.
These practices are not inconsequential. Neither are they convenient. Just
as Jesus invites those who want to follow after him by asking them to deny
themselves and carry a cross,[68] discipleship, as following Jesus by the Spirit,
implies a cost—cruciform living—which changes how life is valued and
lived in such a radical way that losing one's life is truly finding it. This is
an uncomfortable passage, perhaps explaining why this sort of selflessness
is a rarity in a Western culture that privileges—and rewards—acts of self-
preservation. The Spirit invites Christians to lay down their lives for others
for the sake of justice, but in doing so, a life to the full is found, a life worth
living and giving away. This death entails dying to the version of the world
and ourselves that we had, to a new life in which our heart is changed and
from which we embody a different and more just way of living in the world.

Finally, invoking the Spirit in the cause of freedom must move beyond
piety or prayer into social action. Frederick Douglass said, "We want practi-
cal religion—religion that will do something. When I commenced praying
with my legs, I felt the answer coming down."[69] Over a hundred years later,
in his march in Selma with the Reverend Dr. Martin Luther King Jr., Rabbi
Abraham Joshua Heschel recounts: "For many of us the march from Selma
to Montgomery was about protest and prayer. Legs are not lips and walking is not kneeling. And yet our legs uttered songs. Even without words,
our march was worship. I felt my legs were praying."[70] Both quotes make
the connection between prayer and social action, spirituality and praxis.

67. Copeland, *Enfleshing Freedom*, 128 (emphasis in original).

68. Mark 8:34.

69. Douglass, "Speech."

70. Heschel, "Following."

Commitment meets consequence in the fact of the flesh. The Spirit empowers and emboldens, moving and compelling bodies into liberative action. James instructs, "So faith by itself, if it has no deeds, is dead."[71] By contrast, the Spirit animates, makes alive, and attaches flesh to bodies; the Spirit is the verb of liberation. Where the Spirit is, there is freedom; where there is freedom, there is the Spirit. In response, what else can one do than announce that Pentecost comes, again and again, to set free, break loose, and bring about otherwise possibilities? Political Pentecost requires praying with one's legs until all are free. This is what it means, what it feels like, to enflesh freedom.

71. James 2:17.

Conclusion

In a short time, God began to manifest His power and soon the building could not contain the people. Now the meetings continue all day and into the night and the fire is kindling all over the city and surrounding towns. Proud, well-dressed preachers come in to "investigate." Soon their high looks are replaced with wonder, then conviction comes, and very often you will find them in a short time wallowing on the dirty floor, asking God to forgive them and make them as little children.

—*WILLIAM J. SEYMOUR, THE AZUSA PAPERS*

Introduction

WHEN I SET OUT TO WRITE a dissertation on the affective and ritualistic contours of Pentecostal experience, I did not account fully for where the "me-search in the research" would take me. Neither did I realize how much of myself is tied to, shaped by, and invested in the subject matter. I did not anticipate how exploring my childhood experiences in a tradition that led to estrangement in conversation with my experiences at TFAM's biannual conference would affect me so deeply. But it has shown me that freedom is possible without conformity, and that liberation is always an act of the Spirit. Indeed, my lack of understanding also kept me from addressing what it is about Pentecostalism that still moves me. These stories and ex-amples underscore the limiting and liberative nature of Pentecostalism. Its theological malleability is a great strength and weakness. And I, like many, can testify to this tension.

One cannot account for the emergence of Pentecostalism in the US without understanding the history, politics, and fleshy factors that pro-duced it. Without the songs and cries of the enslaved, the camp meetings of the nineteenth century, and the events at Azusa, there would be no Pentecostal movement. Donna Harraway writes: "It matters what matters we use to think other matters with; it matters what stories we tell to tell other stories with; it matters what knots knot knots, what thoughts think thoughts, what descriptions describe descriptions, what ties tie ties. It matters what stories make worlds, what worlds make stories."[1] Thus, this project is about Pentecostalism as informed by Black, queer, and other voices often silent or rendered invisible. Without this representation, Pentecostalism is simply one tradition among many co-opted and appropriated for the ongoing colonial projects of the modern Western world.

Ironically, given the appropriation, Pentecostalism continues to boom around the world, particularly in the Global South and in parts of Asia. What can account for this growth? Donald Miller writes "Their [Pentecostals] worship is extremely vibrant. . . . One reason these churches are growing is because they are able to integrate mind and body in their religious experiences, and they're being incredibly creative in responding to the needs of their people."[2] Mind and body integration and an awareness of the needs of the people—here we see a Pentecostal spirituality and praxis of liberation. Without a doubt, the staunch individualism rampant in Western culture creates a consumeristic and self-reserved approach to spiritual experience, which severs ties between individuals and communities. This is nowhere more obvious than the language of a "personal" relationship with God and Jesus as one's "personal" Savior. This individualism is mirrored in the current state of American politics. It is the opinion of the author that part of liberative Pentecostal spirituality is becoming affectively aware, once again, to the interconnectedness between God, others, and ourselves. This interconnectedness is modeled in the rituals of the church—in the singing, the preaching, and outreach.

My hope for this project is that the claims I have made have been clear. As I look back over the chapters of this work, I see three themes that continue to appear, sometimes tacitly and other times explicitly: 1) Pentecostalism is not a typical theological framework and actually works against the grain of modern Western norms, such as rationalism, while at the same time offering a flexible structure for Pentecostals to bend and mold with their practices. This is nowhere clearer than in the variations of the idiom "Don't make it a doctrine." Pentecostalism, I argue, cannot be tamed by

1. Haraway, *Staying with the Trouble*, 35.
2. Brody, "Global Impact of Pentecostalism."

theory, nor is it subject to the standards of orthodoxy. For this reason, it sits outside of reformed traditions. There are also countless Pentecostal denominations, likely because there are myriad ways of experiencing God and articulating those experiences. Its plasticity is both its greatest strength and weakness. 2) The Pentecostal movement began as an extension of Black experience, thought, life, and expression. Beginning with the transmission of African cosmologies into Christianity through the horrific Middle Passage and institution of slavery, the enslaved injected cultural practices into slave-holding religion. The spirituals and the blue note are the sounds produced over and against the violent, unjust practice of slavocracy. Yet, these contributions are the foundation for American music.

Moreover, the notion of race factored greatly in William Seymour's vision at Azusa Street. It is important for this project to name the racialized history of religion in the US generally and Pentecostalism in the US particularly. And because of the intersectionality of issues of race, gender, and sexuality, it is important to consider how these issues can shape and be shaped by Pentecostalism. 3) Pentecostalism, when taking into account the social ramifications of its development, and the social milieu in which it was birthed, can be a liberative praxis. I say "can be" to acknowledge that, like many other traditions, it can also be used for non-liberative, even legalistic, practices. I have tried to underscore the connection between the work of the Holy Spirit and freedom in various vignettes and examples, in the Scriptures, at Pentecost, in hush harbors, at Azusa Street, and finally at TFAM. My theological interpretation of the Scripture "Where the Spirit of the Lord is, there is freedom" is foundational to these claims.

Chapter 1 sought to establish the theoretical framework for the entire project. Theories of affect and ritual studies offer a multifaceted approach to theorize Pentecostalism. Theories of affect are generative to think with, especially within, the ecstatic, emotive repertoires of Pentecostal worship. Furthermore, exploring ritual as repetitive bodily movements, actions, and gestures solidifies the relationship between feeling and doing. A most apt metaphor for this relationship is dancing, which is a recurring theme throughout the project. Dance serves as a metaphor and praxis, bringing together spirituality, feeling, movement, and performance.

After offering histories of theories of affect and ritual studies, I moved to consider how the two broad fields can inform theorizing around Pentecostal worship. Music, singing, dancing, shouting, and emotive preaching make Pentecostal worship a dynamic experience. Affects focus on feeling, which shapes our understanding of the world and our place within it. Ritual is complementary and offers a way of learning bodily languages through practices that make sense of the world and practitioners' place within it.

Chapter 2 turned to the connection between Blackness, sound, and dance-possible epistemologies. There is a reciprocal relationship between sound and affect: sound produces feeling and feeling produces sound. I chose three vignettes to explore sound and the Spirit: Pentecost and the upper room in Acts 2, the spirituals produced by the enslaved in the Southern US, and at the Azusa Street Revival. One aspect of all three examples is how the Spirit appeals to the senses—the medium of the message is sensate, i.e., what is heard, felt, and registered in bodies.

In the upper room narrative, the Spirit appears with a sound of a mighty rushing wind. Of course, the name *pneuma* connotes wind or breath, so the wordplay is obvious. The Spirit's activity in the upper room empowers the disciples in the room by equipping them with the ability to speak previously unknown languages. The role of the Spirit in this story is to bring the message of God to those living around Jerusalem, those living in diaspora. God speaks to them in their own tongue. This is both an intimate and inclusive act. The Spirit seeks to make all people free. In the spirituals, the enslaved produced a sound previously unsung: the blue note. The blue note, like the Spirit, disrupts the norms of conventional European music. By flattening intervals, the blue note embodies the sounds of suffering and also otherwise possibilities outside of the musical conventions. In hush harbors, the enslaved encountered the Spirit, who gave birth to expressions and methods of subverting the music and theology of the time in the fight for freedom. Finally, the road to Azusa was marked by other histories and sounds—tongues, shouting, ecstatic worship, and the language of social holiness—which was a transmission of Seymour's vision. I attend to the events leading up to Azusa and trace how the short-lived movement gave birth to a global movement. The revival which brought thousands upon thousands of visitors to Los Angeles was a prophetic movement that did not separate spiritual experiences from social consequences. The heritage of the Pentecostal movement, as born at 312 Azusa Street, has a legacy of subverting racial and gender norms. Once again, I contend it is the Holy Spirit, and ecstatic awareness of that presence, which leads to social action.

Chapter 3 addressed gender, sexuality, and inclusion in Pentecostalism. While many Pentecostal churches and denominations are not open and affirming, that is, inclusive to LGBTQ+ people, I argue that such inclusivity is another example of the locus of the Spirit's movement toward liberation. Simply put, the connection between the Spirit and liberation does not exclude based on who one loves or how gender is understood and expressed. But this connection is not espoused or embodied by most Pentecostal churches. A dilemma emerges, then, for people who must choose between living in the closet, i.e., conforming, and living authentically, risking alienation and ostracization. The cost of this decision, either way, is someone's happiness. Thus, using Sara Ahmed's work on the affective and scripted nature of happiness, I unsettled the notion that a good life is a happy life. In fact, happiness often functions as a veneer of conformity through the language of modesty, decency, and purity. What is needed, instead, is what queer liberation theologian Marcella Althaus-Reid calls an indecent theology, a rejection of objects of happiness in order to find acceptance, purpose, and new joy. Insofar as happiness involves the propagation of oppressive norms, joy is an act, is the spirit, of resistance.

The Fellowship of Affirming Ministries (TFAM) is an example of a Pentecostal tradition modeling LGBTQ+ inclusion. Bishop Yvette Flunder's pioneering work with TFAM is evidenced in the gospel of radical inclusivity, which focuses on those most marginalized, both by society and faith traditions, because of their gender and sexuality. This gospel is the good news that everyone is welcome at the table. The community alone is responsible for and able to shape the theology and ethics of the group. If it is not liberative or life giving, it is not the good news. I turned from TFAM to explore further the intersectionality of gender, sexuality, and race in queer womanist theologizing. What we find in Pamela Lightsey and Yvette Flunder, in the womanist tradition of Alice Walker, Katie Cannon, bell hooks, et al., is a framework for how LGBTQ+ bodies belong to the body of Christ and claim that body as queer. Such a claim is consonant with M. Shawn Copeland's work on redefining theological anthropology by locating God's presence (in Christ) in Black—and queer—women's bodies. What Copeland calls "enfleshing freedom" features in the fourth and final chapter.

Chapter 4 is the final chapter, shifting the conversation to the Holy Spirit's role in what the Reverend Dr. William J. Barber II calls "political Pentecost." Important to my arguments is that spiritual experience must never be confined to or separated (severed) from social action, that is, political life. Try as many may, the two spheres are inseparable and mutually-reinforcing. Efforts to bifurcate the two are futile and potentially damaging. Political Pentecost is both an invitation and annunciation that the Spirit comes to disrupt the world as it is and reorder it in more liberative ways; that where the Spirit is, there is the work of liberation.

Akin to Barber's vision of a political Pentecost is Flunder's assertion of TFAM as a "third Pentecost." Like the Spirit in the upper room, and at Azusa, TFAM is the fresh wind bringing God's message of freedom, justice, equality, equity, and inclusion into the church and world. Third, or political, Pentecost is affective and embodied. Therefore, I engage the work of Brian Massumi and Sara Ahmed vis-à-vis the politics of affect. Understanding that affects attach bodies to ideas, objects, and others through resonance and feeling, offers one explanation for the rise of affective politics, which shapes and orients bodies by stoking fear and anxiety through media and political rallies (rituals). What is needed, thus, are counter rituals that recue bodies toward hope and otherwise possibilities through rituals of protest.

I demonstrated the relationship between religious experience and social action in the mystical life and writings of Howard Thurman in what he deems the inwardness and outwardness of religion. The inwardness of religion is the individual's initial recognition and experience of God in their personhood (body) and the outwardness is the response that always follows. This inward/outward dynamic shows that religious experience is never severed from the social, from suffering, but is the impetus which brings together the separation of inner and outer life to a vanishing point. Finally, I explored Ashon Crawley's Blackpentecost in conversation with M. Shawn Copeland's concept of enfleshing freedom. Any liberative work must be grounded in the fact of the flesh, given that the flesh and body is the locus of oppression. I argued that invoking the Spirit, through breath, Black breath, becomes a way of announcing Pentecost and becoming aware of and open to otherwise possibilities. When the Spirit is invoked, situations change, because people are transformed. In that way, through prayer and worship, Pentecost is always coming afresh and anew. The important work is to become attuned to the Spirit of liberation, the God of life, and to let that unstoppable force of freedom move bodies into motion/action.

I want to offer a few clarifications as to the scope and intent of this project. There are likely exclusions and areas, ideas, and events left unaddressed. First, this is not a systematic Pentecostal theology nor a comprehensive history of Pentecostal movements. I have chosen the events, thinkers, and histories that are pertinent to this project. For example, I explored the spirituals but did not address white gospel (Southern) or how some white Pentecostal churches may parallel the Black aesthetics of

Pentecostal worship. My hope is in future projects to explore and critique white Pentecostal movements, especially those that use giftedness (charisma) to market and accumulate large amounts of wealth. Pentecostalism and profit through capitalism is a subject worthy of more attention than a chapter or section in a chapter.

Second, this project does not address postcolonial/decolonial liturgy and theology but theologizes as it traces the genesis of the Pentecostal movement as birthed at Azusa Street. While there is certainly some overlap between colonialism and the spread of Western ideas and norms, especially within Christianity, I have focused instead on Pentecostalism as its own cosmology of ideas, customs, practices, and rituals within the context of the United States. There is much to learn, however, from Cláudio Carvalhaes's *Liturgy in Postcolonial Perspectives: Only One Is Holy*, as well as the work he and others have done on the role of worship in social change around the world.[3] It is important to consider the factors that have caused Pentecostalism to grow and spread with zeal, making it the fastest-growing part of Christianity in the world.

Finally, I explored the liberative contours of the Holy Spirit without delving too far into the discourse of liberation theologies. One exception, of course, is James Cone's work, as it is pertinent to the context and scope of this project. What I hope came across was that liberation theology is not something that developed in the twentieth century, but it is the very core and essence of the message of God as found in the Scriptures and embodied in Jesus of Nazareth. It is for this reason that I looked at the Spirit's work in creation and Pentecost; wherever the Spirit is, we can expect two things: chaos and the work of liberation.[4] The Spirit is the tension, the cognitive dissonance, and the sustaining force of resistance. This should give Christians hope in the face of fear and resiliency in the long, slow work of justice. And what better way to be encouraged, to be strengthened, than to encounter viscerally the Spirit in worship? What else can stir up hope than to remember that the Spirit of the living God—the same Spirit that raised Christ from the dead—indwells all people?

I offer this benediction as an ending:

---

3. See also Carvalhaes, *What's Worship Got to Do*; Carvalhaes, *Eucharist and Globalization: Redrawing the Borders of Eucharistic Hospitality*; Carvalhaes, *Liturgies from Below: Prayers from People at the Ends of the World*; Miller and Yamamori, *Global Pentecostalism*.

4. Catherine Keller notes that the Spirit is already present in Gen 1 before God begins to bring order out of chaos rather than creation *ex nihilo* (Keller, *Face of the Deep*, 3–24).

May you encounter the God of liberation, who stirs up trouble,
the one who is able to do exceedingly, abundantly
above all that can be asked or imagined,
the one in whom we live and move and have our being.

May you remember Jesus, the brother of the living,
who walked in the line of prophetic witness,
who stood up for the poor and oppressed,
who on a cross hung in solidarity,
because the world always silences its prophets,
the one death could not kill.

And may you embody the Spirit, the wind and breath of God,
who makes alive and free,
a ferocious force for justice,
the verb for liberation,
the vibrations of goodness and love,
who brings about freedom in every age. Amen.

Bibliography

Adkins, Amey Victoria. "Symposium Introduction." Syndicate, Oct. 16, 2017. https://syndicate.network/symposia/theology/blackpentecostal-breath/.

Ahmed, Sara. *The Cultural Politics of Emotion*. New York: Routledge, 2014.

———. *The Promise of Happiness*. Durham, NC: Duke University Press, 2010.

———. *Queer Phenomenology: Orientations, Objects, Others*. Durham, NC: Duke University Press, 2006.

Alexander, Estrelda. *Black Fire: One Hundred Years of African American Pentecostalism*. Downers Grove, IL: IVP Academic, 2011.

Alexander, Michelle. *The New Jim Crow: Mass Incarceration in the Age of Colorblindness*. New York: New, 2020.

Althaus-Reid, Marcella. *Indecent Theology: Theological Perversions in Sex, Gender and Politics*. London: Routledge, 2000.

———. *The Queer God*. London: Routledge, 2007.

Althusser, Louis. *On the Reproduction of Capitalism: Ideology and Ideological State Apparatuses*. Translated by G. M. Goshgarian. London: Verso, 2014.

Augustine. *The Retractions*. Translated by Mary Inez Bogan RSM. Washington, DC: Catholic University of America Press, 1968.

Barber, William J., II. "Rev. Barber: These Times Require a New Language and a New Fusion Coalition." ThinkProgress, Jan. 30, 2017. https://archive.thinkprogress.org/rev-barber-these-times-require-a-new-language-and-a-new-fusion-coalition-c741b9eb1b47/.

Bartleman, Frank. *How Pentecost Came to Los Angeles: As It Was in the Beginning*. Los Angeles: Bartleman, 1925.

BBC. "Form 696: 'Racist Police Form' to Be Scrapped in London." *BBC*, Nov. 10, 2017. https://www.bbc.com/news/uk-41946915.

Bell, Catherine M. *Ritual Theory, Ritual Practice*. New York: Oxford University Press, 2010.

Bennett, Joshua. *Being Property Once Myself: Blackness and the End of Man*. Cambridge, MA: Belknap, 2020.

Berlant, Lauren Gail, and Kathleen Stewart. *The Hundreds*. Durham, NC: Duke University Press, 2019. https://www.dukeupress.edu/Assets/PubMaterials/978-1-4780-0288-8_601.pdf.

Biale, David. "The God with Breasts: El Shaddai in the Bible." *History of Religions* 21 (Feb. 1982) 240–56. https://www.jstor.org/stable/1062160.

Boisseron, Bénédicte. *Afro-Dog: Blackness and the Animal Question*. New York: Columbia University Press, 2018.

Bostic, Joy R. *African American Female Mysticism: Nineteenth-Century Religious Activism*. Black Religion/Womanist Thought/Social Justice. London: Palgrave Macmillan, 2016.

Bourdieu, Pierre. *Outline of a Theory of Practice*. Cambridge: Cambridge University Press, 2010.

Bray, Karen, and Stephen D. Moore. *Religion, Emotion, Sensation: Affect Theories and Theologies*. New York: Fordham University Press, 2020.

Britannica, The Editors of Encyclopædia. "Nicene Creed." *Encylopaedia Britannica*, Sept. 3, 2022. https://www.britannica.com/topic/Nicene-Creed.

Brody, Ambrosia Viramontes. "The Global Impact of Pentecostalism." USC News, July 23, 2014. https://news.usc.edu/31221/the-global-impact-of-pentecostalism/.

Brennan, Teresa. *The Transmission of Affect*. Ithaca, NY: Cornell University Press, 2014.

Brown, Robert McAfee. *Spirituality and Liberation: Overcoming the Great Fallacy*. Philadelphia: Westminster, 1988.

Campbell, Randolph B. *An Empire for Slavery: The Peculiar Institution in Texas, 1821–1865*. Baton Rouge: Louisiana State University Press, 1991.

Cannon, Katie Geneva. *Black Womanist Ethics*. Eugene, OR: Wipf and Stock, 2006.

Carter, Christopher. "Blood in the Soil: The Racial, Racist, and Religious Dimensions of Environmentalism." In *The Bloomsbury Handbook of Religion and Nature: The Elements*, edited by Whitney Bauman and Laura Hobgood, Bloomsbury Handbooks in Religion, 45–62. New York: Bloomsbury, 2018.

———. "How Does It Feel to Be the Problem? Affect Theory and White Domination." Syndicate, Oct. 30, 2017. https://syndicate.network/symposia/philosophy/religious-affects/.

Carvalhaes, Cláudio. *Eucharist and Globalization: Redrawing the Borders of Eucharistic Hospitality*. Eugene, OR: Pickwick, 2013.

———. *Liturgies from Below: Prayers from People at the Ends of the World*. Nashville: Abingdon, 2020.

———. *Liturgy in Postcolonial Perspectives: Only One Is Holy*. Basingstoke, NH: Palgrave Macmillan, 2015.

———. *What's Worship Got to Do with It? Interpreting Life Liturgically*. Eugene, OR: Cascade, 2018.

Casselberry, Judith, and Elizabeth A. Pritchard. *Spirit on the Move: Black Women and Pentecostalism in Africa and the Diaspora*. Durham, NC: Duke University Press, 2019.

Castelo, Daniel. *Pentecostalism as a Christian Mystical Tradition*. Grand Rapids: Eerdmans, 2017.

Chen, Mel Y. *Animacies: Biopolitics, Racial Mattering, and Queer Affect*. Durham, NC: Duke University Press, 2012.

Cleveland, Christena. *Christ Our Black Mother Speaks: A Collection of Art, Essays, Questions and Practices to Deepen Our Connection to the Dark Divine Feminine*. N.p.: Cleveland, 2019.

Coates, Ta-Nehisi. *Between the World and Me*. New York: One World, 2015.

Collins, Patricia Hill. *Black Feminist Thought: Knowledge, Consciousness, and the Politics of Empowerment*. New York: Routledge, 2015.

Columbia Law School. "Kimberlé Crenshaw on Intersectionality, More than Two Decades Later." Columbia Law School, June 8, 2017. https://www.law.columbia.edu/news/archive/kimberle-crenshaw-intersectionality-more-two-decades-later.

Cone, James H. *A Black Theology of Liberation*. Maryknoll, NY: Orbis, 2017.

———. *The Spirituals and the Blues: An Interpretation*. Maryknoll, NY: Orbis, 1992.

———. "Theology's Great Sin: Silence in the Face of White Supremacy." *Black Theology*, 2 (2004) 139–52. https://doi.org/10.1558/blth.2.2.139.36027.

Copeland, M. Shawn. *Enfleshing Freedom: Body, Race, and Human Being*. Minneapolis: Fortress, 2009.

———. "Reading/Hearing/Imagining Blackpentecostal Breath: The Aesthetics of Possibility." Syndicate, Oct. 26, 2017. https://syndicate.network/symposia/theology/blackpentecostal-breath/.

Cox, Harvey Gallagher. *Fire from Heaven: The Rise of Pentecostal Spirituality and the Reshaping of Religion in the Twenty-First Century*. Reading, MA: Addison-Wesley, 1995.

Crawley, Ashon T. *Blackpentecostal Breath: The Aesthetics of Possibility*. New York: Fordham University Press, 2017.

———. *The Lonely Letters*. Durham, NC: Duke University Press, 2020.

Crenshaw, Kimberlé. "Demarginalizing the Intersection of Race and Sex: A Black Feminist Critique of Antidiscrimination Doctrine, Feminist Theory and Antiracist Politics." *University of Chicago Legal Forum* (1989) 139–67. https://chicagounbound.uchicago.edu/uclf/vol1989/iss1/8/?utm_source=chicagounbound.uchicago.edu/uclf/vol1989/iss1/8&utm_medium=PDF&utm_campaign=PDFCoverPages.

Daly, Mary F. *Beyond God the Father: Toward a Philosophy of Women's Liberation*. Boston: Beacon, 1974.

Douglas, Kelly Brown. *Black Bodies and the Black Church: A Blues Slant*. New York: Palgrave Macmillan, 2014.

Douglass, Frederick. *Narrative of the Life of Frederick Douglass: An American Slave*. New York: Simon & Schuster, 2004.

———. "Speech." In *Proceedings of the Yearly Meeting of the Friends of Human Progress, Held at Waterloo, Seneca Co., NY, the 3d, 4th and 5th of June, 1859*, by Friends of Human Progress, 8. Rochester, NY: Hebard & Co., 1859.

Driver, Tom F. *Liberating Rites: Understanding the Transformative Power of Ritual*. Boulder, CO: Westview, 1998.

Du Bois, William Edward Burghardt. *The Souls of Black Folk*. New York: Dover, 1994.

Editors, History.com. "Great Awakening." History, Mar. 7, 2018; updated Sept. 20, 2019. https://www.history.com/topics/british-history/great-awakening#section_3.

Educational CyberPlayground. "Listening to Hard Rock—Heavy Metal Music—Can Cause Harm—Mozart Is Better." Educational CyberPlayground, multiple dates. https://edu-cyberpg.com/Music/Mice_and_Music_Experiment_Mo.html. Accessed April 22, 2020.

Edwards, Denis. *Deep Incarnation: God's Redemptive Suffering with Creatures*. Maryknoll, NY: Orbis, 2019.

Flunder, Yvette A. "Bishop Yvette Flunder on the 'Third Pentecost.'" YouTube, May 13, 2019. https://www.youtube.com/watch?v=rDSU6SZA7Pc&list=WL&index=4&t=240s.

———. *Where the Edge Gathers: Building a Community of Radical Inclusion*. Cleveland: Pilgrim, 2005.

Frederick, Candice. "On Black Aesthetics: The Black Arts Movement." New York Public Library, July 15, 2016. https://www.nypl.org/blog/2016/07/15/black-aesthetics-bam.

Freire, Paulo. *Pedagogy of the Oppressed.* Translated by Myra B. Ramos. New York: Seabury, 1970.

Fox 2. "Hands Up Don't Shoot." YouTube, Aug. 19, 2014. https://www.youtube.com/watch?v=8YsDKrEbcO4.

Gibbs, Anna. "Contagious Feelings: Pauline Hanson and the Epidemiology of Affect." *Australian Humanities Review* 24 (Dec. 2001). www.australianhumanitiesreview.org.

Goodall, Jane. "Primate Spirituality." In *The Encyclopedia of Religion and Nature,* edited by Bron Tayler, 1303–6. New York: Continuum, 2005.

Graham, Martha. *Blood Memory: An Autobiography.* Collingdale, PA: Diane, 1999.

———. "Martha Graham Reflects on Her Art and a Life in Dance." *New York Times,* Mar. 31, 1985. https://archive.nytimes.com/www.nytimes.com/library/arts/033185graham.html.

Grimes, Ronald L. *Beginnings in Ritual Studies.* Lanham, MD: University Press of America, 1982.

———. *The Craft of Ritual Studies.* Oxford Ritual Studies. Oxford, UK: Oxford University Press, 2014.

———. *Ritual Criticism: Case Studies in Its Practice, Essays on Its Theory.* Waterloo, Can.: Ritual Studies International, 2014.

———. *Ritual, Media, and Conflict.* New York: Oxford University Press, 2011.

Gutiérrez, Gustavo. *A Theology of Liberation: History, Politics, and Salvation.* Translated by Caridad Inda and John Eagleson. 15th rev. ed. Maryknoll, NY: Orbis, 2018.

Haraway, Donna Jeanne. *Staying with the Trouble: Making Kin in the Chthulucene.* Durham, NC: Duke University Press, 2016.

Heschel, Susannah. "Following in My Father's Footsteps: Selma 40 Years Later." Vox, Apr. 4, 2005. https://www.dartmouth.edu/~vox/0405/0404/heschel.html. Site discontinued.

Hollenweger, Walter J. "Pentecostalism and Black Power." *Theology Today* 30 (Oct. 1973) 228–38. https://doi.org/10.1177/004057367303000303.

hooks, bell. *Feminist Theory: From Margin to Center.* New York: Routledge, 2015.

Hurston, Zora Neale. *The Sanctified Church.* Berkley, CA: Turtle Island, 1984.

Isasi-Díaz, Ada María. *Mujerista Theology: A Theology for the Twenty-First Century.* Maryknoll, NY: Orbis, 1996.

Jackson, Zakiyyah Iman. *Becoming Human: Matter and Meaning in an Antiblack World.* New York: New York University Press, 2020.

James, Robin. *The Sonic Episteme: Acoustic Resonance, Neoliberalism, and Biopolitics.* Durham, NC: Duke University Press, 2019.

Jennings, Theodore W. "On Ritual Knowledge." *Journal of Religion* 62 (Apr. 1982) 111–27. https://www.jstor.org/stable/1203176.

———. "Ritual Studies and Liturgical Theology: An Invitation to Dialogue." *Journal of Religion* 67 (Jan. 1987) 35–56. https://www.jstor.org/stable/44368318.

Jennings, Willie James. *Acts.* Belief: A Theological Commentary on the Bible. Louisville, KY: Westminster John Knox, 2017.

Johns, Cheryl Bridges. *Pentecostal Formation: A Pedagogy among the Oppressed.* Eugene, OR: Wipf & Stock, 2010.

Johnson, Elizabeth A. *Ask the Beasts: Darwin and the God of Love.* London: Bloomsbury, 2015.

Julian of Norwich. *Revelations of Divine Love*. Edited and translated by Kaya Oakes. Mineola, NY: Ixia, 2019.

Keller, Catherine. *The Face of the Deep: A Theology of Becoming*. London: Routledge, 2021.

Kim, Claire Jean Kim. *Dangerous Crossings: Race, Species, and Nature in a Multicultural Age*. New York: Cambridge University Press, 2015.

Klassen, Pamela E. "Ritual." In *The Oxford Handbook of Religion and Emotion*, edited by John Corrigan. Printed from Oxford Handbooks Online, 2014. https://doi. org/10.1093/oxfordhb/9780195170214.003.0009.

Kotrosits, Maia. *Rethinking Early Christian Identity: Affect, Violence, and Belonging*. Minneapolis: Augsburg Fortress, 2015.

Lewin, Ellen. *Filled with the Spirit: Sexuality, Gender, and Radical Inclusivity in a Black Pentecostal Church Coalition*. Chicago: University of Chicago Press, 2018.

Lewis, Scott B. "William J. Seymour: Follower of the 'Evening Light.'" *Wesleyan Theological Journal* 39 (Fall 2004) 167–83.

Light, Gordon. "Draw the Circle Wide." In *Common Praise*, edited by Anglican Church of Canada, #418. Toronto: Anglican Book Centre, 1998.

Lightsey, Pamela R. *Our Lives Matter: A Womanist Queer Theology*. Eugene, OR: Pickwick, 2015.

Los Angeles Times. "Weird Babel of Tongues: New Sect of Fanatics Is Breaking Loose." *Los Angeles Times*, Apr. 18, 1906. https://latimes.newspapers.com/clip/84304061/ the-los-angeles-times/.

———. "Women with Men Embrace." *Los Angeles Times*, Sept. 3, 1906. https://latimes. newspapers.com/clip/111726668/women-with-men-embrace-la-times-sep/.

Massumi, Brian. *Politics of Affect*. Cambridge, UK: Polity, 2015. https://s3.amazonaws. com/arena-attachments/682183/8f09ee372f5bed9c0251e2c6174058d3.pdf.

Miller, Donald Eugene., and Tetsunao Yamamori. *Global Pentecostalism: The New Face of Christian Social Engagement*. Berkeley: University of California Press, 2007.

Moss, Otis. *Blue Note Preaching in a Post-Soul World: Finding Hope in an Age of Despair*. Louisville, KY: Westminster John Knox, 2015.

Moten, Fred. *In the Break: The Aesthetics of Black Radical Tradition*. Minneapolis: University of Minnesota Press, 2003.

Myskja, A., and M. Lindbaek. "How Does Music Affect the Human Body?" [Article in Norwegian.] U.S. National Library of Medicine, Apr. 10, 2000. https://www.ncbi. nlm.nih.gov/pubmed/10863350.

Nelson, Douglas. "For Such a Time as This: The Story of Bishop William J. Seymour and the Azusa Street Revival." PhD diss., University of Birmingham, 1981.

Oates, Stephen B. *Let the Trumpet Sound: A Life of Martin Luther King, Jr*. New York: HarperPerennial, 2014.

Okiji, Fumi. *Jazz as Critique: Adorno and Black Expression Revisited*. Stanford, CA: Stanford University Press, 2018.

Parham, Charles. *The Everlasting Gospel*. Baxter City, KS: Apostolic Faith Bible College Press, 1911.

———. *The Sermons of Charles F. Parham*. New York: Garland, 1985.

Parham, Sarah E. *The Life of Charles F. Parham, Founder of the Apostolic Faith Movement*. New York: Garland, 1985.

Péguy, Charles. *Notre Jeunesse*. Paris: Gallimard, 1933.

Peretti, Burton W. *Lift Every Voice: The History of African American Music*. Lanham, MD: Rowman & Littlefield, 2009.

Pinn, Anthony B. *Introducing African American Religion*. London: Routledge, 2013.

Pitts, Walter F. *Old Ship of Zion: The Afro-Baptist Ritual in the African Diaspora*. New York: Oxford University Press, 1997.

Plate, S. Brent. *A History of Religion in 5 1/2 Objects: Bringing the Spiritual to Its Senses*. Boston: Beacon, 2015.

Pollard, Alton B. *Mysticism and Social Change: The Social Witness of Howard Thurman*. New York: Lang, 1992.

Rambo, Shelly L. *Spirit and Trauma: A Theology of Remaining*. Louisville, KY: Westminster John Knox, 2010.

Rand, Erin J. *Reclaiming Queer: Activist and Academic Rhetorics of Resistance*. Tuscaloosa: University of Alabama Press, 2014.

Randolph, Peter. *Sketches of Slave Life*. Charleston, SC: Nabu, 2010.

Rauschenbusch, Walter. *Christianity and the Social Crisis in the 21st Century: The Classic That Woke up the Church*. Edited by Paul Raushenbush. New York: HarperOne, 2007.

Rivers, Clarence Jos. *Soulfull Worship*. N.p.: Rivers, 1974.

Robinson, Cedric J. *The Terms of Order: Political Science and the Myth of Leadership*. Chapel Hill: University of North Carolina Press, 2016.

Schaefer, Donovan O. *The Evolution of Affect Theory: The Humanities, the Sciences, and the Study of Power*. Cambridge: Cambridge University Press, 2019.

———. *Religious Affects: Animality, Evolution, and Power*. Durham, NC: Duke University Press, 2015.

Scheve, Christian von. "An Interview with Donovan Schaefer on Religious Affects." *Affective Societies*, Nov. 28, 2016. https://affective-societies.de/2016/interviews-portraits/an-interview-with-donovan-schaefer-on-religious-affects/.

Sedgwick, Eve Kosofsky, and Adam Frank. "Shame in the Cybernetic Fold: Reading Silvan Tomkins." *Critical Inquiry* 21 (1995) 496–522. https://doi.org/10.1086/448761.

———. *Touching Feeling: Affect, Pedagogy, Performativity*. Durham, NC: Duke University Press, 2003.

Sedgwick, Eve Kosofsky, and Michael D. Snediker. "Queer Little Gods: A Conversation." *Massachusetts Review* 49 (Apr. 2008) 194–218.

Seymour, William J. *The Doctrines and Discipline of the Azusa Street Apostolic Faith Mission of Los Angeles, California*. Pensacola, FL: Christian Life, 2000.

Shakur, Assata. *Assata: An Autobiography*. London: Books, 2014.

Sherwood, Harriet. "Religion in US 'Worth More Than Google and Apple Combined.'" *Church and State*, Jan. 15, 2016. http://churchandstate.org.uk/2016/09/religion-in-us-worth-more-than-google-and-apple-combined/?fbclid=IwAR15l36JLAar4aap5Mz4L5xwHopzscq-AyR--DKiF3R7FZKww-YNvrbCMA8.

Shukla, Aditya. "The Social Psychology of Heavy Metal & Rock Music: Research on Metalheads." *Cognition Today*, Mar. 10, 2019; updated Sept. 19, 2022. https://cognitiontoday.com/2019/03/the-social-psychology-of-heavy-metal-rock-music-research-on-metalheads/.

Simply Tomas: The Collection. "'Yes Lord' Praise at Pentecostal Temple COGIC—Memphis, TN." YouTube, 1990. https://www.youtube.com/watch?v=vuisScVJphg.

Smith, James K. A. *Thinking in Tongues: Pentecostal Contributions to Christian Philosophy*. Grand Rapids: Eerdmans, 2010.

Söelle, Dorothee. *On Earth as in Heaven: A Liberation Spirituality of Sharing*. Louisville, KY: Westminster/John Knox, 1993.

Somé, Malidoma Patrice. *Ritual: Power, Healing, and Community*. London: Arkana, 1998.

Stephenson, Christopher A. *Types of Pentecostal Theology: Method, System, Spirit.* New York: Oxford University Press, 2016.

Stewart, Kathleen. *Ordinary Affects.* Durham, NC: Duke University Press, 2007.

Synan, Vinson. *The Holiness-Pentecostal Tradition: Charismatic Movements in the Twentieth Century.* Grand Rapids: Eerdmans, 2000.

TFAM. "About Us." TFAM, n.d. https://www.radicallyinclusive.org/about-us. Accessed May 31, 2020.

Tickle, Phyllis. *The Age of the Spirit: How the Ghost of an Ancient Controversy Is Shaping the Church.* Grand Rapids: Baker, 2014.

Thompson, Marie, and Ian D. Biddle. *Sound, Music, Affect: Theorizing Sonic Experience.* London: Bloomsbury Academic, 2013.

Thurman, Howard. *The Creative Encounter: An Interpretation of Religion and the Social Witness.* Richmond, IN: Friends United, 1997.

———. *Disciplines of the Spirit.* Richmond, IN: Friends United, 2003.

———. *Jesus and the Disinherited.* Boston: Beacon, 1996.

———. *The Luminous Darkness: A Personal Interpretation of the Anatomy of Segregation and the Ground of Hope.* Richmond, IN: Friends United, 1989.

———. *With Head and Heart: The Autobiography of Howard Thurman.* Boston: Mariner, 1981.

Tomkins, Silvan S. *Exploring Affect: The Selected Writings of Silvan S. Tomkins.* Edited by E. Virginia Demos. Studies in Emotion and Social Interaction. Cambridge: Cambridge University Press, 1995.

Van der Haak, Bregtje, and Richard Vijgen. "Atlas of Pentecostalism: An Expanding Record of the Fastest Growing Religion in the World." Atlas of Pentecostalism, July 29, 2018. http://atlasofpentecostalism.net/atlas.pdf.

Vox. "Grime: London's Latest Music Export." YouTube, June 8, 2017. https://www.youtube.com/watch?v=Am2sYBhg_hM.

Walker, Alice. *In Search of Our Mothers' Gardens: Womanist Prose.* New York: Harcourt, 1983.

Watts, Shea. "Ritualizing Bodies: Exploring Religious and Political Affects." *Berkley Journal of Religion and Theology* 4 (Sept. 2018) 33–52.

Webb, Stephen H. *The Divine Voice: Christian Proclamation and the Theology of Sound.* Eugene, OR: Wipf & Stock, 2011.

Welker, Keith M. "Music as an Emotion Regulation Strategy: An Examination of Genres of Music and Their Roles in Emotion Regulation." *Psychology of Music* 47 (Oct. 2017). https://www.researchgate.net/publication/320639925_Music_as_an_emotion_regulation_strategy_An_examination_of_genres_of_music_and_their_roles_in_emotion_regulation.

Williamson, Jenn. Review of *Summary of Sketches of Slave Life: Or, Illustrations of the "Peculiar Institution,"* by Peter Randolph. Documenting the American South, n.d. https://docsouth.unc.edu/neh/randol55/summary.html. Accessed Aug. 4, 2020.

Wynter, Sylvia. "Unsettling the Coloniality of Being/Power/Truth/Freedom: Towards the Human, After Man, Its Overrepresentation—An Argument." *CR: The New Centennial Review* 3 (2003) 257–337. https://doi.org/10.1353/ncr.2004.0015.

Index